LIVING OFF THE WEST

LIVING OFF THE WEST

Gorbachev's Secret Agenda and
Why It Will Fail

SOL SANDERS

MADISON BOOKS
Lanham • New York • London

Published by Madison Books
4720 Boston Way
Lanham, Maryland 20706

3 Henrietta Street
London WC2E 8LU England

Distributed by National Book Network

Library of Congress Cataloging-in-Publication Data

Sanders, Sol W.
  Living off the West / by Sol W. Sanders.
  p.   cm.
  Includes bibliographical references.
  1. Soviet Union—Economic policy—1917-
2. Soviet Union—Foreign economic relations—
United States.   3. United States,—Foreign economic
relations—Soviet Union.   4. Soviet Union—Foreign
economic relations.   I. Title.

HC335.S3625 1990
337.47073—dc20   90-5735 CIP

ISBN 0-8191-7679-6

British Cataloging in Publication Information Available

CONTENTS

KEEPING UP WITH A WHIRLWIND

In the two and a half years since this research and writing project began, the Soviet Union and Central Europe have been caught in a vortex of events that have challenged serious interpretation and provided a media carnival.

Still, little has happened that has not embellished, rather than destroyed, the basic hypothesis with which I had worked: The Soviet Union has always been far more dependent on foreign economic support than conventional wisdom has been willing to acknowledge. And, in fact, the Communist experiment which defied natural law has survived only through periodic transfers of resources from the West, duplicating an earlier Russian historic phenomenon.

A section of the Soviet elite, perhaps a minority, grouped around Mikhail Gorbachev, has understood this essential ingredient of Soviet survival. At the same time it has appreciated that, as never before, the Moscow state needed a new and larger transfusion from the West. That could only be accomplished by a radical restructuring of the Soviet Union, to allay Western suspicions in order to bring forth that possibility, and to prepare a Soviet patient so as not to reject the transplant (to slightly change my medical metaphor). Communist experiments in the post-World War II period had several times demonstrated that it would have to be such a teeth-rattling "reform" as to put into jeopardy the very existence of the system, a truly great gamble in the tradition of the first Bolshevik ideologue, V.I. Lenin.

Yet, it was a part of my hypothesis, that the end result, the prospects for success, was dubious at best. The modern industrial societies were distancing themselves from the leading Marxist-Leninist society at a more and more rapid pace. Nowhere was that more apparent than in the military sciences. And I hypothesized that the chief motivation for the attempted restructuring was, indeed, the diminishing relative power of the Soviet military establishment—despite its startling past accomplishments. Gorbachev and his allies saw, precisely, that the schizophrenia of the dual track civilian-military economy and society could no longer be maintained. Increasingly, the sciences of war and material civilian progress were merging in the West. And even when it was overtaken by periods of a relaxation in its defenses, the industrial world led by the U.S., Western Europe, and Japan was making the most contemporary methods of war-making obsolete through their development of civilian or dual-purpose innovative technology.

Added to all of this was the vast panoply of Gorbachev's "non-logical" problems:

- The general confusion that such an attempted renovation would produce on the old system before something new was born.
- The growing cognizance among the Soviet elite of the depth of the problems produced by their seventy-year-old demands on society by an ideology enforced by terror.
- The outbreak of age-old racial, ethnic, and caste differences in the Soviet empire which the failure to produce a Communist social conciousness, "a Soviet man", had left behind.

That is why Gorbachev, himself a creature of the system, has played a totally opportunistic game, moving back and forth across the chessboard in contradictory plays to perpetuate and extend his power. His erratic behavior often has put into question for many observers whether there was a strategy at all. When he failed in his effort to initially work through a Communist Party bureaucracy, recreated in his own image as his predecessors had done, because of the built-in obstruction of the self-aggrandizing bureaucrats, he turned to rebuilding a powerful state apparatus outside the Party. He seemed to be threatening that most sacrosanct of all Communist dogmas, the paramountcy of the Party. And at this writing he has become the most powerful dictator backed by pseudo-constitutional trappings since Stalin, whether he is to exercise that power through the bureaucracy—his most ardent declared enemy of reform—or by a return to Party control now that he has grasped the state organs.

Yet through all these gyrations one formula has been repeated over and over in recent months: For every success in consolidating his personal power, Gorbachev has had to retreat from real economic reform. *Perestroika*, insofar as it means renewing the Soviet economy, is about where it stood five years ago when he initiated the process. If there is even the psychological plus of a new intellectual opening and willingness among some of the population to accept reform, an openness in the media unprecedented in Soviet history, its effects may well be canceled out by the growing exasperation at the shortages and failures and a despair that after so much talk, so little in the ordinary life of Soviet citizens has changed.

If one omits—and it is a very large omission from his perspective—Gorbachev's consolidation of domestic political power, it is only abroad where his tactics appear to have paid off handsomely in strategic gains. He has convinced a significant portion of the leadership of the North Atlantic Treaty Organization alliance that he does indeed want to end the forty-five years of post–World War II confrontation. NATO's will to continue to sacrifice and to cooperate for a common defense is being deeply eroded. The rationale may be that the Soviets have finally learned that they can no longer disproportionately devote their resources and energies to an aggressive military machine and are scaling it down. The beginnings of a Soviet withdrawal in Central Europe are said to be a proof of that, rather than being seen as a tactical withdrawal necessitated by the new kinds of warfare that the new technologies would bring into play.

And from this new attitude, particularly in Europe, but rapidly spreading among American leadership, Gorbachev may yet extract massive aid for his economy. In Central Europe, he apparently is willing to barter German reunification—the trump cards he still holds in his hand despite the near collapse of the East German regime brought on by Gorbachev's own unwillingness to continue to back the Communist hardliners. It would be an exchange for massive economic help from a reunited Germany. I have laid out here the historical and contemporary reasons why this may be forthcoming.

But just as the depth of the economic rot in the Soviet Union after seventy years is only beginning to become clear, the recognition of the cost of resuscitation of the Soviet Zone of Germany is mounting daily. And whether even the incredibly productive West German economy can undertake the rebuilding of East Germany with a concomitant continuation of its crucial role as the major foreign supplier and the high-tech transmission belt from the West for the Soviet economy remains to be seen.

As I write, we are at this very moment at a crucial point in the drama: Gorbachev now has accumulated virtually total political power in the Soviet Union. He has, at least, a benign relationship with his former enemies in the West. Some of his intimates—and his apologists in the West—tell us that only such power would permit a Soviet leader to make the painful decisions necessary to begin the turnaround of the Soviet economy and society. That is a siren song which has been sung by too many twentieth century dictatorships that have ended in disaster. But the test is still to come.

With Marxism in full retreat as an explanation of man's motivations and a blueprint for his dreams and aspirations, nothing could be so farcical as an attempt to explain what is happening today in the Soviet Union simply and only in terms of economic determinism. The profound rebellion of the human spirit in the Marxist-Leninist states—or what is left of them— in Central Europe, and the confusion and disorder in the Soviet Union, give testimony that not only does man not live by bread alone—he cannot earn his bread in the modern world with a system that ignores human values.

Yet, there is a powerful economic argument: For half a millennium, the rulers of Muscovy—first the czars in the European family of nations, and then the Communists in the wider world—have tried to rule over an equal, contemporary, nation-state. An essentially backward country could not sustain such an effort without enormous economic and social distortion. Insofar as the endeavor was successful, it was made by starving the Russian-Soviet peoples in an attempt to export food and raw materials, which were exchanged for more advanced, often the latest, imported technologies, as well as the goods and factories with which to make them. Frequently, this technology was accompanied by foreign managers and engineers, or, in the case of agriculture, by peasant German cultivators themselves, to modernize the economy. Cyclically, however, within a generation, because of basic societal conditions in the country, this industrial plant would again become moribund.

In the current world economy in which rapidly advancing technologies, service industries, and communications play a major role, the industrial societies of the West need neither Soviet food nor raw materials; in fact, the United States and Western Europe can and do ship enormous quantities of subsidized surplus foods at bargain prices to the Soviets. (In the late nineteenth century, Siberian butter was a delicacy enjoyed in the more fashionable houses of Western Europe. In September 1989 the United States sold the Soviet Union $80.9 million worth of surplus butter—subsidized by the American taxpayer at approximately 25 cents a pound.)

The increasingly rapid transformation of technology and its innovations make virtually all raw materials fungible. Within a decade, spun glass filaments have virtually replaced copper wire in new telephone transmission lines; rubber sheets with new waterproof adhesives replace the old copper flashings on roofs; cheaper aluminum increasingly replaces more traditional copper functions, and copper as a commodity has suffered.

The Stalinist system and its residual problems are a monument to what man can do to build great physical enterprises, no matter how fundamentally incorrect the ideology that inspires them, and regardless of the human sacrifice. (Jawaharlal Nehru was fond of saying that the bloated state-owned enterprises he created with the help of Soviet planners were the temples—the pyramids of modern India. Alas, how right he was, in indicating their less than maximum economic benefit.) No one has described better than today's Soviet econometric critics the waste and the chaos of the Stalinist economic system—to say nothing of its moral failures and the price extracted from the Soviet people. It is not clear, however, that these same Soviet critics are, as they appear in the West, converts to capitalist methodology and Western humanist morality.

The econometricians among the Western Sovietologists maintain that external trade for the Soviet Union is less than 4 percent of the gross national product—perhaps slightly more if one can believe the new calculations that are being made about the total Soviet economy being much smaller than is usually supposed. Such a quantitative evaluation is ludicrous because few individuals have to go very far in everyday life to realize that measuring only the quantity of the elements of our existence vastly understates their value. (Or, perhaps we should stand Hegel on his head—if a qualitative change is great enough, it is a quantitative change!)

The Soviet system is intrinsically stagnant. The continuing testimony of non-Soviet critics of the system in Central Europe imposed on their countries constantly provides new evidence for that conclusion. There have been almost cyclical subcrises within what, if judged by any West European or American standards, has been the permanent Soviet economic crisis. These crises were obscured by the bizarre political drama of the regime, particularly the nightmare years of Stalin's rule.

The Soviet regime survived these crises principally because of transfers of technology, capital, goods, and management techniques from the West. Although they might have appeared relatively insignificant from the Western point of view, they were critical to the Soviets.

Today the Soviet system faces another of those crises—the most critical in the history of the regime. Having lived on its capital for seventy years, there is little left in the civilian economy to maintain even the minimal living standards inflicted on the population. (A look at the architectural plant of Moscow or Leningrad in which the overwhelming majority of buildings are pre-1914 supports this point; émigré engineers and plant managers relate similar conditions in the manufacturing plant. They have worked in what by Western standards are incredibly antiquated plants, which are still in use.)

Finally, the wall between the two parallel economies in the Stalinist model—the military-space economy that received whatever it needed at any cost to build the strongest military machine in the world, and the civilian economy that got what, if anything, was left—has broken down. For it was a model and not reality.

The reality today is that there are gaping holes in that Chinese wall that divided the two parts of the model, which made it increasingly difficult for the military to keep abreast of a rapidly changing world of technology. After a short period of rebuilding its strength, the West may be dithering in maintaining its military potential in contrast with the Soviets who continue to maximize their military force. Nevertheless, technology is racing along in the civilian sector in the West; much of it involves what the strategists call "dual use," which means that it is applicable to both civilian and military purposes. It promises to leave the Soviet military, to say nothing of its civilian economy, far behind as the two technologies increasingly merge.

I believe that it is that sense of a widening gap—on the military side—which has provided the main motivation for Soviet leadership, headed by Mikhail Gorbachev and his supporters, to try a radical restructuring of their system. The hidden agenda is to persuade the West, once again, to give the Soviet state a transfusion of wealth that may enable the Soviets to continue to play a superpower role, far beyond the means of an essentially third world economy.

The Soviets have been most successful in secreting their military strategies and abilities (imagine a military structure that has a special command for disinformation!). This deception makes it difficult to know if there is evidence for an argument that we have entered a new Russian-Soviet era. And the long history of Soviet duplicity and malevolence toward the outside world does place the burden of proof on those who would argue that fundamental changes have been made in the Soviet Spartan lifestyle from which there is no turning back.

All of this begs important questions. What is the real reason that Gorbachev and the Soviet "new thinkers" have asked for aid from the West? The next question is, of course, not only whether enough of a "transfusion" will be forthcoming from the West, but whether the patient is not too ill to take the blood. And what is the probability that a sick and dying Soviet regime may not try to use its only remaining asset—its military strength—in a last desperate attempt to resuscitate its system?

In those pages, I have tried to lay out why I believe Gorbachev's heritage in the Soviet Union is too poor to accomplish his ends. He will ultimately fail as he has to face still graver options than those which for the most part he has dodged until now: Namely, whether the Soviets would have to abandon its superpower role with its enormous economic drain for military expenditures and imperial ties, and accept the poor, backward, and ravished society and economy for what it is if the living standards of its people are to be improved. That is not a decision that any Soviet leader has been willing to make—or, if you will, that for centuries Russian rulers have been willing to make. Can Gorbachev or his successor do that now? If not, then much of the current euphoria as I write is short-lived, for it would mean that we are not to escape from the toils of history nor is an inevitable march toward more democratic institutions taking place in the Soviet Union. And, with a still powerful if frustrated regime armed with the terrible weaponry of modern war, we are in great danger.

New York City
March 15, 1990

CHAPTER 1

POTEMKIN LIVES

Fooling the West about Aims and Motives

N on-Communist Western intellectuals have deceived themselves about the fundamental nature of the Soviet regime with disastrous consequences in at least four historical periods—immediately after the October Revolution, in the mid-1930s during the days of the Popular Front Against Fascism (a social democratic-left liberal-Communist alliance), at the time of the cobelligerency with the West against the Axis during World War II, and again during the détente of the 1970s. These periods of optimism in the West about the nature of Soviet society, or what was presumed to be its evolving character, have each ended with a sudden, dramatically contradictory act by Moscow—the forced collectivization of the 1930s, the Moscow Trials of supposed spies and "wreckers," the Hitler-Stalin Pact, the betrayals in Central and Eastern Europe of the Yalta agreements for liberation from the Nazis, and, most recently, the invasion of Afghanistan. (Remember the incredibly naive statement of President Jimmy Carter, after news of the invasion, that he had learned more about the nature of communism in the last twenty-four hours than in the rest of his life!)

A discussion of the enormously complex background that dictated Western attitudes in each of these rather arbitrary demarcations that I have chosen, admittedly would necessitate a series of other books.[1] Briefly stated, however, the initial revolution by social democrats and Russian

European-style liberals, which was followed by their Bolshevik successors in imperial Russia, found many non-Socialist Western sympathizers, among them someone as prominent as President Woodrow Wilson of the United States. Wilson, like many Western intellectuals, had long considered the imperial Russian regime the quintessential reactionary influence on the world scene. He not only welcomed its overthrow but also sought to prevent a conservative alliance that would destroy it.

Again in the 1930s, the growing menace of Hitler's Germany, the promise of a new era with the promulgation of the ultraliberal 1937 (Stalin) Soviet Constitution (ironically, announced virtually as the Show Trials began) convinced intellectuals in Europe and America, particularly those left-of-center, that common cause could be made with the Soviets against the growing Nazi-Fascist menace. An interview with Stalin by H.G. Wells, the noted 1930s British historian and novelist and one of the most prescient of pre-World War II writers and thinkers, demonstrates the incredible mental gymnastics that permitted Western rationalizations of the terror regime in the Soviet Union. Wells said after the interview: "I have never met a man (Stalin) more candid, fair, and honest . . . No one is afraid of him and everybody trusts him." "Good Old Uncle Joe" was not the bitter, sarcastic slogan that it became later in the Cold War. During World War II, the American public and its leaders, including the clever and often cynical politician President Franklin Delano Roosevelt, persuaded themselves that Stalin and the Soviet totalitarian system could be manipulated for Western benefit. No one summed up the disappointments of another period of self-deception, Richard Nixon's détente in the 1970s, so well as Henry A. Kissinger, its principal author:

> Under the doctrine of assured destruction, nuclear war became not a military problem but one of engineering. It depended on the theoretical calculations of the amount of economic and industrial damage that one needed to inflict on the other side . . . It was a general theory that suffered two drawbacks: One was that the Soviets did not believe it, and the other is that we have not yet bred a race of supermen that can implement it. While we were building assured destruction capabilities, the Soviet Union was building forces for traditional military missions capable of destroying the military forces of the United States.

Historical analogies are odious, we are told by some historiographers. But it is less than idle speculation that we should use this past experience as a guide in examining the dilemma presented by the current drama in the Soviet Union. Certainly, we are entering an entirely new period in Soviet—and Russian—history. And, perhaps, so much of the past cultural overburden will be shed that the regime and the culture will be transformed into a willing and capable partner for world peace and prosperity.

Certainly, some spectacular unprecedented events are taking place. A young and dynamic leadership has assumed command. A new openness has gripped the Soviet media. Unprecedented criticism of the past has appeared.[2] Soviet President and Communist Party Chief Mikhail Gorbachev has not only promised a basically new approach, "a second revolution," to many problems explicit and implicit in seventy years of Soviet history, but also has advertised an economic crisis of catastrophic dimensions. He has repeatedly identified public lethargy (and demoralization because of past Communist policies and failures) as the embittered opposition to be overcome. That is very far from the traditional Marxist-Leninist denunciation of "class enemies" as the source of all political and economic woes for the regime.

Foreigners and foreign cooperation have been welcomed into the Soviet Union as at no time since World War II—perhaps not since the New Economic Policy (NEP) era of the early 1920s. Then, of course, Soviet leader V.I. Lenin endorsed a temporary return to capitalism and welcomed foreign investors to save the regime and the post-civil war economy. Today Soviet spokesmen have admitted their backwardness in cultural and political, as well as economic, fields and called on the West for a mutually beneficial program to improve their benighted society. Most important of all, Gorbachev has initiated a new period of détente with the West, and has made unilateral concessions in arms negotiations that have been enthusiastically accepted in the West, particularly in Western Europe.

To many in the West, what Gorbachev and his followers call "new thinking" is the fulfillment of a perennial Western dream among left-of-center and even conservative intellectuals that the Bolshevik regime, at long last, might "mature," moderate its revolutionary aims and institutions, and become a genuinely peaceful and cooperative partner in the world community. For these observers, and they range from Russian historian and diplomat George F. Kennan[3] to journalists like the economics columnist Hobart Rowen of *The Washington Post*,[4] the message for the West is that it must "help" Gorbachev in his excruciatingly difficult task of reforming Soviet society. Not to do so, we are told, could result in

Gorbachev's failure, the collapse of his "revolution from above,"[5] and a consequent return to belligerence toward the outside world.

One U.S. organization, specializing in looking at Central European and Soviet affairs, presents the case for an activist policy toward Gorbachev:

> Viewed historically, current Soviet attitudes toward foreign affairs, which suggest a more realistic Soviet adaptation to the international environment, may be interpreted as confirmation of a patient Western policy combining military strength and political flexibility. Ironically, many of the contemporary Soviet statements on "mutual security" and "interdependence" echo prevailing Western views of the early 1970s. In response to a series of aggressive projections of political military power by the USSR in the mid- to late-1970s, culminating in the invasion of Afghanistan, the West, and especially the US, quickly shed this rhetoric, downplaying arms control and collaborative security approaches. In certain ways, the West remains transfixed by the image of Soviet power that developed during the late 1970s, while the Soviets themselves are adopting approaches comparable to those widespread in the West in the early 1970s. To break this cycle, both must adapt creatively to the break that the Gorbachev leadership is making with important aspects of the Soviet past.[6]

Yet, it is important to know that the authors and a great majority of the signatories of the "Report" are long-term advocates of a softer line toward Moscow, and for years fought the very program of "combining military strength and political flexibility" they now endorse retroactively.

> A "wait and see" attitude by the West would consciously forfeit opportunities to encourage Soviet adaptation to international conditions . . . a Western failure to respond creatively to the opportunities offered by the new directions in Soviet policy would indicate indifference as to the fate of Gorbachev's policy . . . The West should explore every possibility—consistent with its own interest—to engage Soviet leadership in the effort to improve East-West relations. . . .[7]

If, indeed, this dilemma exists—and it is clear that there is increasing pressure on Western and U.S. leadership to accept this analysis—how does Western leadership go about examining the situation in the Soviet Union with its constant avalanche of press reports and speculations? Is the fundamental nature of the Soviet regime changed? Is there no turning back, as we are often told by Western expert and newsman alike, even by some genuine Soviet opponents of the regime, no way that tried and true tools of traditional Soviet totalitarianism can be reinstituted? Or is history repeating itself? May these not be like previous "reforms" that turned out, in the end, to be relatively minor adjustments of the Soviet tyranny and its threat to world peace?[7]

Or, worse still, may not a genuine attempt at reform be turned back—as has so often happened in Russian history—by the magnitude and seeming impossibility of the task? Is it not possible that Soviet repression, using the latest techniques, may move to a new plateau of sophistication in dealing with dissent? Could Moscow not be repeating the patterns of the 1930s when it developed the techniques of totalitarianism, never seen before in their sophistication, that were borrowed by the Nazis and ended in the intimidation of the German people, the death camps, and the other horrors of our age?

If we are to examine these critical issues for the West, then we must shelve our completely explicable "hopes" and examine the realities of the current situation insofar as that is possible. All of our speculations basically can be reduced to three categories.

• Who is Gorbachev, who are his supporters, and what can we deduce about his motivations? Given the history of the still highly centralized power structure in the Soviet Union, the personality and motivations of the leader and his clique are paramount.

• What are Gorbachev's possibilities of success given these aims? That is, after defining the nature of *perestroika*, we must examine the odds of Gorbachev's achieving a "revolutionary" readjustment of Soviet society—one that would benefit the West.

• Finally, and by far the most difficult to prognosticate, if Gorbachev were to "fail," what are the likely Soviet options and their consequences for the West? Failure, of course, would have to be defined in Soviet, not Western, terms; hence, we have completed the circle, back to the leadership's motivations as well as Gorbachev's actions.

There is a further exercise that any such analysis requires. It is necessary to invoke two basic sets of historical memories if we are to place the Soviet events of the moment in perspective. The most obvious, perhaps, but the one most often forgotten in the enthusiastic and optimistic view of present events, is the very nature of the Soviet regime in the past, peculiar to it as to none other. John Dziak has, perhaps, put it best—simply and concisely—when he calls the Soviet regime "the counterintelligence state."[8] The Communists, building on czarist traditions, have devoted more time, energy, and resources than any other regime in history to presenting a false image of reality to both their own people and the outside world. There is little evidence that the mechanism and experience in deception constructed over the past sixty years, again so well described by Dziak, has been destroyed, and it has yet to be determined how far its potential power has been eroded.

It perhaps took an artist in the monumental Russian tradition like Solzhenitsyn to dramatize the history of the Soviet horrors and make them common currency in the West, to once and for all end the flirtation of Western intellectuals with the grotesque myth of the "progressive" nature of the Soviet regime.[9] But it is important to remind ourselves—it is often forgotten even by many anti-Communists over the years and often virtually unknown to younger, less knowledgeable non-Communists— that the detailed transgressions against humanity of the Soviet regime were recorded in a vast literature even as they were happening. In the 1930s and 1940s, an international group including such names as Eugene Lyons, Isaac Don Levine, Victor Serge, Max Eastman, Arthur Koestler, and dozens of others in the West (often at great cost to their reputations among their fellow intellectuals and writers), and *samizdat* (underground) writers in the East (often at the risk of their very lives), exposed the real conditions inside that vast prison called the Soviet Union.

Most of the current historical "revelations" of the Soviet press add little to that body of fact and opinion. In fact, we have the travesty of the officially sanctioned Soviet "dissident" press often borrowing wholesale from such writings. And we have the testament of defectors and émigrés that the Soviet people, themselves, always believed far less of the official history than might be imagined by those outside.

I hasten to add that this is not, of course, to assign everything that is said or is reported from the Soviet Union to conspiracy or disinformation. Nor is it intended to minimize the obvious enormous confusion in all aspects of Soviet society today, because this confusion is likely to increase whatever the direction of developments. Nor can one doubt the sincerity of millions of Soviet citizens who would like to build and enjoy a new, free, and prosperous society modeled on the West.

It is a fact, however, that Gorbachev and his ruling group spring from the heart of "the state security organs." And we must assume that it expresses that ruling clique's most sophisticated view of the inadequacies of the Soviet system at the moment they defend many of its basic premises. It is not paranoia, then, nor a heightened sense of the conspiratorial in modern international relations to attribute to the category of disinformation and manipulation reported events, published or personally presented analysis, or the public persona of Soviet officials that is pleasing to the West.

But what about *glasnost*, the new era of openness and ostensibly unfettered criticism in the Soviet media and by Soviet spokesmen, both inside and outside the Communist Party and the government apparatus? Any explanation must start with the word, *glasnost*, and consider the difficulty of translating Russian words and concepts into politically meaningful modern American language. "The difference between Russia and America is simple and dramatic," says Richard Lourie, an American translator of Russian writing.[10]

> For us, history is a subject, a black-and-white newsreel; for them [the Soviets] it is a tank on their street, a search of their apartments by strangers with power. In the Soviet Union nearly every life has been touched directly, branded, by the great historical spasms of revolution, war and terror. . . . The only luxuries in Russia are emotional. In the zone of feelings that exists apart from the state and history, the Russians have developed a cult of spontaneity and sincerity. . . . Today, even more than *glasnost* or *perestroika*, the operative word is *normalno*, meaning "normal, regular," and is the usual answer to "How are things?" It is a wistful, ironic word, containing all the pain that came before and all the hope of what might yet come to pass, the great dream of the present, a "normal" society.

The word, *glasnost*, is an old word in Russian. Walter Laqueur points out that it figured prominently in the writings of Russian nineteenth century reformers, and was used extensively by Lenin, and even Stalin. Its meaning is apparently difficult to render easily in English. Laqueur says:

> The reason is that *glasnost* is not exactly freedom of speech, or the kind of cultural or political freedom known in the West, but a specially Russian phenomenon: the attempt to combine a non-democratic or anti-democratic mode of government with a certain degree of cultural freedom, with accountability (especially on the lower levels of the administration) and with "transparency." Although it can be and has been interpreted as a step toward

democracy, in itself it is not the same thing as democracy; if there were democratic freedoms there would be no need for *glasnost* as a discrete element in the political system.[11]

The French Soviet scholar Françoise Thom writes that:

At the beginning *glasnost* had one objective: To make the Soviets more credible both internally and externally by reducing the difference in what was said officially and what everyone was able to perceive in daily life. The Soviet ideologues have finally become aware that the situation was shameful for them: No one in the Soviet Union had any confidence in the media, foreign radio transmissions and rumors were the principal sources of information. It was necessary to do something radical about it. *Glasnost* was installed internally in the fastest way possible because there a Soviet [citizen] had the elements for a comparison, he could see the lie. Regarding representations to the West, there was no reason to worry, because the man in the street did not have the means to verify the allegations in the media. That is why until now the Gorbachevian "franchise" concerns the problems of Soviet society. The descriptions of the West remain caricatures in the best traditional Communist fashion. Thus one could read in the press recently that the rights of man are not respected in Sweden, that husbands in the West beat their wives, that the Americans live in terror of the FBI and they build concentration camps, that sorcery and black magic are practiced in France and the United States. They continue the daily refrain about drugs and racism in the West, police persecution against thousands of pacifists and "dissidents": in the cliches about "the silver world" and attacks against the American "military-industrial complex," and most recently, careful elaborations about all the Western nuclear plant accidents which give the impression that there is at least one Chernobyl a week in the United States or in Europe. Does that mean that nothing has changed in the presentation of the Western world [in the Soviet media]? It is necessary, in their own words, "to create an ideological immunity to the effects of hostile propaganda." One of the theoreticians of *perestroika*, A. Iacovlev, openly says: "The world of today has become smaller from the point of view of communications, and always more interdependent. To believe that it is possible to create, in this world, a niche or a corner cut off from external influences and to hold on to it passively, is not only to fall into an illusion, but it is also to condemn oneself to defeat. We must be active ourselves, to take offensive positions which guarantee us not only an absolute priority in our mission but reinforce systematically our influence in the outside world."[12]

The French scholar points out that the new Soviet propaganda line is simply to use techniques and stratagems to control the general line of discussion. She quotes the well-known Soviet propagandist Vladimir Pozner, a frequent Soviet "newsman" invited to appear on American discussion programs:

To obliterate or explain badly the mechanism of some of their [Western] failures—and there are some—we have to create skepticism [in the minds of our] listeners. . . . The only place where we often fall down is the slowness of our reactions. If we are the first to release the news, they [in the West] comment on it in their manner. But it is sufficient to get ahead of the West in order to disarm them immediately. Until now the General Secretary of our Central Committee speaks of restructuring, that means to me a return to Leninist principles of propaganda and agitation.[13]

That means, Thom says, that, for example:

Glasnost has as its goal in the West to channel Russian nationalism in the direction desired by the Party. That's why [for example] when Japanese explain their territorial complaints [against the Soviet Union] in a TV relay program, this kind of program is all the better for Soviet propaganda.[14]

Perhaps the editors of *Pravda* said it best in an editorial:

It is clear that *Pravda* cannot transform itself into a harvester of ethnographic information, nor a dry recreation of events. We work in a journal of the Party and we are proud that our essential work has been and remains propaganda for the international politics of the Communist Party of the USSR and of the Soviet state.[15]

The basic problem for an effective intellectual liberalization of the Soviet Union is the unique role of the Communist Party, enshrined in all the constitutions, laws, propaganda, fiction, ideological writing, and politics of the country for almost the entire existence of the regime. Vladimir Fadeev, editor of a Leningrad literary magazine (literary magazines have always been at the forefront of political discussions and the setting of new propaganda lines), came close to delineating it in early 1989.

Fadeev stops short of calling for a multiparty system, but he indicts the monopoly of power of the Communist Party and accuses its members and leadership of defeating Gorbachev's efforts at economic reform. Further-more, he says:

> The party has nothing at all to counterbalance a cult of personality like that of Stalin. The people cannot interfere. We are thinking now of Brezhnev as awful, but ten years ago, everyone was quoting him, too. Couldn't we make those mistakes again? There is still no guarantee that another person like that won't appear on the horizon.[16]

The contradiction, of course, is that while he writes against the opponents of Gorbachev and Gorbachev's program, he fears that a cult of personality may grow around Gorbachev that will threaten freedom again.

What is missing, perhaps, more than anything else in the Soviet scene that would begin to produce what its would-be reformers call "a normal society" is the rule of law. During the Stalin period, there were two systems of legality. One, purely theoretical and totally illusory, was the so-called 1937 Stalin Constitution that promised Soviet citizens rights similar to legal institutions in the West. It was one of the great ironies of the time that almost coincidentally with its annunciation, Stalin's NKVD secret police were herding hundreds of thousands of citizens into concentration camps, usually on trumped-up accusations and often with scant, if any, administrative hearing, much less a court procedure. The show trials of the famous old Bolsheviks were fabricated as the Soviet press is now busy revealing. The reason that the participants were willing to go along involves a complex weave of intimidation, drugs, threats to family and friends, and—for the Westerner—that most mysterious logic, the old revolutionary's loyalty to "the revolution" even when it was committing criminal offenses against him personally. Arthur Koestler, himself once a true believer, perhaps describes it best in his novel *Darkness at Noon*.

The KGB has now been attacked publicly in the Council of the People's Deputies, which is the new Soviet imitation of Western parliaments, and its secrecy has been decried even by some of its own spokesmen. Given the history of its crimes, however, and the history of Russian and Soviet secret police high intrigue for at least two centuries, establishing a rule of law would, under the best conditions, be difficult. Western societies with long histories of a legal tradition built on freedom know how fragile legality is—even in a free system with those traditions.

Are the Gorbachev "reformers" actually seeking such a rule of law? It bodes ill that the man chosen by Gorbachev to reform the Soviet penal system is Aleksandr Sukharev. Sukharev, despite the accolades he has received in *The New York Times, Newsweek*, and elsewhere in the Western press for his liberal pronouncements on the formulation of new Soviet law, is a traditional Stalinist *apparatchik*. As minister of justice for the Russian Federated Republic and deputy justice minister for the USSR, he sent a number of the most prominent dissidents, including Iurii Orlov, Anatolii Koriagin, and Natan Sharansky, to the *gulag*. He led the Association of Soviet Lawyers who justified the banishment and harassment of Andrei Sakharov. And he had the temerity to deny to *New Times* in April 1987 that the concept of political prisoner had ever existed in the country. An American attorney, who follows the struggle for law in the Soviet Union, writes:

> Legal reform requires legal accountability for those who helped send Mr. Sakharov to Gorki [internal exile] and Mr. Sharanksy to the *gulag*. Failing to distinguish between reformers and those who persecuted them makes that impossible—preserving neo-stalinist and neutralizing pressure for change, keeping the Soviet Union closed and the world less safe.[17]

On April 19, 1989, the front page of *Pravda* printed a text of a decree signed by Gorbachev amending Soviet law in relation to "state crimes." Although the law may decrease penalties in some instances for "anti-state activities," which has been a catchall to indict political dissenters, the new law is so vague and so comprehensive that it permits the regime a free hand. Article 11 (1) Insulting or Defaming State Organs and Public Organizations says: "The public insulting or defamation of the USSR supreme organs of state power and government . . . or officials appointed, elected, or approved in offices of the USSR Congress of People's Deputies or the USSR Supreme Soviet, or public organizations . . . is punishable by deprivation of freedom for a period of up to three years." Article 70 could bring a sentence of ten years for "public calls for the overthrow of the Soviet state and social system for its change . . . involving the use of material assets or technical means from . . . organizations" overseas. The article can be used against people who use "technical equipment . . . for mass duplication," receiving terms up to seven years.[18] Bohdan Horyn, a leading member of the Ukrainian Helsinki Union, stated that "the publication of this decree on April 11, 1989, signifies a total reversal to antidemocratic methods in our political and social life. . . . The West has closed its eyes to this unlawful highhandedness. . . ."[19]

Another foreign correspondent in Moscow defines the complexity of the bureaucratic problem:

Legal reformers and scholars complain that the model legislation they prepare disappears quickly into a mysterious bureaucratic maze, to be mutilated by anonymous party officials opposed to *glasnost* and *perestroika*. It is doubtful that such a secretive unaccountable legislative process will ultimately generate laws that truly foster and safeguard human rights. Evidence that this process fails to protect basic rights can be found in two decrees regulating public demonstrations, ratified by the Supreme Soviet in the fall [1988] . . . These laws have been used repeatedly to prohibit and punish public demonstrations by unofficial groups, even if the state purposes are not political. . . . Equally troublesome is another law that regulates the behavior of the Ministry of Internal Affairs troops (special police often referred to as the militia). Among other things, the law empowers the militia to "gain entry to residential buildings and the premises of enterprises, organizations and institutions in pursuit of persons suspected of having committed a crime." . . . The militia are provided broad, unchecked power to engaged in unreasonable searches and seizures for an indefinitely long period after an alleged crime is committed, and seriously threatening the Soviet constitutional right to inviolability of the home.[20]

Perhaps it is all best summed up by an American reporter talking with some young Soviets, serving as apprentice lawyers in an exchange program in the United States:

Hanging ominously over the interns on their visit here, however, is the crushing weight of Russian history in this century—the terrors, and wars and repressions Irina Savelyeva speaks of with chilling detachment as "the river of blood." Lenin may have been the first Soviet lawyer, but no one can number the thousands who vanished with their clients in the Stalinist purges, and there are times when the rule of law in the Soviet Union seems as distant as the moon. "In our country now you never know what will happen next month," says Mikhail Barschevsky. "I think it is very hard to make these changes."[21]

The realization of how very different is the nature of Soviet society from anything in the West comes to a visitor slowly, even in the exotic

environs of Moscow. One lovely May evening in 1988, two news correspondent companions and I, after spending a good part of the afternoon
obtaining directions with harried and secretive telephone calls, set off with
an address to find what had been touted to us as a "dissidents' seminar."
With great difficulty, we finally found the address. More accurately, a taxi
driver, whom we had hailed in the street, found it (with the help of a few
packages of American cigarettes held up to capture his attention. One
learns quickly that although the taxi driver is required to report comings
and goings of foreigners to the KGB, if one hails a cab rather than take
one of those waiting in front of the hotel, he likely will not be a full-time
informer).

We entered the Khrushchev era apartment house—what Muscovites call
"instant slums"—and smelled the strong stench of rotting potatoes coming from the basement. We mounted two flights of stairs into a small
apartment where the two rooms were packed with what we learned later
were attendees from seven Russian cities as well as Moscow. In one room,
with a small Sony public address system going so those in the second
room and in the hallway could hear, we listened to the speakers deliver
their "papers" and the discussions that followed each one. The seminar
was chaired by two well-known Soviet academics—a man and a woman—
both of whom had served sentences in the *gulag* for their activities.

The interpreter, who was quickly provided for me and my friends, was
a Russian priest in full Orthodox regalia. As the evening wore on, we
heard papers on unemployment and the lack of government services for
the handicapped (delivered by a paraplegic who ambulated on a kind of
skateboard contraption), and a paper on the homeless, who have a
particular problem because they are sent to special prisons in the *gulag*
and then cannot get an internal passport issued by local authorities. As
the speakers droned on in the overheated room, and the discussion became
quite argumentative on fine points of econometric calculations, I turned
to the priest and began another conversation. He gave me his name, a
well-known Jewish family name, and I immediately began to speculate on
what his real functions were in this group. He said that he was an ethnic
Jew, showed me his internal Soviet passport that still carried that designa-
tion, and explained that he had once been a professor at a large Russian
university. When he had converted to Orthodoxy (his son, incidentally,
was a refusenik trying to get permission to emigrate to Israel), he was
given a church near Moscow. Because of his association with the dissi-

dents, however, he had been dismissed from his parish by the hierarchy, and now he and his wife were living off the proceeds of the sale of an extensive library he had had as a professor. Still suspicious that a Jew and an Orthodox priest (in full regalia) would be at a dissidents' meeting, I said to the priest, "Father, you know we hear in the West that the Russian Church is heavily infiltrated by the KGB. . . ." The priest replied, "Oh, do you want to hear about that?" and proceeded to give a twenty-minute lecture to me and my colleagues on KGB infiltration of the church. His estimate, he said, is that at least 40 percent of the priests are either KGB agents or informers. "We know them," he said, "and we speak frankly to each other. You must not misunderstand; most of them believe in God and are Christians. They say unless they cooperate with the security organs, the Church will be destroyed, and Christ's mission will not be done in Mother Russia. I tell them that they cannot serve two masters." The priest had told me that he was subject to repeated questioning sessions, that the KGB went over his biographical material again and again. "They want to know everything; they function on the assumption that they may at some time or other use every bit of information," he said. When the seminar was over, I approached one of the chairmen who had arranged for us to come. He was harassed, a little frantic, saying, "We must clear this place immediately. We must go." As we moved out of the apartment, I asked what would be the result of the seminar. He said that there had been a high official of the KGB attending this evening. "He is sympathetic to us," he said, "and promises to try to have the papers published."

My principle conclusion from the events of this bizarre evening is that the depth of the penetration of the seventy-year-old internal espionage of the Communists, which, of course, built on the czarist secret police, is almost incomprehensible to foreigners. It seems unlikely that any facet, certainly no facet of educated Soviet life, has been exempt, nor is it possible for a Soviet professional, whatever his politics, not to have some relationship to the security organs, either as a victim, a collaborator, or somewhere in between. The very multiplicity of the security forces is a key. Besides the KGB, there is the *Rabkrin*, the Workers' and Peasants' Inspectorate or People's Control, descended from an organization created by Lenin to control the Bolshevik elite; the Ministry of Interior; the Central Organ of the Press, the OBHSS, or Socialist Fraud Squad; and the *GRU*, or the Chief Intelligence Directorate of the General Staff of the

Soviet Army, known as the Unit 44388 (which conducts most of the industrial espionage abroad). Police surveillance and intervention in the lives of the Soviet citizen took on such enormous importance that it is impossible for someone from the outside to comprehend it.

> In the beginning, in order to rule, Lenin divided everything in Russia that was capable of being divided, and ever since the Communists have continued faithfully to carry out the instructions of the great founder of the first proletarian state. . . . In shape and form, Soviet power is everywhere duplicated, from the planning of rocket launchings into space to the organization for burial of Soviet citizens, from the management of diplomatic missions abroad to lunatic asylums. . . .[22]

Andrei Sinyavsky, exiled from the Soviet Union in 1974 after he became a cause célèbre for Western intellectuals, speaks sarcastically in the novel *Good Night* of foreigners who master Russian. He asks how they could ever truly grasp the meaning of "being tailed," "denunciations," and "prisons." Equally important, it is difficult for an American or a West European to appreciate the magnitude of the deception that official Soviet policy has conducted during the past seventy years in every aspect of Soviet life.

For example, Soviet Chief Cartographer Viktor R. Iashchenko has admitted that since Stalin's time, Soviet maps have distorted everything purposely from the location of cities to street maps of Moscow. Iashchenko said this was done on the orders of the secret police when mapmaking was put under the control of the NKVD (the predecessor of the KGB). "Roads and cities were moved. City districts were tilted. Streets and houses were incorrectly indicated. For example, on a tourist map of Moscow, only the contours of the capital are accurate."[23] Iashchenko's admission and his promise to produce new and correct maps is a part of the campaign. But that campaign is not without its contradictions—so great that one must still ask how sincere and long lasting such professions of "the new thinking" really are. For example, on September 29, 1989, Moscow's Lenin Library announced it was opening most of its collection of restricted works, including the writings of proscribed early Bolsheviks such as Leon Trotsky and Nikolai Bukharin, czarist officials and generals, and so forth. Yet, in August, libraries in some Soviet cities were being ordered to remove from their shelves the writings of former Communist

Party Chairmen Leonid Brezhnev and Konstantin Chernenko, Viktor Grishin, longtime party ideologue, and other recent Soviet leaders. "Librarians were reportedly told to clear from the shelves the documents of the four Communist Party congresses over which Brezhnev presided, and to tell readers who inquired that the volumes had been checked out."[24] The whole "cleansing" had taken on such proportions that during the summer of 1988, secondary schools in the Soviet Union had to cancel examinations in history because they had studied from books which the Gorbachev regime considered false, particularly in their treatment of Brezhnev.

Nor has the KGB intrigue and false information stopped. During the *glasnost* years, the Kremlin started a disinformation campaign in the Third World, initiating it as it has done often in the past with *Blitz*, which is the Soviet-line weekly in Bombay. The accusation was that the disease AIDS was, in fact, a form of American germ warfare that had escaped from experimental test tubes to infect the world. The "evidence," the transmission belts in pro-Soviet media, the personnel in some instances, were the same as those that had been used thirty-five years earlier to spread the canard that the United States had waged germ warfare in the Korean War. In the fall of 1988, a Commission for International Cooperation in Humanitarian Problems and Human Rights appeared on the Soviet and world scene.

> One Radio Liberty researcher maintained that the Commission was the "brainchild" of the CPSU's Propaganda Department. He noted that Andrei Grachev, then head of the international information subdepartment in the CPSU (Communist Party of the Soviet Union) Propaganda Department, and now deputy chief of the CPSU International Department, addressed the Commission's constituent session. In the year after its creation, the Burlatskii Commission received positive attention from the Soviet press. It also was able to obtain official sanction to send delegates to the Netherlands and Vienna, which met with Western government officials and human rights groups."[25]

The whole structure of Soviet cultural life has been built up on a network of these controls and suppression and propaganda organizations. Whether the Gorbachev regime would publish the works of Solzhenitsyn, and which ones, writing originally smuggled to the West, illustrates the depth of the intrigue and confusion. Demands for Solzhenitsyn's works to be published inside the Soviet Union have come from opposite ends of the literary world—from the westernizers and from the Nationalist-Slavo-philes. But some of the same bureaucrats of the official Writers' Union, who decide who can and cannot be published, have reversed themselves several times on Solzhenitsyn. Vitalii Korotich, editor of one of the most sensational of the new sources of criticism, *Ogonyek*, has nevertheless opposed Solzhenitsyn because he says if he were to return to the Soviet Union, he would be a rallying point for the Right in Soviet political life. But, one wonders, what is the real role of Korotich, himself? At a meeting sponsored by the British Foreign Office to discuss *perestroika* in the spring of 1989, I heard Korotich speak to a group of seminar participants. He had come to London ostensibly to report on the situation before a visit from Gorbachev. That day, however, he had spent an hour and a half with Prime Minister Margaret Thatcher, which is a little more than an ordinary journalist's interview, and he obviously was an unofficial advance man for the Soviet leader. He spoke in his usual rat-a-tat-tat stream-of-conscious-ness dialogue that bowls over foreign visitors. (I had earlier visited him in his office in Moscow.) After he had spoken for some time, he was asked—in one of the few interruptions his style permitted—for some autobio-graphical detail. He told us that he had been a surgeon and a poet in his native Ukraine. In the Brezhnev era, he had become the head of the Ukrainian Writers' Union, but had trouble with the censor after having written some pieces in praise of Brezhnev, which he now regretted. He had been removed from the Ukrainian Writers' Union and for nine years he had "lived as a freelance," and then had become editor of *Ogonyek*. As one of my colleagues said at the time, "If you believe that, you believe in the tooth fairy." It has long been considered a given in Western intelligence circles that Soviet newsmen, especially those sent abroad, were either cadre or informants for the KGB. And that seems to apply to the "reformist" journalists, or many of them, especially those closest to Gorbachev.

The tortuous intrigues of the Writers' Union, which is actually a government arm—composed of Communist bureaucrats and largely hack writers—that decides who may or may not be published, are illustrated in its recent attempt to gain respectability through the International PEN. The latter is a legitimate international association of writers in the West that has often been at odds with Soviet censorship and suppression.

Tatiana Tolstaya, a descendant of the Russian nineteenth century writer Leo Tolstoy, and a writer herself, does not believe a real change has taken place:

> The old guard is strong there and why is it so? I think it is connected with the fact that in our country a writer is an over-estimated person, a sort of prophet. It sounds crazy but it existed for centuries in Russia. And so writers, such important personages, are taken into the Central Committee. So many of the secretaries of the Writers' Union are at the same time members of the government. And this old guard is only interested in taking bad writers that will help them to keep their comfortable positions.[26]

According to Miss Tolstaya the Soviet propagandist pulled a coup in 1988 when the Writers' Union organized a Soviet chapter of PEN.

> There were two lists, [Egor] Vinogradov's [a well-known and highly respected critic] list and [Writers' Union First Secretary Vladimir] Karpov's list. Karpov took over Vinogradov's list because he saw it had in it the right people to whitewash the union's black deeds. After all, he is clever enough to know the list can't be all the king's men. So some writers agreed to join, but to join Vinogradov's PEN, not Karpov's. Others didn't know a thing; they just awoke and they were on the PEN list. This is a serious matter in our country, if you fight for someone or raise your voice then you yourself may be in trouble. May be not, may be, but a writer should think twice whether to join PEN, because it can be trouble. So the idea of having a Soviet PEN depends upon who will be in this chapter, and how these people intend to behave. Otherwise it is just to please the West.

But the censorship, the cultural "opportunism," the intrigue in artistic circles, is also a reflection of the general problem of a crippled civilian economy where shortages are manipulated by the Communist bureaucracy. Thane Gustafson writes in a depressing review of how little the new "openness" really means:

> Management of the media in Moscow involves much more than simple censorship and administrative control. It rests on an elaborate system of graduated incentives and rewards that is built into the core of the command economy and the system of one-party rule. Even if Gorbachev abolished

Glavlit [the office of the censor which dates back to Lenin's day] tomorrow, *glasnost* would still not be safe.

The foundation of the system is the manipulation of scarcity. Take paper, for example, the most basic stuff of publishing. The United States produces 15 times more paper than the Soviet Union—a startling measure, incidentally, of the Soviet obsession with heavy industry. Since paper is scarce, it is allocated centrally, and state bureaucracies bargain hard among themselves to get their share, which they then dole out to their own publishing houses. (Thus the Defense Ministry is in the publishing business, as is the nuclear power industry, and of course the Party itself. *Goskomizdat*, the State Committee for Publishing, complains that it is able to get its hands on only about 16 percent of the total supply.) The potential for control in this rationing system is obvious, as are the obstacles to any real liberalization. . . . In short, the power of the state over the media remains intact. Indeed, in some ways it is growing stronger all the time. The most important event of the last 20 years has been the spread of television to virtually every Soviet home. Initially, for lack of relay stations and satellites, the broadcasting system was regionally based and offered a good deal of local programming in local languages. But since the Soviets have developed a modern satellite network and television has become highly centralized, beaming Moscow's perspective—largely in the Russian language—across the entire country.[27]

Gustafson admits that there is some new freedom that arises from the confusion in new legislation and some intrepidness on the part of some Soviet media personnel.

So the tap of media control leaks a bit. Still nobody seriously doubts that the leadership could squeeze *glasnost* shut if it really wanted to. . . . But why should they? Why lose Soviet audiences all over again and abandon the battle for public opinion to the BBC, Radio Liberty, and the Moscow rumor mill? After all, as Laqueur points out, czarist experience offers a precedent: a large degree of cultural freedom coexisted very well with authoritarianism.

Andrei Navrozov, an émigré poet, asks is it any wonder then that for his fellow poet, Irina Ratushinskaia . . .

"Never believe them, never fear them, never ask them for anything" was the key lesson in the poet's schooling, which began with her arrest in 1982 on a charge of "anti-Soviet agitation." Judging by Ratushinskaya's public utterances, it seems she is not about to unlearn that lesson now—as the wishful,

ever wishful West reads a desperate faith into her former captors' every pose, including the pose of clemency that they struck announcing her release in October 1986. That particular pose, she understands, was timed to coincide with the Reykjavík summit. "It's nonsense to talk about limited human rights," Ratushinskaya recently told an interviewer, "it's like limited breath." Indeed, is it not nonsense to talk about human rights at all—as if these were a natural phenomenon, more or less limited under different regional conditions? Would it not be more accurate to say that human rights have never been limited in Soviet Russia—for the simple reason that they have never existed in Soviet Russia? Half-intuitively, half-rationally, Ratushinskaya knows, it seems, that what has existed is a succession of tactical decisions, made by the rulers of totalitarian Russia in their seventy-year effort to deceive and disarm the West. As part of Lenin's New Economic Policy, Stalin's New Constitution, Khrushchev's New Liberalism, and the present-day New Openness have all done their job. What they have done is to give the individual even a tiny grain of genuine freedom—which is, and has always been, the ability to defend himself against tyranny. Like it or not, the totalitarian order is immutable, and only its visible features—from criminal justice to poetry, from Ratushinskaya's arrest to her release—vary to suit its propaganda needs of the moment.[28]

And, again, one wonders about larger cultural values that blunt the effort at reform. The popular poet Evgenii Evtushenko, a survivor in the system although an early anti-Stalinist and an outspoken critic of Soviet official and unofficial anti-Semitism, says:

So much material has now been published in our media unmasking the total war against the people which took place at that [Stalin's] time that even if nine-tenths of it were exaggerated, it should be sufficient to cure all naiveté. But some people prefer to stay blind. They love not Stalin but their blindness.

Often one hears, from unexpected sources, a kind of Russian fatalism that almost celebrates intellectual suffering. It views the incredible excesses of the Soviet regime as a terrible and excruciating experience that somehow must be resolved into the totality of life instead of evoking—as would be the Western reaction—bitterness and a demand for expiation, justice, or even revenge. That is an important aspect of Pasternak's *Dr. Zhivago*, and may explain why it was a relatively early "reappraisal" permitted under *glasnost*, and why the film has been shown in the Soviet Union. After all,

does the film not in the end, say that all that transpired was somehow a great suffering that produced the grand achievements of the regime; the final crescendo of the long search for Lara's daughter finds her amidst the gargantuan background of one of the great Stalinist hydroelectric developments!

Or, consider an anecdote from an article written by two special correspondents for *Izvestia* from Paris, an interview with the exiled poet and Nobel prize winner Joseph Brodsky: " 'Now that your work is gradually getting back to your motherland, don't you somehow have a desire to return?' He stood there pale, tired, polite. 'No . . .' 'But what about No country, or churchyard do I wish to choose . . .' 'Only to the churchyard, perhaps.' 'Suppose that instead of getting a private invitation, you were to be invited by the Writers' Union?' 'Even less reason.' He [Brodsky] paused for a moment. 'It's not a matter of resentment. . . . No. No one's to blame for anything. Neither you nor I, much less We. . . . Blame is not only by the extent of one's direct involvement, but by the standard of each individual's conscience. We, each one of us living in our own time, are all implicated in everything that happens.' "

Sergei Grigoriants, one of the most important Russian dissidents, makes a similar point:

> The movement which began, indeed in Moscow, in the 1960s and early 1970s was a human-rights movement and it was a movement of individuals. It was a movement of Moscow intellectuals, which attracted worldwide attention. It was a wonderful movement, filled with personal self-sacrifice, but it was never a mass movement. . . . Throughout history, as now, there have always been some wonderful Russian individual persons who have led the way, but unfortunately, there is no base for a Russian national democratic mass movement. I hope that this fact will not prove to be tragic; but it's dangerous and alarming.[29]

In the poverty and degradation of Soviet economic life, it may be that cultural values such as freedom of expression are of less interest to a population that has never known them. Laqueur writes: "It is not at all certain how much spontaneous interest there is in glasnost outside a few big cities. It could well be that the majority of the population is far more concerned with better food supplies and housing and in a general improvement of living conditions than in a discussion of Stalin and Stalinism. *Repentance*, Tengiz Abuldze's now famous movie about the Stalin period, has been seen by two million residents of Moscow but by only another six million outside the capital; truly popular Soviet films are watched by eighty million or more."[30]

There is another aspect of *glasnost*, a very practical one, that necessitates that Gorbachev and his supporters in the Soviet elite consider introducing a modicum of veracity into their society. It is simply the proposition that "truth," in at least some areas, is absolutely necessary for modern industrial society to function. In a landmark article on statistical methodology (which obviously goes much further afield), published in 1987[31] in a Soviet publication, whose thesis has been replicated hundreds of times since in other places and in conversations with Westerners, two Russian economists lay out the basic problem: "The distortion of the product volumes has spread to estimates of productivity and capital and from them to all the accounts figures."

In other words, the authors go on to argue, what originally began in the regime as a simple effort to exaggerate production results, has turned into a nightmare of distortion for those who would want to know what is really happening in the economy. "The principle cause of the commodity-supply imbalance (the population has more money than there are necessary goods for sale)"—the long-camouflaged Soviet inflation—is the result of this data falsification, the statisticians continue. They lament the growing mediocrity of economists and economic thinking in the Soviet Union, the usurpation of econometrics to the goals of central planning, and relate in some detail the history of the (losing) battle since the 1920s to maintain honest statistics. They show how all of this, in more recent years, has masked a modest increase in productivity despite claims of enormous gains.

The authors argue that negative trends actually appeared in the economy—not in the mid-1970s as is generally assumed in official Soviet literature and much that has been written in the West—but actually fifteen years earlier. The authors conclude on the pessimistic note that a reconstruction of all statistics is inevitable for without it the "revolutionary" changes in the Soviet economy now being called for by Gorbachev will not be possible. But, realistically, they question whether that will be possible given the multiplicity of distortions. In other words, even with all the goodwill and the effort of those trying to set it right, it may never be possible to know with any accuracy what actually happened in the

Soviet economy. "False figures are become deeply imbedded, and there are sufficiently many people with an interest in preserving them. There are not as yet any completely finished procedures of true accounting."[32]

Unless we are to believe that the overwhelming bulk of new technical information about the Soviet economy now being published inside the country today is total disinformation, much that has been written about the Soviet economy in the past by Western experts now must be greatly revised, if not completely discarded. For decades Western scholars of the Soviet economy used Moscow's statistics, for, obviously, in a police state there were no others. They attempted to make adjustments that they thought necessary to correct the obvious and premeditated distortions. But it is now clear that, in addition to the outrageous propaganda contained in the statistical publications, there was a growing element of confusion on the part of Soviet economists and propagandists themselves who had lost touch with the reality around them.

All this leads one to the inevitable conclusion that, along with other revisionist approaches to the Soviet economy, it is increasingly necessary to question the conventional wisdom that has long maintained the marginality of Soviet dependence on the outside world. I believe that there has been an underestimation of not only the extent to which the Soviets have been dependent on imported Western technology but also of their dependence on Western trade and capital transfers.[33]

With the spread of Soviet-style economics and planning to much of the world outside the old Russian Empire, and its widely documented failures there, it becomes increasingly clear that stagnation was always an innate part of the system. One of the most incisive critics of the Communist system precisely because he once held a very high position in it, the Yugoslav Milovan Djilas, puts it simply and well:

> The Soviet leaders' attempt to reform the system is not inspired by some noble realization that the system is universally poorly regarded abroad, but by strict necessity. They have come to realize what other Communists in Yugoslavia, Poland, Hungary, Czechoslovakia, and China realized earlier— namely that Communism doesn't work. It won't work at the economic level nor at the level of satisfying what are human needs and liberties. Put all these factors side by side with the rapid growth of technological advance of the Western and modern worlds and you cannot help realizing that Communism is a 19th century relic and a prescription for disaster. . . . They (the Soviet

rulers) realize that Stalinism, the 'command economy,' and the conservative bureaucracy have made the system a permanent loser vis-à-vis the variously mixed economies of the world.[34]

What one can now deduce is that the system in the Soviet Union even before World War II produced virtually cyclical economic crises, obscured, perhaps, by the drama of what a modern contemporary person in the West can only call the bizarre political history of the Soviets. It is my contention that this permanent economic crisis that has exploded repeatedly in subcrises, has been remedied if only temporarily, by "transfusions" from the West, to a greater extent than has been realized by foreign Soviet specialists. These transfusions of wealth permitted the Soviet patient to live on beyond the merits of the system itself.

The impact of these "transfusions" has been underestimated by conventional wisdom and understated by most of the scholars for a number of reasons: Again they have been obscured by the drama—and the morbidly romantic aspects of Soviet (and Russian) history, which is a tale of misery and suffering like no other. If Stalin said he was "building socialism in one country," and if the sacrifices of the Soviet people were enormous, and if there were gigantic results (at whatever cost in human suffering), was one not to conclude that it had been done without a significant foreign component?

Through the decades, Soviet propaganda (backed up by Russian nationalism) has steadily droned on in Western ears (echoed by fellow-traveling voices in the West) about the autarchic nature of the Soviet economy, so long and so insistently that even the most thorough scholars (forced to rely on Soviet materials) were mesmerized, to a greater or lesser degree, into accepting it. Furthermore, with no empirical evidence except that generated by "cooked" Soviet statistics and their extrapolations and analysis by economists outside, many of whom had no more than academic knowledge of the Soviet Union, a false econometric picture of the economy[35] was presented that ignored anecdotal evidence of the importance of Western technology, trade, and even finance to the Soviet system.[36]

As Antony Sutton has demonstrated in his monumental record on transfer of technology from the West to the Soviets,[37] the "transfusion" that took place during the NEP in the 1920s undoubtedly saved the Soviet regime from collapse. In the early 1930s, American machine tools shipments—at times 75 percent of U.S. exports—and American engineers and engineering companies were essential in helping Stalin build "socialism in one country." The German-Soviet exchanges during the brief period of the Hitler-Stalin Pact were of great importance to both sides.[38] America's never repaid $13 billion (a minimal estimate in 1939 dollars) in lend-lease and other wartime and postwar deliveries of war and industrial goods to the Soviet Union, while admittedly playing a smaller part in the war, were critical to rebuilding the USSR after World War II. The rape of Central Europe after World War II, particularly Germany's contribution to Soviet aircraft and space developments and Czechoslovakia's contribution as a then world class industrial power, particularly in machine tools, played an enormous role in Soviet growth in the 1950s. And crucial shipments of equipment during détente helped through another crisis, particularly in ground transport.[39] An enormous work awaits the scholars who will have to winnow the new information coming from Moscow.[40] It is certain to produce a revisionist look at the external relations of the Soviet economy just as it already has forced a revision sharply upward of statistics regarding the amounts of Soviet resources going into the military,[41] as so many of the shibboleths of Soviet apologists in the West have melted in the new glare of Moscow's own self-criticism.

The present economic crisis and relevant statistics now appearing in current Soviet literature as a result of Gorbachev's *glasnost* must be seen as only the latest in the long series of these crises. It is certainly the most complex, convoluted, and, perhaps, the most critical crisis for the system since the 1920s. But arranging the necessary Western transfer of resources is still the most urgent priority of Soviet strategy in overcoming it. That is obviously the message of all the twists and turns of Soviet economic criticism and attempts at new policy-making in the years since 1985 when Gorbachev became general secretary of the Communist Party of the USSR. It also explains greatly the contradictions in Kremlin policy and motivates much that is said and done by Gorbachev and other Soviet leaders.

These two guidelines—the continued and fantastically successful use of Soviet traditional arts of deception, and the high priority given desperately needed resource transfers from the West—are the framework by which to judge the true aims of current Soviet policy. The way in which those objectives could be satisfied, the probabilities that they will, and the possible alternatives for Soviet policy if they are not, are the subject of this book. It goes without saying that we are in a world of fast-moving events and difficult speculation. The new Soviet experiment, however, is so important to the rest of the world that we have an obligation to make a leap into the unknown.

CHAPTER 2

SYSTEMIC OR CULTURAL

How Much Communist, How Much Russian?

A Soviet émigré scientist, in the United States for only a few months, tells a familiar story: He worked in the Soviet Union in an electronic research laboratory attached to a Soviet plant that produced computers. One day he and his partners in the laboratory were given an Australian-made American personal computer to examine and study. The émigré scientist avows that when he and his laboratory colleagues broke the machine down, they found nothing that surprised them. They understood the methodology of its designers; they examined the parts and found nothing surprising; and they could take it apart and put it back together again, as well as operate it, of course, without difficulty. As so often in talks with Soviet émigré engineers, scientists, and scholars, one is reminded that the level of theoretical Soviet science is extremely high in many areas, and that, perhaps correctly, Russians often claim that the average Soviet engineer may be better trained than his U.S. counterpart, at least at the theoretical level.

The émigré scientist pointed out, however, that the Soviet plant in which he worked could not duplicate the computer on a production line. They could not reproduce the reliability of the American-Australian product, which is the reason that every Soviet scientist and engineer wants to have a foreign-made personal computer—the reason that he rejects the idea of using a machine made in his own country. Why were the Soviet

27

machines unreliable? There were many reasons. For example, it was impossible to persuade the Soviet engineers who worked in his laboratory to wear the "mittens" over their shoes when they came into the laboratory. Those cloth bags were intended to prevent dirt on the shoes from producing dust and thereby faults in the equipment that they were building—ostensibly in a dust-free environment. The equipment produced was, therefore, unreliable and anyone who needed the services of a personal computer in the Soviet Union would prefer to have a foreign-made one, although it might not be a particularly advanced machine in Western terms—not on the "cutting edge" of state-of-the-art Western technology.

Of course, our émigré scientist said, there was also the simple problem that "people in my country have forgotten how to work." Why should an engineer wipe his feet if he received the same relatively low salary, and, perhaps more important, found little to buy with it, whether or not he worked assiduously, and whether or not he wiped his feet? All he really had to do to collect his salary was turn up at the laboratory for a minimum workday. That problem, my émigré interlocutor said, could be termed "systemic"—a product of the Communist system that for seventy years has destroyed the initiative and the conscientiousness of the Soviet worker. At least that was his analysis. For if that were not true, why was it that Soviet scientists and engineers who emigrate to the United States, Israel, and other parts of the West generally so often succeed quickly in a different work environment?

The question repeatedly presents itself: What part of the current politicoeconomic crisis in the USSR should be ascribed to the effects of that failed system of modern political and economic organization—communism? And what part is the long historical cultural tradition in the lands ruled by Moscow? How much of today's problem is that of a society that has always followed at some distance the physical progress of the West?

Undoubtedly, this is one of those insolvable conundrums of history, and is no less explicable, perhaps, than that old question of why the industrial revolution was born in the West and not in the more advanced societies of Asia. Karl-August Wittfogel, the German anti-Stalinist Marxist historian and philosopher, a longtime acquaintance before his death in 1989, ascribed it to the peculiar nature of the Oriental ecosystems that had to harness vast resources for irrigated agriculture under an authoritarian system.[1] But even so, it has absorbed the energies and intellectual talents of many scholars—and amateurs—in the field of Russian/Soviet history. There is a basic corollary at issue: To what extent has a historical "break" occurred between the pre-Communist society and that which followed the October Revolution that brought the Bolsheviks to power?

In recent years the famous debate between Russian novelist-historian Alexander Solzhenitsyn and Harvard historian Richard Pipes is archetypical. Pipes, a Polish-born American historian, generally maintains that the drive of Soviet imperialism, particularly in the post-World War II period, builds basically on the traditions of Russian colonialism and its aggressive nature in the pre-Soviet centuries. Solzhenitsyn, in many ways a Russian traditionalist, sees the Soviet totalitarian system as a complete break with the Russia of Christianity, humanitarianism, and what so-called Communist reformers today call "a normal society." Therefore, this logic runs, the ambitions of a Communist regime for worldwide conquest are an aberration on the Russian past. Mikhail S. Bernstam of the Hoover Institution writes:

> Intellectuals habitually blame Communist massacres on despotic precedents that they can easily find in the historical records of any country.
> But Solzhenitsyn points out that Russia makes an especially difficult case for these theoreticians of historical continuity. Russia was for all practical purposes a capitalist country, although most peasants did not own their land until the Stolypin agrarian reform of 1906–10. However, most economic and social relations were based on laissez-faire individual transactions, and the general trend of the development of the country was toward universal freedom.[2]

A quite contradictory point of view is presented in a letter criticizing another author. Pipes writes:

> David Moro's enthusiasm for Russian nationalism rests on two misconceptions: The first assumes that Communism is somehow antithetical to Russia's national spirit and traditions. . . . The Communist regime has never achieved anything close to a majority of popular support.[3] But its main base of support in 1917–20 were areas populated by Great Russians, and the Communists managed early to adapt themselves to Russian political culture, with its stress on autocracy, politicized justice, and socioeconomic leveling. For many decades now the Kremlin has extolled Russia's past, imposed the Russian

language on the rest of the population, and insisted on Russian ethnic preponderance in the Party, security, and military establishments. . . . Second, Moro idealizes beyond recognition the spirit of Russian nationalism. Born in the Middle Ages, of a sense of religious exclusiveness, it has always been driven by xenophobia. Patriotism, defined as love of one's country that does not disparage other nations, is confined in the Soviet Union to Westernizing intelligentsia, who are constantly attacked by the "Russianists." The Soviet government tolerates conservative-nationalist associations and publications while it persecutes those of pro-Western and democratic orientation precisely because the former present no threat. In his *Letter to Soviet Leaders*, to which Moro refers, Solzhenitsyn, a leading spokesman of the "Russianists," was quite willing to have the Communist Party stay in power in Russia.[4]

Although this intellectual argument—and so many other subsidiary differing interpretations associated with it that dip deep into the history of the civilization of Eastern Europe—may be academic and abstruse, it reflects basic attitudes that will affect the outcome of the current crisis. That will be true even if it does no more than frame the problems posed in both Mikhail Gorbachev's and the reformers' efforts to remodel the Soviet system. They will have to constantly draw on these arguments in their difficult and often desperate search for a new model for Soviet-Russian society.

It is, therefore, essential for those of us trying to unravel the mysteries of current Soviet political and economic problems to examine, at least superficially, this long debate over Russia's relation to the world and particularly to Western Europe. That relationship into modern times has variously been characterized as that of "a privileged colony."[5] Or, ". . . since Russia lacks the basic potential—educated, that is to say, free men in numbers approaching our [Western] own—it can never catch up on its own. . . ."[6]

Although it soon becomes obvious to the viewer of current Soviet events that this is a debate ultimately without issue—that it is one of those questions that cannot finally be decided—it is equally evident to the most superficial reader of Russia's history that pre-Soviet conditions existed that dictated a quite different development for that society than those that influenced Western Europe. The first, of course, is geography. Nowhere, not in the vastness of midcontinent North America, nor in Australia, nor in the huge Indian subcontinent does one encounter that vast stretch of plain that rises in the east beyond the Urals, themselves less than a major barrier to the winds and migrants, and then stretches into Europe to the Baltic Sea. That vast expanse from time immemorial has seen an incredible ebb and flow of waves of invaders from Central and East Asia and from Scandinavia, sweeping new races and cultures and new sets of overlords into the European areas of the Soviet Union.[7] No wonder that if there is what has been called "the Russian soul"—a peculiarly Russian psyche and worldview—it is often said to be one that abhors and fears societal disorder and chaos more than it is concerned with questions of freedom and personal liberty.

In one of those great "might-have-beens" of history, the origins of what is seen in the West as the Russian state could have led to a development perhaps not so dissimilar to what took place in Western or at least Central Europe. The emergence of the Kievan Rus state in what is today the European Soviet Union (the Ukraine) was a development similar to many that occurred, if much earlier, in Western Europe. Under Norse leadership (Varangarians) but with strong cultural and economic ties to Byzantium in Constantinople—Christianity was adopted shortly before A.D. 1000— Kievan Rus began to establish in the vast Eurasian plain a society akin to others in Europe in the ninth and tenth centuries. There were matrimonial as well as trade ties between the Kievan Rus and the Germans and French, including a Kievan princess who became the mother of Philip I of France. The internal splintering of the kingdom in the next two centuries, however, and its conquest in 1238 by the Mongol Hordes, broke the growing ties with Byzantium and with the West.

The 250 years of the Tatar Yoke over the Russian principalities— although it could be argued that they interfered little in daily Russian life after the conquest—had an enormous impact. There was widespread devastation during the early conquest, depriving the Russian center for centuries of much of their best agricultural land in the south and south-eastern corner of Europe, and pushing the center of Russian culture into the poorer northern areas. This was to accentuate its isolation. The tribute payments to the Mongol overlords impoverished and dislocated the economy, and cultural norms were eroded. (The Mongols sold the grand dukedoms to the highest Russian bidders; perhaps the beginning of the vast corruption that has dominated Russian history into modern times.) The long period of Mongol pressure on the Russian principalities, "no doubt, contributed something to the general harshness of the age and to the burdensome and exacting nature of the centralizing Muscovite state which emerged out of this painful background."[8]

But the Mongol Yoke was only one of the threats to Muscovy on the vast unprotected Eurasian plain. From the West, after A.D. 1000 came the push of Catholic cultures—the Lithuanians (united with Poland for a time) by 1462 had constructed a state that included many of the Russian principalities shattered by the Mongol invasion. Later Swedish and German pressures often denied Moscow access to the Baltic in the fifteenth and sixteenth centuries, limiting any relationship with the great commerce of the Hanseatic League and Western Europe.

These pressures not only resulted in a virulent Russian xenophobia but also in the development of an elaborate defensive theory of the special role of the Russian state and its culture centered around its Orthodox religion vis-à-vis the West. By the nineteenth century this ethos would form the nucleus of the so-called Slavophile movement—a Russian mirror image of German and other romanticism in the West.

> The etymological meaning of "Slavophilism" is "love of Slavs." In Russian historical literature, however, this term has come to be applied in a narrow sense to a group of ideologists belonging to the conservative nobility, whose outlook became formed in the late 1830s in opposition to the trend known as "Westernism." Moreover, Slavophilism denoted in this case not so much a feeling of solidarity with brother Slavs as a cultivation of the native and primarily Slavic elements in the social life and culture of Russia. . . . The central issue of Slavophile ideology was Russia's relationship to Western Europe, which the Slavophiles examined in the light of an all-embracing philosophy of history. . . . The fabric of European civilization, [Petr] Kirevesky argued, was made up of three strands: Christianity, the young barbarian races who destroyed the Roman Empire, and the classical heritage. Russia's exclusion from the Roman heritage was the essential feature distinguishing her from the West. . . . Kirevesky . . . saw ancient Rome as a rationalist civilization that represented "the triumph of naked and pure reason relying on itself alone and recognizing nothing above or outside itself." . . . The juridical rationalism of the Roman state had appeared to hold society together, but it had actually torn apart its organic and unifying bonds. . . . Having inherited this pagan rationalism, Western Europe found its evolution bound to be a constant struggle of mutually antagonistic interests; Russia, on the other hand, had been spared this fatal heritage and was therefore established on purely Christian principles that were in complete harmony with the spirit of the Slavic peasant commune.[9]

The Russian enmity with the West was enhanced in her relations with her smaller—if more advanced—neighbors to the West by their growing fear of Moscow's potential as a major player in European affairs. Repeatedly, the rulers of Poland and the Baltic states appealed to their neighbors in Western Europe to deny Moscow access to their higher technologies and trade possibilities, which they saw as contributing to the Russians' military potential. Yet, a long procession of West Europeans from the sixteenth century on went to Russia at the request of the czars as artisans, entrepreneurs, and traders to build up the primitive Muscovy economy. The dearth of knowledge was reflected in a letter from Ivan IV (the Terrible) to Elizabeth I of England in 1566: "From Italy and England we need master builders, who can construct for us fortresses, bastions, and palaces, also surgeons and apothecaries, also master craftsmen who understand how to prospect for and mine gold and silver." Earlier, however, when Ivan had sent a Saxon as his agent to recruit specialists, the 120 doctors, teachers, artists, and technicians who accepted his invitation were caught by the authorities of the Hanseatic League and the Livonian Order of Knights and prohibited from traveling to Moscow.

Still, others did come at the czars' invitations. By the middle of the seventeenth century, there were so many foreigners living in Moscow that they were forced into "a New Foreign Quarter." One historian has estimated that two-thirds of the czar's servitors at the end of the seventeenth century were of foreign extraction. By 1665 this enclave for the foreigners, a model little village along Western European contemporary standards, constituted one-fifth of the entire area of Moscow. It represented a veritable microcosm of Western Europe, including a German school, four Protestant churches, European-style mansions and broad streets—the only paved streets in the Russian capital—with over two hundred households. Their segregation was as much a function of the Russian xenophobia as an attempt to provide the Westerners with accommodations that would keep them in Moscow. Their treatment was a function of the ambivalence of the Kremlin toward foreigners that has dogged Russian society down to our day. The Russians wanted Dutch and Swedish ironmasters to teach advanced skills to apprentices, but they did not want foreigners to infect Russians with ideas alien to the Russian tradition. Even in the earlier Kievan Rus, the Orthodox bishops had warned the Russians against contamination from the Catholic West, prescribing ablutions for those who ate or otherwise associated with the Westerners.

As the new Russian state expanded around Muscovy, however, it wanted the best of both worlds—to advance materially with the help of the West, but to keep its cultural and "moral" distance from the Europeans. The Russian government turned to foreign merchants for building local factories because they had pressing need for industrial products—mainly for military purposes—but these transplants were an entirely different development from the industrialization that was beginning to take place as a result of indigenous economic forces in the West.[10] "Literally, the Russian state hoped to use foreigners to bridge the technological gap between Russia and the West in order to consolidate and perpetuate—by maintaining military might and political independence—major elements of the cultural chasm existing between the two civilizations."[11]

The culmination of the early attempts to import Western technologies to Russia was the celebrated efforts of Peter the Great (1672–1725). The amazing career of this Russian ruler is one of the romantic legends of all modern history—appearing to the outside world, as he did to his own people at the time, as either a superhero or the Antichrist. His so-called Grand Embassy of 250 courtiers that traveled through Europe is legendary. In March 1697, with Peter ostensibly traveling incognito at its head, it set out on an extended visit to the Baltic provinces and then to Western Europe and the Hapsburg Empire. It was the culmination of his curiosity about the West that developed when he was a child playing in the New Foreign Quarter. Peter set out to learn as much as he could from the West about navigation and other technical skills. During parts of his trip, he pretended to be a commoner in an attempt to more specifically understand Western processes like boatbuilding. He had to end his trip after eighteen months to return to Moscow to stem a rebellion of the *strl'tsy*—the traditional Russian military. The rebellion was partly a result of the growing number of foreigners whom he had recruited for his military in an attempt to modernize the army and build the first Russian navy. Peter, and his immediate predecessors:

> . . . were interested in using foreign officers to improve the fighting quality of the armies, but the *strl'tsy*, professional elements of the army who enjoyed good pay and extensive peacetime trade and artisan privileges, justifiably saw this "modernization" as a threat to their established position. So they

emerged in the 17th century as a reactionary element opposed not only to the army reform but also to any form of Westernization, and their sentiments were sometimes expressed in armed clashes with foreign soldiers.[12]

Nevertheless, on his grand tour, Peter recruited altogether more than 750 Europeans, particularly Dutchmen, with offers of advantageous employment, high salaries, and religious toleration—and what was later to be called extraterritoriality.

Throughout the centuries, however, there has been no consensus among Russian historians about Peter's real role in the country's history. It is clear that he accelerated "Westernization." And his victory in The Great Northern War against Sweden, which destroyed that country's military power, opened the Baltic to the Russians and made the Russians one of the arbiters in the European scene. But Peter's reforms were less "revolutionary" than the mythology indicates.

> Peter gave clear definition to the goal toward which his predecessors had already moved in halting steps—the goal of raising the country's productive capacity. . . . The results of his activity were very great: he gave his people the widest possible opportunity for material and cultural association with the entire civilized world. But one must not overestimate these results. Under Peter, education affected only the upper strata of society, and even there only to a small extent: the mass of the people retained their old outlook.[13]

Just as Peter's construction, at an enormous cost of human life, of his "window on the West"—the city and new capital, St. Petersburg—established the dichotomy that Moscow and that city were to represent in modern Russian history, so Peter also inaugurated the great debate in Russian intellectual history and its society:

> "The ideological schism"—*ideologicheskii raskol*, the word *raskol*, schism, harking back to the great religious schism in the sixties in the seventeenth century—between the conception of Russia as a part of Europe and of Muscovy as a world of her own, neither Europe nor Asia. . . . (This actual formula was coined much later by the historian Kavelin in the writing on Peter in 1866.) . . . Thenceforward, above all in the great controversies between the Westerners and the Slavophiles, this question is regarded as fundamental in the historic-philosophical disquisitions on the relation of Russia to Europe, on the place of Russia in the world, on the meaning of

"national culture" or "national spirit" or orthodoxy, the *mir* (the village commune) or of governmental power. . . . This prolonged public debate has as its central theme: . . . Can a centralized, dictatorial government impose successfully from above, radical changes, or a revolution, especially at extreme speed and by violent means?[14]

It is self-evident that the argument has come down right to our day, through the centuries of czarist rule and through the seventy years of Soviet communism. Although Gorbachev has denied it in some contexts, he, himself, has spoken of a revolution from above in his attempt to reorder the Communist system.

Peter's answer to the question was clear: "Is not everything done by compulsion?," he asked rhetorically in his edict of 1723 that established the rules for a mercantilist state—rules that were to dictate the basic attitudes of the Russian government toward commerce and industry into the nineteenth century. "Already much thanksgiving is heard for what has already borne fruit. And such is not to be accomplished in manufacturing by propositions alone, but must be compelled, and aided with instruction, machines, and all manner of means; and one must be like a good manager, with compulsion in part."[15] Part and parcel of this compulsion was the beginning in Peter's time of a transfer of the already existing rural serfdom—an agricultural worker in bondage—to manufacturing. An example was that Peter's attempt to produce linen textile manufacturing (for cloth to be used for military uniforms) ended with one monopoly producer who used 641 serf homesteads for his labor force. An edict of 1721 permitted merchants to purchase inhabited hamlets for factories and workshops.

By the time of his death, Peter had created approximately 200 industrial plants, many of them successful. By 1714, Russia was, for example, the largest producer of iron in the world. Narva, Riga, Reval, Vyborg—the Baltic ports—handled Russian commerce ten times greater than it had been a half century earlier. But Peter's reforms had not created what Richard Pipes has called "the missing bourgeoisie" for the czarist regime. This trade was almost completely in the hands of foreign merchants and the nobility. Soon after Peter's death in 1725 the commerce commission of the Czar's Privy Council recognized that the whole of Peter's effort to build Russian industry had failed—or at least had failed to reward the Russian nobility. Peter's manufacturing enterprises, themselves, began to collapse one after the other until hardly twenty were left by the mid-eighteenth century.[16]

Why? One historian, after giving all the reasons that capitalism did not progress in Russia in the sixteenth and seventeenth centuries and indicating that they were not problems exclusive to that country, sums up his answer this way:

> Capitalism is above all a series of social relationships resting upon certain technological foundation. . . . Certainly Russia in the 16th and 17th centuries lacked neither capital nor access to the most modern industrial techniques of Western Europe. . . . The answer to this question may lie in the "third factor" in a country's capitalist development, namely the state of class relationships in that society. Capitalism, as a mode of production, does not attain great strength until the disintegration of feudalism reaches an advance stage. . . . At the base of the entire movement from a feudal-agrarian to a bourgeois-industrial order is the separation of the agricultural worker—whether slave, serf or yeoman peasant—from the land which is simultaneously the means of his livelihood and the source of his economic backwardness. Such dispossession of the peasants by their social betters usually follows in the wake of technological developments in agriculture which make it possible to feed large groups of people no longer engaged in farming. . . . Based on this analysis, we conclude that *serfdom* was the main barrier to extensive capitalist development in Russia during this period. . . . Thus Russian manufacturing lacked broad opportunities for growth. . . . Manufacturers relied upon royal patronage and privileges, and accepted ascribed serfs for unskilled labor. . . . The sovereign was himself a vigorous entrepreneur who used his absolute political authority to advance private economic interest; even in the area of "private enterprise," property rights were uncertain and the state played a key supervisory role.[17]

Ironically, it was a reversal of this government role that finished off the Russian entrepreneurial class in 1762 when Peter III revoked his grandfather Peter the Great's edict. Merchants were forbidden to use serfs as laborers, and the nobility was allowed shortly thereafter by Catherine, Peter's successor, to start manufacturing operations on their estates, except in St. Petersburg and Moscow. The cumulative effect of these reforms was to deny the merchants cheap labor and to shift manufacturing back to the rural areas and the villages. By the beginning of the nineteenth century, most trade in Russia—mostly agricultural produce—was conducted by peasants who did not have to pay the onerous taxes of the merchants organized in guilds. When again in the 1880s, the Ministry of Finance began to promote large-scale industry, the situation again resembled that of the Petrine period—state initiative, foreign capital, and management. The great surge of industrial development in the last decade of the nineteenth century, unparalleled in Russia and perhaps with no equal anywhere else in the world, was nevertheless propelled by these outside influences. This policy developed out of the recognition by Czar Alexander II, after the defeat of Russia at Sevastopol in the Crimean War in 1855, that Russian society and the economy had to be reorganized. Alexander had to find a way to fund the costs of the Russian military which absorbed one-quarter, and sometimes one-third, of the national budget.

Throughout the rest of the nineteenth century, the problem of the ambitions of the czars to be a leading European (and latterly an Asian) power with the economy of a country far less developed than its rivals in Western Europe, was the central one for Russian policy. The need to build the economy of a vastly undeveloped country compared with its rivals and allies in the West drove the Russians to borrow heavily—deficits that by the end of the century had reached 3.5 billion rubles with one-third of this amount being held in the West. The interest payments were financed by heavy grain exports which, in turn, required a rapid expansion of foreign-financed railroads to move them to ports. The ministers of finance under the last three czars, particularly Sergei Witte, were able to develop a "system" to pursue these goals which, while viable, was precarious. It further impoverished the peasantry and risked collapse under the threat of war and famine.

> While the buckles held, the very fabric of the Russian economy went to pieces in the great famine of 1891. The state had taken everything from the peasants who had no surplus whatever to guard against crop failures. And to add insult to injury: German and Austrian diplomats sneered that Russia was too poor to be a great power; a civilized state did not suffer disastrous famines.[18]

Paradoxically, this heavy government borrowing had another side effect on Russian development that would play a significant role in events leading up to the revolution in 1917. The shortage of capital might have been compensated by foreigners but for the myriad obstacles erected by the government itself. "On the whole, foreign investors remained indifferent. If they invested in Russia, they preferred government bonds, for unlike private citizens the Russian government scrupulously paid its debts and paid them in gold. Foreign loans, if obtained at all, were thus channeled through the government, which made them at once a pawn of power politics. Foreign governments would always try to influence Russian foreign policy by manipulating the sluices of foreign credit."[19] It is perhaps this ghost, more than any other, that dogs those Soviet leaders today who would borrow heavily in the West to finance *perestroika* and a rapid increase in the standard of living. After 1892, with the arrival at the helm of Russian imperial finances of Sergei Witte, a brilliant Baltic German who would in modern terms be called a technocrat, "the Witte system" evolved.

> Considering the fact that Witte's policy was one of state capitalism, one would look in vain for a complex and detailed modern "plan of industrialization." The basic pattern remained a simple one. Extensive railroad construction would stimulate the growth of the metallurgical and fuel industries supplying rails and other equipment. In turn, the expansion of the heavy industries would create favorable conditions for the growth of the light industries. In the end, the new vigor of the industrial and urban segment of the population would raise rural production and prosperity as well.[20]

Despite the fact that Witte was a hard-nosed former railroad bureaucrat whose view of Russia and the world's problems was largely technocratic and realistic, he, too, shared a dream of the Kremlin's mission. Proposing the gigantic Trans-Siberian Railway project to the czar, replete with a blueprint for a long-term attack on imperial China prepared by a Slavophile Mongolian (Buriat) subject of the czar, Witte philosophized on the global mission of the Russian state:

> Standing on the confines of two such different worlds [Europe and Asia], Russia none the less represents a world apart. Her independent place in the family of peoples and her special role in world history are determined both by her geographical position and in particular, by the original character of her political and cultural development, a development which has been achieved through the living interaction and harmonious combination of three elements that have manifested their full creative power only in Russia. These elements are: first, Orthodoxy, preserving in purity the true spirit of Christianity, as the basis of education and upbringing; secondly, autocracy

as the basis of state life; thirdly, the Russian national spirit, as the basis of the internal cohesiveness of their state, a national spirit that creates a strong inward center, closely united yet free from nationalistic exclusiveness, possessed of a vast capacity for friendly companionship and cooperation with the most diverse races and peoples. It is on these bases that the whole edifice of Russian power has been built up, and it is therefore impossible for Russia to be fused with the West.[21]

It certainly can be argued that this idea of a Russian mission was not all that different in spirit from other nineteenth century imperialists (for example, Cecil Rhodes and Britain's role in Africa). But what is striking is the idea that Russia, for all its Christianity and humanism, is wholly distinguishable from the West.

Whatever the philosophical motivations, by 1900, France, seeking an ally in Europe to oppose the growing power of Bismarck's Prussia, found the czar. And by 1900 one-quarter of all French foreign investment was in Russia with the French banking houses availing themselves of the fat commissions doled out by the Russian government. Witte would set a pattern for later Soviet traders and their "active measures" when, by manipulating the Paris stock exchange through the use of Russian gold holdings abroad, he secured unusually favorable terms for the loans. Again, anticipating Soviet clandestine activity in our times, he literally bought pro-Russian sentiments in the French press. Yet, the basic insecurity of Russian exports and the poverty at home made the situation more and more desperate. In 1894 world prices for grain had fallen to such an extent that the value of Russia's agricultural exports were half of what they had been in the 1870s at a time when Witte was trying to boost industrial imports to speed the industrialization. And this meant that despite a recent famine Witte was exporting 15 percent of the Russian grain crop compared with only 5 percent a decade earlier. He was helped by the weather and new agricultural exports—Siberian eggs and butter of good quality, sugar from the Ukraine, timber, and flax.

But Witte finally succumbed to the intrigues around the czar and criticisms from the court and others that Russia, despite the vast network of railroads that had been built, was becoming poorer.

Witte's regime as a whole had been a remarkable accomplishment. He had made ends meet in state finance, and, in addition, through industrialization had strengthened and expanded the economy of Russia. Even by modern standards, his work for the economic advance of Russia, though eclipsed by Soviet drive, stands out as a monument to Russian state ambition. This was the way in which he longed, so vainly, for the remainder of his life, to have his accomplishments viewed.[22]

What Witte—and others before and after him—tried to do was to build a Russian state that was no longer an economic laggard in the world of the European family.

If the Russian government . . . failed to put the country on its feet, Witte's argument implied, then its subjects would have no chance whatsoever of catching up and rebuilding that deeper sovereignty, that native originality, which would permit their country to hold its own in the cultural, economic, and political competition of the modern world. Without power, native creativity in any field of human endeavor could not unfold to its fullest potential. And yet any "artificial" effort to hasten these results was bound . . . to lead to more suffering, ill will, and renewed weakness.[23]

This summary by a sympathetic historian could well be voiced by an observer in the late 1980s after looking back over the wreckage of the seventy years of Soviet revolutionary history.

CHAPTER 3

THE NEW ECONOMIC
POLICY (NEP)

Two Short Steps Backward,
One Long Step Forward

The British historian H.G. Wells, traveling through the Soviet Union in 1920, three years after the Bolshevik Revolution, saw "an unparalleled example of civilization in a state of complete collapse; the railway tracks were rusting and becoming gradually unusable, the cities were falling into ruin."[1] The combination of Communist economic theory and practice and a grueling civil war, heaped on the traditional problems of the Russian imperial economy, had brought the society to a near standstill. Most factories and mines were deserted, consumer goods, fuel, and food were exhausted. Worse still for the Bolsheviks, the once prorevolutionary workers and sailors at the important naval base of Kronstadt near St. Petersburg had revolted, this time against the Bolshevik leadership—the most devastating proof of the failure of the regime by its own standards. "Kronstadt" would resound down through the years of Communist conspiracy around the world as the synonym for dedicated revolutionary loyalists breaking with the false gods of Marxist-Leninism.[2] In the West, there was every expectation that—after the Allied government's failure with the half-hearted military interventions and support for incompetent and reactionary opponents of the Communists—the regime was falling of its own accord.

V.I. Lenin, the brilliant strategist and tactician of the Bolshevik leadership, in a decision analyzed and debated over and over again in socialist circles ever since, suddenly reversed course. In March 1921 he announced the "New Economic Policy" (the NEP). The new domestic policy sought to permit the peasant-farmers to produce again by going back to taking a percentage of their production in kind rather than by relying on the increasingly arbitrary requisitions that often had not even left seed for replanting and had aggravated famine conditions. In an effort to restart commerce and rehabilitate the urban economy, the new policy permitted the reemergence of markets that had been expropriated in the bid to build socialism as soon as possible in "the new society." Furthermore,

> If it was all right to tap the resources and initiative of the *domestic* bourgeoisie in the interests of socialist construction, then what was wrong in principle with tapping the resources and initiative of the *foreign* bourgeoisie as well? Since one could not overthrow the international bourgeoisie, might not one exploit *them* and enlist *their* help, too, in the rebuilding of the Russian economy?[3]

At the Party conference in May 1921, Lenin insisted that the NEP had been adopted "seriously and for a long time" and the conference concurred by a resolution that described the NEP as "established for a long period to be measured in terms of years." At the same time, Lenin referred to it as "a retreat," later on as a "defeat and a retreat—for a new attack," and as a sympathetic historian has said, ". . . such a description seemed to encourage the view of NEP as a temporary evil to be overcome as quickly as possible, a blot to be erased from the party escutcheon. [Even though] [A]t the end of 1921 Lenin was still speaking of the need for further retreat."[4] But in February 1922, Lenin talked of the "concessions to capitalists" being at an end and that was repeated at the Eleventh Party Conference a month later in a more formal way. That did not happen for several years, and, in fact, some aspects of the NEP stretched on into the 1930s.

For the Bolsheviks of that day, the fundamental ideological problem of governance was—as it had been from the outset of their plotting for a socialist revolution in imperial Russia—that of reconciling the predictions of Karl Marx that socialism and communism would come through the natural and inevitable final development of the capitalist system. Obviously, it would occur first in the most developed industrialized countries of Western Europe and the United States, rather than in the most primitive major European society, czarist Russia. The Bolsheviks' surprisingly successful usurpation of power in Russia and their attempts to create socialism from the top down were increasingly isolated. It was not a part of the world revolution that the world socialist community had foreseen and hoped would evolve in Germany and the West and "excuse" their forced implementation of Marxian theory in Petrograd. In the shadows was the fear, expressed in earlier exile by Lenin himself, that failure of the world revolution might lead to the development of "Asiatic despotism" in Russia. This term refers to a vague Marxist concept of special economic conditions in the nonindustrial world, particularly Asia, to which Marx had alluded in some of his writings.[5]

Gorbachev's "reform" attempts have renewed interest in analysis of the NEP, and the obvious comparisons to current dilemmas of the Soviet policymakers. The question is whether Gorbachev's *perestroika* is not another version of the NEP and, therefore, a retreat from socialism, or even another admission that socialist economics do not work. Until very recently in orthodox Marxist philosophical and historical circles, there was no possibility of regarding the NEP other than as a dead end and aberration that had preceded Stalin's successful (however painful) industrialization of the Soviet Union. Furthermore, with the increasing awareness of the depth of the problems of the Soviet economy, there is the same argument on a vaster scale, about whether socialist orthodoxy must be abandoned for decades, not just years, as under the NEP—or, indeed, whether a socialist orthodoxy exists.

A key turning point in this discussion came in November 1988 when Gorbachev, in a major speech on the seventieth anniversary of the Bolshevik Revolution, began the official "rehabilitation" of the reputation of Nikolai Bukharin, one of the most popular and intellectual of the early Bolsheviks. Bukharin, like Lenin, had been an advocate of the most inflexible socialist policies in the early Bolshevik days in power. But, before others in the Party, he had turned to advocating a more gradualist approach, particularly toward agriculture and the peasantry. By 1929 Bukharin had become a bitter enemy of Stalin. In 1934, Stalin, in a seeming effort to reconcile old enemies, sent Bukharin abroad to Paris as a former president of the Comintern—the Communist international organization headquartered in Moscow—to cultivate Western fellow travelers and French intellectuals sympathetic to the Soviet regime. A former German comrade in the Comintern, writes:

> An old friend was describing the struggles of the defeated German Commu-
> nists, hopeless and despairing, and accused Stalin of the disaster that had
> befallen the revolutionary movement in Germany. "Some fine day he will
> hang us all," Bukharin sighed, his face reflecting the despondency of his
> words. . . . Sad and resigned, he rejected all suggestions to stay in France
> where he would enjoy freedom to continue his scientific work. That would
> be desertion, but no way out. "You can free yourself from force and coercion
> but not from yourself. The generation that has made the revolution in Russia
> has to go its road to the end, whatever that end may be."[6]

When Stalin, as general secretary of the Communist Party, called him to return to Russia, he went. And in 1938 he became one of the most spectacular of the old Bolsheviks charged in the famous "show trials" with having been a traitor, a saboteur, and so forth. Bukharin, the model for Arthur Koestler's attempt to examine the psychology of the old revolution- aries in his novel *Darkness at Noon* has recently been lionized by Soviet and some Western intellectuals as a symbol of the "liberal" aspects of the regime, often referred to as Leninist principles. But the fact remains that Bukharin's, Lenin's, and even some of Stalin's opponents' attitudes toward basic economic arguments, as well as moral and political values, shifted quickly back and forth during the turbulent early years of the regime. And defining "Leninist" values becomes, at best, a highly debatable exercise.

Whatever the motivations for initiating it, and whatever Lenin, already ill and dying, would have done later with the NEP had he survived, it did accomplish its tactical purposes amazingly well. The NEP, along with massive shipments of food relief—organized primarily by Herbert Hoover, who would later be the U.S. president, to alleviate the post-civil war famine conditions throughout the country—helped stave off total collapse of the Soviet domestic agricultural and consumer economy. And the NEP laid the basis for a new effort to rehabilitate Russian industry and to begin the vast new industrialization that would take place in the 1930s. It provided a necessary transfusion from the West to jump-start the idle plants and mines that the Soviets had inherited from the remarkable industrialization of the late czarist period, largely in good condition but devoid of their managers and workers.

It is impossible to quantify adequately the foreign investment and technology that flowed into the Soviet Union as a result of the NEP. But there is a wealth of anecdotal material to indicate just how important it was for the resuscitation of the economy and the society. The most difficult part to quantify of the massive assistance that developed from the West is that which came from Germany under the terms of the secret Rapallo Treaty of 1921. According to this treaty, the Bolsheviks' hospitality for a reemerging German military force (manufacturing of arms and transport including aircraft, training grounds, and so forth) was swapped by the Bolshevik state for trade and investment from German industry. In the post-World War I depression and the subsequent runaway inflation of Weimar Germany, "Krupp, the AEG, the 'Steel King' Otto Wolff of Cologne, the Linke-Hoffman works (leading manufacturers of rails and rolling stock), all of these concerns were able to maintain their position principally by exporting industrial plant and equipment to the Soviet Union," says one German author who has written authoritatively on the subject.[7] There were at least 2,000 German engineers who went to the Soviet Union to restart the czarist plants. These included the German aircraft designer Hugo Junkers who inaugurated the Soviet aircraft industry when he transferred his Desau plant from Germany as a result of the Versailles prohibition against aircraft manufacture in postwar Germany. These engineers and other Westerners were extremely important for, contrary to popular misconception, the Russian capital plant had suffered relatively little damage during the Civil War except in the Don Bas region in the Ukraine. They failed to function because of the flight of their skilled personnel and workmen and the utopian socialist formulas of the early Bolshevik rule that destroyed what was left of the fabric of the czarist economy.

Despite the fact that the United States did not recognize the regime, American businessmen were also ready to accept Lenin's invitation to do business. Standard Oil took a drilling concession on the Amur River. The International General Electric Company sold over $20 million worth of equipment between 1921 and 1925, a part of what would eventually be $37 million worth of machinery sold in this period by various American firms. An English company retook the Lena Goldfields with a "concession" from Lenin, although another British firm had only a few years earlier been expropriated by the Soviets. (By 1930, the Soviets again took the company after it had invested machinery, railways, dredgers, and so

forth, and Moscow put some of its engineers on trial for "sabotage"!)
SKF, the famous Swedish ballbearing manufacturer, provided a pilot
factory. Trans-Siberian Cables, which was a subsidiary of the Great
Northern Telegraph Company, a Danish company, brought the wireless
to the Communists after Lenin had read about it in the Western press—
and was shortly expelled from the country after its installation was
completed. By September 1927 the Soviets had granted 156 concessions
to foreign companies, including almost all branches of the prerevolutionary economy.

In much of the literature about Soviet economic development, these
foreign concessions, if mentioned at all, have been relegated to a very
minor role in the history of the development of the Soviet industrial and
war machine. But an incredibly thorough and methodologically conservative three-volume study by Antony Sutton, a British economist working
in the Hoover Institution, Stanford University, has revealed the enormity
of the technological transfer, by implication the transfer of capital, and
the importance of these transfers in restarting the prerevolutionary czarist
industrial plant.[8]

An example of how these transfers came about can be seen in the
resuscitation of the czarist railways. There had been a well-established
machine-building industry in czarist days, largely dependent on the spectacular expansion of the railroad system in the last decade of the nineteenth
century and the early years of the twentieth century. By 1923, half the
machine-building plant in Petrograd, which, besides Moscow and the
Ukraine, was where it was located prerevolution, was idle. A licensing and
training agreement with Metropolitan Vickers of Great Britain was signed
in 1927. A technical assistance agreement was signed in 1926 with
Gasmotoren-Fabrik Deutz AG of Germany for motors, stationary engines,
and compressors. The imperial Russian branch of Westinghouse Air Brake
Works, nationalized in 1925 after a protracted and artificially induced
labor dispute with its employees, became an important component of the
new Soviet Gomza machine-building trust. Although the Soviets at that
time had locomotive capacity that was not used, they purchased through
intermediaries a locomotive plant in southern Sweden to have access to
Western technology. In 1921 and 1922 the Soviets used Estonian machine-building plants to repair 2,000 "sick" locomotives with contracts
negotiated with Krupp of Germany and Vickers-Armstrong of Great
Britain, and financed by Deutsche Bank in Germany. The Baldwin Loco-

motive Works in the United States in 1929, together with fifteen other companies, made an agreement to sell and finance its products and send engineers to the Soviet Union on a revolving credit basis. Although czarist designers had been pioneers in diesel traction design, Soviet management could not restart the technology because the design engineers had fled the country, so in 1932 it imported General Electric technology, which supplied the basis for Soviet railway technology down to the present time.

In addition to these out-and-out business arrangements with the Soviets, as Sutton has noted, there were important if less tangible "arms length" arrangements, particularly in the United States, which had not recognized the regime and did not do so until Franklin D. Roosevelt entered the White House in 1933. These were individuals or organizations, put together either by the Russians themselves or, in many instances, by radical sympathizers and businessmen in America, that extended technological and financial aid to various parts of the Soviet economy. Sutton sums up:

> The process by which the Tsarist machine-building industry was restarted is quite obvious. A great number of the plants were physically intact after the Revolution; skilled labor and engineering personnel were missing. Both had been dispersed by the political upheaval . . . the restored Tsarist machine-building industry was on the way to modernization at the end of the decade [1920s]. Construction of new plants was on the drawing boards of top American and German companies.[9]

Yet, while the NEP and its associated policies, confused as they were, had saved the Soviet economy from collapse, they had not provided the stimulus for the growth into a modern industrial state, which was the ambitious aim of the Bolsheviks. Ironically, after seeing the demise of their dreams of "a world revolution," as one after another of the putsch socialist regimes collapsed in Western and Central Europe, the Russian leadership began to believe that it was possible to use the West to create such a regime in the Soviet world. And the Bolshevik leaders believed that they saw "evidence" for this in a "scientific" examination of the world economic picture in the aftermath of the Great War.

"For the world economy to be restored, Russian raw materials must be utilized," Lenin said when capturing this mood in 1920. "You cannot get along without them—that is economically true. It is admitted even by . . .

a student of economics who regards things from a purely bourgeois standpoint. That man is Keynes. . . ." That is how Lenin, and his closest advisers, saw the post-World War I world in 1920.[10] And the flip side of the argument was that "it would be absolutely ridiculous, fantastic, and utopian to hope that we can achieve complete economic independence." It was this thinking—the hope of mutually profitable cooperation (the Bolsheviks called it "integration" in their interminable discussions on Marxist theory)—that had led to the granting of the NEP concessions. The most important international element in the NEP program, therefore, was an idea that had originated in the negotiations for the separate treaty with imperial Germany at Brest in 1918.

A Lenin protégé, Grigorii Sokolnikov, an economist and younger than most of the Bolshevik leaders, became the spokesman for this new line as Commissar of Finance in 1922.

> Our point of view is as follows: capitalism is not experiencing any kind of industrial recovery and cannot manage without us. All Europe is crying out about this, and anyone who follows the European press . . . says that France, Germany, and England are wailing about the fact that they cannot escape from the economic crisis unless Russia plays a part . . . That is why they are forced to come to an agreement with us.[11]

In April 1922, when the major powers met in Genoa to discuss the issue of czarist Russian debts with Soviet representatives, they were unwilling to accept a swap of Moscow's debt recognition for new credits to the revolutionary government. There was some talk of a swap of British credits for an oil concession to the Royal Dutch Shell group in the Baku region. But the Belgians and the French, with more to lose, held out for restitution of their expropriated properties. And U.S. pressure was also being applied on all the European war debtors, but especially the Soviets, through the British and the French. A second round of talks in The Hague in May also failed to strike a deal in which a set of foreign investments would be swapped for new credits. It was during these failed negotiations that the two pariah regimes—defeated Germany and revolutionary Russia—made a deal. The Soviet regime signed its secret pact with the German Weimar Republic at Rapallo, near Genoa, for the raw materials swap against German industrial goods and facilities for the German army.

Having survived the ultimate crisis years from 1919 to 1924 with the

NEP, with its partial rehabilitation of Russian agriculture, and with its enticement of some essential foreign investment, technology, and management, a new mood appeared in Soviet leadership. As so often happened in the Marxist polemics of the revolutionaries, Leon Trotsky, the chief critic of the integrationists and the NEP, now became the advocate of those policies. For, inevitably, Trotsky's advocacy of world revolution as the only way that the victories of the Bolsheviks in Russia could be preserved and enhanced, had to view some sort of cooperation with the West as the solution. But Bukharin, whose Right opposition line believed in the necessity of compromising with the peasantry at home and moving slowly toward socialism, also argued for some kind of integrationist policy with the West. The emerging giant figure of Josef Stalin, who, through his growing control over the Communist Party apparatus, was moving toward absolute power, initially placed himself between these two ideological positions. In fact, the argument between Bukharin and Trotsky permitted Stalin to take a middle ground at least temporarily for political gain, which gave him the opportunity to consolidate his growing power by arguing for "socialism in one country."

Stalin argued that despite the failure of world revolution, socialism could be built in one country—the Union of Soviet Socialist Republics, with its huge size, population, and enormous raw materials and manpower resources. Acting in the Party behind the scenes, Stalin was able to seize control from Party opponents, who seemed to be more knowledgeable and to have larger popular followings than he. By playing one of his enemies against another, final victory came on December 27, 1927, when the Party Congress condemned all deviations from the central Party line, with Stalin, as general secretary of the Party, dictating that line. Stalin offered the Party a sweeping program that promised to achieve all the Bolshevik goals. And the same Party Congress that endorsed his bid for power brought the NEP to an end and inaugurated the regime of the five-year plans.

Lenin had been fascinated by Germany's wartime economy and its plans as early as 1918. The first long-term plan for electrification was drawn in 1920, but its original wildly optimistic goals were put aside very quickly, and the whole plan remained simply another policy planning document. In 1927, Soviet economists began to develop the first Five-Year Plan to incorporate all the country's productive capacity, attempting to use every resource for industrialization. Optimal and initial variable figures were adopted as goals. Coal would double, and oil and iron ore production would increase five times. Then, in December 1929, the entire plan was suddenly given only four years for implementation, and on February 4, 1931, Stalin talked about the possibility of completing decisive parts of the plan in three years. The country was urged on in a kind of hysterical call for work and production; Stalin warned that if the Soviet Union did not complete in ten years what other countries had taken fifty years to accomplish, the Soviet state would be crushed. The figures increasingly became meaningless.

As two émigré Soviet historians have commented:

> But the country could not ignore reality. . . . The only quota that was met on time was the employment index. . . . The rapid growth of the urban population led to a catastrophic worsening of the housing situation. Food supplies for the cities were severely strained. . . . All records for "consumer asceticism" were surpassed during those years in the villages, which literally starved to death. . . . In April 1929 bread was rationed. By the end of the year rationing was extended to all foodstuffs, then to manufactured goods. . . . Prices never stopped climbing, wages rose nominally, and production quotas constantly increased. . . . In April 1929, when work on the first five-year plan was just starting, Stalin was already preparing his scapegoats. . . . he declared wreckers "are sitting now in all branches of our industry."[12]

Nevertheless, in record time and at enormous cost, incredible progress was made on some industrial projects. Stalin's dictum, however, that socialism would be built in one country, and that it was built, even at enormous sacrifices, has been equated with a general belief in the autarchic nature of what was done. The Five-Year Plan, or the part that actually was accomplished, could not have been implemented without foreign assistance. Albert Kahn and Company, an industrial architectural firm, was hired to design plans for buildings worth approximately $2 billion after Soviet engineers visited and studied at its headquarters in Detroit. A dozen of these plans were actually drawn in Detroit, and the rest in the Soviet Union, according to an agreement with the Supreme Economic Council of the USSR.

It was in this model that by the end of the 1920s, Sutton points out, the Soviets believed they had found a better vehicle for transferring Western technology than the earlier concessions awarded foreign investors and traders by Lenin. Moscow used various tactics to legally and semilegally end the 350 foreign concessions. They then moved toward technical assistance agreements with foreign companies, consultants, engineers, and skilled workers. And by 1935, only the Danish telegraph operations, Japanese fishing in Far East waters, and the Standard Oil lease remained on the books.

The history of these concessions and their end is a remarkable story of how the Soviets beguiled foreign investors to transfer machinery, technology, skills, and capital. When the maximum effect had been achieved, Moscow used various tactics to expropriate the concessions. Originally many of these concessions had been written to run for extended periods so that the investor could recover his capital and make a profit. (For example, the Swedish ASEA firm's concession, started in 1927, was to run until 1961; the British Lena Goldfields concession was to run until 1975.) The problems were the same in all the concessions—profits could not be remitted, goods could not be exported, labor difficulties were bedeviling management, credits were not forthcoming, arbitrary taxation or customs were imposed, and so forth. In most instances, the companies themselves and their parent governments were happy to see an end to the entire adventure.

The Soviets, of course, explained these closings by saying that "monopolistic" capital no longer found sufficient profit. Moscow could argue that some of the concessionaires had not fulfilled their agreements on technical grounds. Bukharin, in a speech, put the Soviet strategy bluntly, when he said:

> On the one hand, we admit capitalist elements, we condescend to collaborate with them; on the other hand, our objective is to eliminate them completely (*radicalement*) conquer them, to squash them economically as well as socially. It is a type of collaboration which presumes a furious battle, in which blood may necessarily be spilled.[13]

Despite Soviet treatment of the concessionaires, many of these Western firms were willing to sign technical assistance agreements with the USSR, which may explain more about their Western collaborators than about the Soviets. Sutton identifies approximately 2,200 technical assistance agreements between the Russians and the West in the period from 1929 to 1945, but suggests that the list is almost certainly incomplete. During the first two years of this period, the Russians hired large numbers of foreigners—a Soviet source reported that there were approximately 6,800 engineers of all types in heavy industry in 1932. Another Soviet source says there were 1,700 American engineers alone in this activity. But as Sutton points out, some of these individual engineers were of dispropor-tionate importance to the Soviets. For example, L.A. Swajian, construc-tion engineer for the Ford Motor Company's River Rouge plant, worked in turn as chief engineer for the construction of the Stalingrad Tractor Plant and the Kharkov Tractor Plant. John Calder, another engineer who had held important jobs in Detroit, was Soviet troubleshooter at a half dozen different sites. Many of these engineers were topflight men without whom the huge Soviet designs of the 1930s would have remained paper proposals only.

Sutton believes that the evidence he has accumulated shows that al-though there was considerable stumbling in the period from 1924 to 1928, the decision in 1920 to hire foreign personnel as well as companies made possible the erection of the huge projects of 1930–1932. That led to a new plateau, and possibly some stagnation in the period from 1936 to 1940—although with the drama of the political trials and the enormous loss of skilled personnel that Stalin's murderous policies caused in industry as well as in agriculture and in the military—it is difficult to determine the real extent of growth. Certainly it was a myth perpetrated abroad that the five-year plans and central planning had given the Soviet economy a new route for smooth and continual development.

It was true as the Soviets claimed that these new units that were built with foreign technical and personnel assistance had enormous capacity, unequaled in the home countries of many of the foreign contractor parties. The Urals Elmash *combinat* increased Soviet electrical manufacturing capacity seven times, for example. The KEMZ plant at Kharkov, designed by General Electric, had a turbine capacity two and a half times as great as the huge GE plant at Schenectady, New York. And the Magnitogorsk plant was a replica of the Gary, Indiana, plant of U.S. Steel but was larger. Stalin once bragged that two-thirds of the new Soviet plants were projects in which the Americans had participated, and as much as one-half of the equipment was German-made.

At the same time that these huge industrial plants were being built, what Solzhenitsyn calls the "great backbreaking" was taking place in the Soviet rural areas and in agriculture. In November 1928, an article by

Stalin in *Pravda* announced that there would be industrialization of agriculture. Shortly afterward he called for an official end to the NEP— "either we go back to capitalism or we go forward to socialism." Over the next two months, Stalin moved in a more radical fashion than at any time in the whole revolutionary period. At one fell swoop, the wealthier and more industrious and independent-minded peasants (*kulaks*) were "liquidated"—in many instances they were literally killed and in others they were deported to northern frontier lands or to Siberia where many, if not most, died because of the living conditions. Even Soviet official historians, writing thirty years after the event, acknowledged that the persecutions were without rationale—that is, who was considered a *kulak* and, an even more ambiguous phrase, *kulak* henchman (*podkulachniki*). In some regions 15 to 20 percent of the peasants were deported with perhaps three or four middle-income peasants arrested for every *kulak* deported. The peasantry that remained was stampeded into state farms within a few months by declaring that whoever refused to enter would be considered "an enemy of the state." A system of obligatory deliveries to the state was introduced on the collectives using the state-run machine and tractor stations, acting as a control mechanism and taking another arbitrary portion from the harvest.

During the first four years of collectivization, by official count, yields dropped by as much as 30 percent, and harvests dropped below their prerevolutionary totals. Yet, Stalin viewed the entire effort as a success, for he claimed that marketable produce had doubled, giving political control of the harvest to the Moscow bureaucrats as they had never had it before. The general ruin of the countryside can probably not be exaggerated, however. A famine in 1932 and 1933, never acknowledged by the authorities (even to mention it was a crime against the state), was probably worse than the disaster of 1921 and 1922, which had followed the Revolution and the Civil War. Furthermore, Stalin continued to export grain to pay for the imports of machinery and technicians that were building the industrial plants. Grain exports were as much as twelve times 1928 in the collectivization years of 1930 to 1932. Just as they had for 500 years, the Russian peasant and consumer were paying the cost of importing the best, most modern, and largest Western technological machinery.

All this took place under Stalin's whip, although there was no official answer to such vital questions as what exact form the *kolkhozy* (the state collectives) would take, which land, implements, and animals should be collectivized and which left in individual hands, who would administer the new organizations, where necessary tractors and other equipment would come from, and so forth. "The genocide against the peasants in the Soviet Union was unique not only for its monstrous scale; it was directed against an indigenous population by a government of the same nationality, and in time of peace."[14] Stalin told Winston Churchill that ten million *kulaks* had been killed by the other peasants or sent into Siberia where tens of thousands died because of the conditions of their transfer. Estimates of the cost in lives have been variously placed at between five and ten million. The terror in the rural areas delivered the entire economic life of the country into the hands of Stalin, the dictator, and consolidated his unquestioned political power as well.

The destruction of the leading peasantry and the bureaucratization of Soviet agriculture has had disastrous long-term implications for the food supply. A Soviet scientist returning to Bukovina in 1988, the former Austro-Hungarian breadbasket and then Romanian province ceded to Moscow after World War II, reported a desolate scene replacing the early agricultural plenty he had seen there in 1982.

> What, then, befell this rich district to transform an area of bounty into an abomination of desolation? In the fall of 1983, there was an ecological disaster on the Dnestr River which the central press at the time did not report. The entire Dnestrovsky watershed was poisoned—the Dnestr itself, its tributaries, its derivative ground water, springs and wells, and in addition to the lowlands of the Dnestr, the Dnestrovsky estuary and even the waters of the Black Sea. Wastes from chemical plants also poisoned masses of people and livestock. . . . The barbaric intensification of planting and the mindless application of pesticides in Chernovtsy Province and in neighboring Moldavia have finally led to exhaustion of the *chernozem* or the black-earth layer of the soil. . . . the situation in Chernovtsy appears to define the conditions of virtually the entire Ukrainian and Moldavian Republics. The Soviet Union's "breadbasket" has been turned into a disaster area by bureaucratic loafers.[15]

The destruction of traditional Russian agriculture is at the root of Soviet agricultural problems today, and, for many Western observers, may explain the reason that there is no solution in the medium term, much less the short term, for the problems of Soviet agriculture. The vital but ephemeral cultural thread of a thousand years of peasant-farmer agriculture in which father passes to son love and practical knowledge of the land has been broken in Russia.

CHAPTER 4

GOOD OLD UNCLE JOE

The Postwar Thrust for the Economy

It is one of those ironies of history that the Soviet dictator did not appreciate the attempt in the West to make him a more sympathetic figure. "In his year of supreme triumph, 1945, when Roosevelt confided to him over a dinner table at Yalta that he and Churchill between them called him 'Uncle Joe,' Stalin showed genuine pique."[1] But it was part and parcel of the spirit of the Western democracies, particularly of the United States, that the Americans should give unreserved support to their ally, the Soviet Union, in the joint effort against Hitler's Germany once the Nazi dictator turned on his fellow totalitarian with whom he had so much in common.

In July 1941, when Roosevelt sent his special assistant, Harry Hopkins, to Moscow to tell the Russians that they could expect full American support in their resistance to the Nazis, he had already begun a vast effort that would help the Soviets not only to fight off their aggressors but also eventually enable Moscow to rebuild the Soviet postwar economy. The White House immediately authorized armed convoys to start moving war supplies to Russia's Arctic ports under the Lend-Lease Act, which had been implemented to make the United States all but a belligerent and an ally of the beleaguered British. Even before Averell Harriman, an old hand at looking at the Soviets from his investments in a Soviet manganese concession beginning with the NEP, reached Moscow in September to conclude a formal agreement and find out what the Russians needed for a longer term supply, the Americans had shipped $145 million worth of goods. Washington not only sent armed convoys (the losses were significant) through the North Atlantic route to Murmansk, but built the famous Alcan Highway to Alaska and maintained an air and sea lift into Soviet Asia.

The extent of the American aid to the Soviet Union, first during the wartime arrangements, and then extended through the so-called Pipeline Agreement of October 15, 1945, is estimated to have totaled at least $10.8 billion. But this represents only a part of the total expenditures with subsidiary agreements, some of them somewhat shadowy in their relationship to the war effort and often outside the so-called Lend-Lease Protocols. In toto, the United States shipped more than 14,000 aircraft, almost a half million tanks and trucks (because of the numerous trucks that were carrying Soviet transport, "Studebaker" became a generic Russian word for heavy motorized vehicles), more than a quarter of a million tons of explosives, more than five million registered tons of shipping, another seven thousand marine engines, four million tons of foodstuffs, more than $1 billion in machinery and equipment, two and a half million tons of steel, 800,000 tons of nonferrous metals, a million miles of wire, more than two million tons of petroleum, and more than 800 short tons of chemicals. The postwar "Pipeline Agreement," toward which Moscow eventually repaid $150 million before it lapsed into delinquency, included industrial machinery and spare parts, electrical generating stations, boilers, engines, motors, transformers, machine tools and tools of all varieties, and large quantities of spare parts. Sutton estimates that the Soviets entered the postwar period with at least $1.25 billion worth of the latest U.S. industrial equipment for the rehabilitation of the Soviet postwar peacetime economy.

Furthermore, at the same time that the United States was rushing to Stalin's aid with these official shipments, the Soviets themselves had an elaborate buying mission in the United States. It was mainly a covert operation that solicited and sent to the Soviet Union both political and commercial intelligence, which might have been denied Moscow through regular channels. The Soviet Purchasing Mission (Amtorg) headquartered in Washington (under the direction of both Stalin's principal fabled international government merchant, Anastas Mikoyan, and Mikhail V. Serov, a security organs officer later noted as Nikita Khrushchev's chief enforcer), was pumping enormous quantities of goods, some of it confidential technological and proprietary information, through a network facilitated by the Americans back to Moscow. Much of it was shipped clandestinely through diplomatic pouches to the Soviet Union via the United States' Soviet Asian air lift via a mobilization jumping-off point at Great Falls, Montana. An Arctic program of improving and building Soviet ports and airfields as well as a $12 million program to establish a Northern Siberian Air Route program was undertaken but not included in the main Lend-Lease Protocols, although, as Sutton suggests, the relationship of these Soviet requests to the actual prosecution of the war was "obscure."

> Among the items obtained were designs of industrial plants, special machines, parts and details, photographs and blueprints of technical processes in aviation, arms, oil, submarine building, and many other industries; long-range plans for the development of industrial units, hundreds of maps of the US, the individual states, industrial sites, bridges, descriptions of railroads; reports on the building of cities and highways, and so on.[2]

Werner Keller writes, in his excellent book on Soviet technological dependence on the West:

> From early 1943 strange items of baggage began to arrive at Great Falls [Montana]. Trunks, large and small parcels, wrapped in brown paper, carefully tied with string and "officially sealed" with bright red sealing-wax.
> The Soviets brazenly sent uranium ore to Great Falls. They bought it in Canada and it crossed the frontier, unchecked, in the goods trucks of the Canadian railways. This ore, the exportation of which was strictly prohibited by Washington, . . . [later] made possible the production of the first "Soviet nuclear reactor," an exact copy of Western models.[3]

Soviet official propaganda has spent a good deal of propaganda coinage over the past forty-five years in denigrating lend-lease, the American effort to help them in World War II, and has always dismissed out of hand the role of lend-lease in their postwar rehabilitation. As *glasnost* begins to open other vistas, the extent of American wartime aid in all its ramifications is bound to become more apparent. At the time, Vice President Henry Wallace, an ardent and uninhibited advocate of the wartime collaboration with the Soviets, was surprised, during a wide-ranging trip through the Soviet Union in 1944, to find huge quantities of U.S. goods wherever he went.

In addition to the direct American shipments, there was also U.S.-financed aid through multinational lending agencies. The United Nations Relief and Rehabilitation Administration (UNRRA), largely American financed in its early operations, for example, agreed in 1945 to distribute $250 million worth of goods in the Ukraine and Belorussia—much of it industrial plant and electric power generating equipment, although priority was given to oils and fats. In addition, in 1942 the United Kingdom initiated a program of deliveries to the Soviet Union, free of cost, in which almost 5,000 aircraft were shipped, as well as spares, engines, and airframes. Other British supplies included a thousand tanks, ammunition, nonferrous metals, and industrial diamonds.

Again, it is obviously difficult to quantify the impact of this overall "transfusion" of Western industrial goods and technology into the Soviet economy. (The reader should remember that the figures quoted here represent dollar values of the wartime years, and in 1990s adjusted figures, they would be far greater.) Although the American statistics leave many ambiguities, it is clear that Western industrial goods and technology played a very large role in the Soviet rehabilitation of its industrial machine in the postwar period. This enormous flow of material to the Soviet Union would be followed by a second wave of Western technological and product infusion in the postwar period—the rape of Central Europe and former Japanese-controlled Manchuria by the occupying Soviet forces.

Again, we are in disputed territory: Edward J. Stettinius, U.S. Secretary of State, recalls in his recounting of the Yalta Conference that Stalin lost his generally implacable cool when the question of German reparations arose. Alex Nove, the dean of Western Sovietologists, writing on the economy of the USSR, says:

> There seems little point in entering into arguments about just how much they [the Soviets] did receive, especially as some of the gains took the form of half-shares in joint companies, the value of which (until the practice of such joint companies was abandoned ten years later) is difficult to compute. . . . surely the evidence is overwhelming that the achievement of reconstruction was due above all to the efforts of the Soviet people, though no one would deny that reparations deliveries helped.[4]

Yet a few pages later, Nove writes that "We have seen how, in the very hard first years of peace, the policy was to dismantle and acquire by way of reparations anything that could be taken from an ex-enemy state, even if had now become allied with the Soviet Union." Indeed, there is a vast folklore about the whole effort of the Soviets to remove almost everything that was portable from those parts of Central and Western Europe that they overran after the Nazi defeat. One Russian émigré, a transport engineer attached to the Soviet mission in Berlin, which was transferring plant, tells how Russian superiors would not take a negative answer when he suggested that one metalworking plant was not worth the effort of packing and shipping to the Soviet Union. He was told, with a knowing whisper, that the effort to ship whatever was possible came directly from the *vozhd* (the chief, Stalin).

It was Stalin's henchman, Viacheslav Molotov, the enforcer of the collectivization and foreign minister during the war years, who originally proposed that the allies demand $20 billion in reparations from their former enemies. And it was Stettinius, acting as the secretary of state, who proposed at Yalta that half the reparations should go to the Russians in view of the enormity of the destruction on their territory. But, as with so many other subjects that were discussed at the wartime summits, Stettinius argues that there was never a firm commitment on the part of the Americans for such a transfer.

Whatever the agreements at Yalta, the Soviets pursued their own policy of dismantlement and reparations. In Manchuria, for example, where Soviet troops made a lightning invasion in the summer of 1945 after the war was over in Europe and before the end of the Pacific War, they grabbed the assets created by the Japanese in their puppet state of Manchukuo in Manchuria before the Nationalist troops of President Chiang Kai-shek could arrive to take over the area. These assets, which included large Western-made capital plant as well as Japanese manufactured machinery, have been valued at $800 million.

> It is clear that the Soviet authorities were working on a separate plan, prepared before the long drawn-out discussions in the Allied Control Council had even begun. The plan was in operation at a time when the Western Reparations Agency had only begun to register the individual claims of the participating powers and was tentatively having particular works earmarked for dismantling.[5]

The U.S. Central Intelligence Agency has put a figure of $10 billion on what the Soviets were able to transfer (excluding Manchuria and possibly Finland).

Again, it has been argued by such authoritative commentators as Walter Bedell Smith, former U.S. ambassador to the Soviet Union, and General Lucius Clay, U.S. military governor in Germany, that many, if not most, of the dismantled plants were never effectively used by the Soviets either because of delays in reestablishing them or of other problems. A British writer, J.P. Nettl, who made an intensive study of Soviet policy in Soviet-occupied Germany, disagrees. He argues that the very effective removal of Soviet plants from the path of the Nazi invasion in 1941 to new installations in the Urals had given the Russians considerable experience in just such plant relocations. There is also the argument that much of the capital plant in Germany, and the other European areas where the Russians removed factories, was damaged by allied aerial bombardment. Sutton concludes, after making allowances for all of these factors, that the Soviet gain was nevertheless overwhelming. He points out that there is evidence that the Russians largely moved plants according to a highly detailed plan; in Manchuria, for example, they took a ballbearing plant but left electric furnaces. And Sutton points to a very efficient dismantling and shipping to Russia in January 1945 of a truck assembly plant that the United States had established under lend-lease in Iran by Soviet and American crews.

It should be noted that not only did the Russians remove plants from what was to become the Soviet zone, or later the German Democratic Republic (East Germany), but they also were granted permission by the Allies to remove plants from the Western zones. Although the Russians were obliged under the agreements to deliver commodities to the Western zones, they actually defaulted on this obligation as they did on others as relations among the occupying powers deteriorated. They got the Band-eisenwalzwerk Dinsklaen AG plant, the most efficient hot and cold steel rolling mill on the European continent at the time, from the British zone. From the U.S. zone, they got the Huttenwerk Essen-Borbeck steel mill. A total of 156 plants in the U.S. zone were marked for dismantling and shipment to the Soviets, including a ballbearing plant from Bavaria.

The steelmaking and machinery plant removals pale into relative insignificance in contrast with the treasure trove that the Soviets secured from Nazi Germany's aircraft and space industry.[6] One can excuse Werner Keller his touch of German chauvinism apparent in his graphic descriptions in his book on Western technological transfer through the centuries to the Russians.[7] On October 28, 1946, trainloads of disassembled aircraft and parts, plants, materiel, aviation experts, and aviation industry workers, plans and drawings, and the contents of entire laboratories, left the Soviet zone of Germany for Podberezhye on Lake Moscow, an artificial lake fed by the Volga, which soon began to be called *Malaia Germaniia* (Little Germany). The Soviets had built quarters here to receive materiel salvaged from the Junker & Seibel Works, the Heinkel Works at Oranienburg, and the Messerschmidt Works from Weiner-Neustadt. The German engineers, some of whom had originally been in the Western zones but had gone back to homes or their former plants in the Soviet zone, were astonished to find even the same desks they had used in Germany. Another group of German engineers was put down with the complete Junkers Motor Works from Bernburg on the Saale in Kuibyshev—the wartime capital of the Soviets when Moscow had been evacuated—which would become the first great production center for the Soviet air force. They were also joined by the machine shop of BMW at Eisenbach. Professor Willy Messerschmidt estimated that two-thirds of the Nazi aircraft production industry had been transferred to the Soviet Union. Kidnapped or enticed, the Germans could do little but make the best of a bad bargain, which was to resume, at the standard German rate of workaholic activity, their previous tasks in Germany. Even the Junker test pilots, like Captain Wolfgang Ziese, began to instruct Soviet pilots and engineers. Ziese started teaching with German glider aircraft, test vehicles with swept-back wings, which were preliminary to the development of jet aircraft, which Messerschmidt has already envisaged before the end of the war and for which preliminary production had already begun in Germany. After the initial 6,000 Germans arrived, the Soviets were able to capture two additional German designers, Dr. Siegfried Gunther and Professor Heinz Benz, who were to be used to produce a jet fighter capable of repulsing American heavy B29 bombers. Benz had been the designer of the famous turbojet HE162, the *Volksjager*, put into production by the Nazis in six months near the end of the war. Gunther had been the chief designer for Heinkel's—designer of the first jet aircraft in the world in 1939. (Gunther had applied for work with the Americans but had been refused and decided to go back to East Berlin where his family lived. The Soviet secret service picked him up in forty-eight hours, offered fantastic contracts, and hustled him off to the East in the middle of the night.)

The first models for the new Soviet air force were floated down barges on the Volga to be test-flown under the fuselage of a B29, which had crashed in Soviet Far East territory after raids on Japan and had never been returned to the United States. A new experimental aircraft, the DFS-346, which was successfully test-flown by the Germans, was not so successful when copies were made and flown by the Russians. And it only later became apparent to the Germans—carefully working in separate groups—that the Soviets were intent on creating an entire new fleet of war planes and coming up with them as a dramatic surprise for the United States and the West. The new fighter with jet propulsion of the Junkers-004 and the BMW-003, copies of which had been brought to the Soviet Union from Germany, began to take shape. The German designs were given Russian names. And when the British Rolls Royce announced a jet engine with greater thrust, the Russians bought it and added it to the project. By 1948 these new "wonder fighters," built and manned by Germans, were taking off from an experimental airfield near Moscow. They disappeared—from the German group—to turn up, first at the edge of the American Airlift that ended the blockade of West Berlin, but only formally during the May Day fly-past ceremonies in 1949. The Americans would meet them, face to face, on the Yalu in November 1950 when the planes—now officially dubbed MIGs—appeared in combat. Keller points out that their resemblance to the F86s that Washington sent to Korea to combat the MIGs was not accidental. Both owed their origins to the German swept-back wing designs that the Americans had taken from Messerschmidt designs (saving three years of development time) and the Russians had taken from the files of the Luftwaffe. Adding insult to injury, "Comrade Engineer and Inventor Gurevich modestly recounted how he had designed the plane in an American technical magazine, adding . . . that there are many others who deserve credit. We are now concentrating our attentions on further problems in the building of new aircraft with which to confirm the supremacy of the USSR and do honor to the achievements of the Great Stalin."

The same type of story was repeated in the bomber command. Dr. Brunolf Baade, a German designer who had worked in the United States before he became chief construction engineer at the Junkers works, continued work in Podberezhye on his last project in Germany, the Vo series of jet bombers. In Russia he developed the Ju-287, the first "Russian" jet bomber, ahead of similar developments in other countries. They remodeled its wings, borrowing from the German V-1 pilotless bombers, and gave it a TU (after the Russian aircraft designer Tupolev). By 1954, eight years after their deportation and after many broken promises, the German and Austrian engineers were permitted to return to Germany. (Twenty-five were dead, of whom five committed suicide, and two went mad. Baade was never permitted to leave.)

Other industries and their workers were also seized by the Russians; for example, the most prestigious optical works in the world, Zeiss, with 300 scientists, technicians, and workers was moved into the Soviet Union, as were the glassworks at Jena, and the Oberspree cable works at Nieder-schoenweida.

There are also abundant details on how Finland, which had fought two wars with the Soviet Union by 1945, was required to pay $300 million in gold in reparations, as well as to surrender one-half of its prewar merchant fleet. The Finnish-Soviet reparations have played an enormously important role in the postwar Soviet economy. Finland, because of its historic good relations with the United States and Canada, was permitted to use credits from the United States and Sweden to create major new industries (which in many instances delivered whole new plants to the Soviet Union) and to expand others to meet the requirements of the Soviet reparations program.

The Finns, by all accounts, know more about trading with the Soviets than anyone else. They have had to learn. In the aftermath of World War II—after Finland had joined Germany as a cobelligerent against the Soviets following their own short and catastrophic Winter War to stave off Soviet aggression—Moscow saddled the Finns with an enormous reparations burden.

Not only did the Finns pay that bill, but they developed out of it a booming barter trade with Moscow. At times in the postwar period, they were supplying Moscow with 25 percent of total Soviet imports. During the heyday of the trade, it constituted 27 percent of all Finnish foreign trade. The Finns, fewer than five million in a country that was essentially rural and agrarian until World War II, have a half dozen Finnish world class multinationals. And Finland's booming (if slightly overheated) economy provides one of the highest living standards in Europe. It is a developmental model—the envy of its Scandinavian neighbors, who marvel at its ability to keep the lid on welfare statism.

By 1989 Finland's trade with the Soviet Union was dropping sharply— despite the little country's post-World War II role as one of Russia's main suppliers in the West. And it came at a time when Finland's burgeoning hi-tech exports would seem to be just what the doctors from Novosibirsk ordered for Soviet *perestroika*. The reasons offer an interesting vignette on the USSR's economic troubles—and a cautionary tale for those optimists in the West who ogle potentially rich Soviet markets.

By 1989 Soviet trade was less than 12 percent of Finland's total; West Germany was her largest trading partner, and the majority of her international trade is with other Western nations. Despite this fact, however, the Finns still depend greatly on exports to the Soviets. In 1989 there were approximately 70,000 people in the workforce who owed their jobs to these exports that tend to be labor intensive. (That figure was down from 140,000 just a few years earlier.)

Finland's tough-minded central bank called a halt to Soviet barter exports in the spring of 1988. (The bank's prestigious history and independence dates back to the nineteenth century when the Czar of All the Russias was Finland's Archduke, who accorded the Finns autonomy, including their own currency.) Moscow had run up approximately a billion dollars' worth of mostly interest-free debt against the Finns. The Bank of Finland obviously did not believe that Finland should finance *perestroika*.

It took most of 1988 to get a settlement. Under new arrangements, the Finns would get interest when the permanent trade imbalance went beyond 100 million Soviet rubles. When the amount exceeded 200 million Soviet rubles, Helsinki could convert part of it into other (convertible) currencies. In fact, some of the trade theoretically can now be carried on in Finn markkaa, which is a convertible currency. And the Finns have taken the precaution, in the event that there is something to the unlikely possibility of a convertible ruble, of insuring themselves against a possible Soviet devaluation.

The Finns have previously had limits on the barter imbalance that were not respected, however, and only the Central Bank's blocking $350 million worth of back orders forced the Russians into the new settlement after months of talk and a half dozen negotiating missions back and forth between Moscow and Helsinki. (Those back orders and the stymied trade were also a powerful political lever for the Russians inside the Finnish political economy.) It is an agreement that did not take effect until 1990, and the government announcements were not entirely clear about what happens to the accumulated debt. (One source told me that the Finns would like to sell some of it at discount to Western banks!)

Over the years the Finns have taken a bum rap among many Western anti-Communists for their relations with the Soviets. The truth is that, abandoned by their Western allies twice during the Winter War in 1939 and again in 1945, they have made the best of living next to the "Great Bear," including their commercial relations. "Finlandize," a term bandied about for years as the name for the possibility of Western Europe's knuckling under to Moscow, is a misnomer; it should rather be "Czecho-slovakize"—based on a similar history of a small country (albeit one that has fared far less well) that might have fought for its freedom had it not been left to the Soviets' mercy by its allies.

Yet, the dismantling and reparations program is only part of the story of the economic benefits that the Soviet economy has derived from the domination of Central Europe in the postwar period. It permitted Moscow to make what Nove calls "unequal" trade agreements with the former capitalist countries, all of whom, almost without exception, had had a standard of living and technological development more advanced than the Soviets. Nove says that the extent of the Soviet advantage in these agreements has been exaggerated "by propagandists" in the West, but:

> The fact that two ministers of foreign trade (in Bulgaria and Czechoslovakia) were executed quite specifically for bargaining too hard with the Soviet Union suggests that bargaining was not really equal. After Yugoslavia's defection (1948), Stalin became deeply suspicious of nationalist deviations, and a great many communists in all East European countries were shot or imprisoned for giving too great weight to their countries' national interests.[8]

As is so often the case with Soviet macroeconomic statistics, there is very little evidence in official figures to indicate that there was a flow of resources from the satellites to the Soviet Union. Much can be inferred, however; perhaps at a future date, it will be possible for students of the issue to reassess this aspect of intrabloc trade. Official statistics do reveal that in 1947, for example, three-quarters of all Soviet imports came from the eastern and central European states that Moscow had overrun. The standard reply of Western students of the Soviet economy is that, although it is true that Moscow used the facilities of these economics for transfers of machinery, machine tools, and consumer goods, they were repaid with shipments of Soviet raw materials, often at below world prices.

The general problem of examining what actually took place, particularly in the early postwar years, during the most primitive period of Soviet domination over Central Europe, is best illustrated by a joke current in that area in the 1980s. A foreign trade organization official of one of the Communist Central European countries comes back from a "fraternal" (Communist) country and reports to his boss that he has clinched a highly profitable deal. He boasts that he has sold 500 dogs for 10,000 transferable rubles. The boss compliments him, but then remembers the requirement that trade with another Communist country be balanced according to the dictates of central planning. And the higher official asks the trade negotiator what he was able to get in return. The trader replies that he has been able to purchase 1,000 cats for 5,000 transferable rubles each.[9]

> The lack of knowledge about gains or losses that trade brings about has created some very peculiar defence mechanisms in intra-COMECON trade [inside the Communist Bloc] in the form of bilateral balancing of trade flows, structural bilateralism (balancing trade by each product group), etc. . . . Trading without proper prices over time has been extended to producing for the other COMECON countries without proper prices.[10]

The problem for East Germany and Czechoslovakia was particularly grave in the post-World War II period because, as late as 1945, both had been among the most highly sophisticated industrialized areas of the world. What is now called East Germany was the seat of one of the world's first industrialized areas, which in 1945, under the Nazi war machine, still held world leadership in such leading technological fields as optics, synthetic chemicals, porcelain, and machine tools. Czechoslovakia had, in fact, by putting one-third of its investments into engineering and by the transfer of many industries from Germany during the war, expanded its metallurgical industries under the German Occupation of Bohemia and Moravia by at least 16 percent with a work force of almost half a million men.[11] By 1947 Czechoslovakia was exporting 92 percent of its prewar level and had a positive trade balance. A Communist draft of an industrial policy for the country in 1945 and 1946 foresaw Czechoslovakia's replacing Germany as the chief supplier of industrial equipment to the eastern European countries. Non-Communist members of the Czech government argued, to no avail, that payments problems with the Russians and the unreliability of raw material deliveries made such a strategy less than adequate. For example, Czechoslovakia had depended on Sweden for about half of its iron ore imports before World War II—70 to 80 percent during the war—because Russian supplies were not as good. They also pointed out that the relative success of the quick postwar rehabilitation was a result of massive inflows of capital and technical assistance from the United Nations Relief and Rehabilitation Administration (UNRRA) and the exhaustion of Czech prewar gold reserves, which had been deposited in London at the outbreak of World War II and then released to the postwar government. From 1947 Czechoslovakia began to run a trade deficit with the West while running surpluses with the Soviet Union by its export of metallurgical goods, including machine tools vital to the Soviets. A struggle ensued inside the Czech government in October and November 1947 over this trade and payments problem between the Communists and non-Communist leadership. The Communists in the government insisted on an expansion of the metallurgical industries while the non-Communist economists and planners argued for capital imports from the West, which would permit the country to diversify into new industries. The announcement of the Marshall Plan in June 1947 by the United States brought all these arguments to a head. Despite Molotov's rejection of the Franco-British program of accepting the American offer to the European states in Paris on June 2, the Czech non-Communists hoped that some compromise would be found that would permit them to participate.

A high Czech delegation flew to Moscow and saw Stalin on July 9.

Stalin firstly mentioned that the governments of Yugoslavia, Poland, and Romania all inquired in Moscow before taking their own decision and only then had finalized the decision. Both Stalin as well as Molotov did not conceal from us that they were surprised by the decision of the Czechoslovak government to accept the invitation to Paris. They stressed that the true purpose of the Marshall plan was to form a Western bloc and . . . that the organizers of the Conference would not remain without influence on the political and economic independence of the participants. In view of this situation, the Soviet Union regarded our [Czechoslovakia] participation as a breach in the front of the Slav states, and as an action directed against the Soviet Union. Stalin declared that these were matters on which our [Czechoslovak] friendship with the USSR depended. There was none in the Soviet government who doubted our [Czechoslovak] friendship with the Soviet Union. Our [Czech] participation in Paris would show the peoples of the Soviet Union that we had allowed ourselves to be misused as an instrument against the USSR, and that could not be tolerated either by the

Soviet public or by the Soviet government. Therefore, Stalin believes, we should withdraw our acceptance [of participation in the conference to formulate the European response to the Marshall plan]. We [Czechoslovaks] could justify this by noting that due to the absence of the other Slav peoples and of other East European states, a new situation had arisen and that our participation could be directed against friendship with the USSR and our other allies. [12]

The repeated call on Slav solidarity in this internal Czech government dispatch sounds hollow and artificial in the 1990s. But in the embittered post-World War II atmosphere in which Czechoslovakia had suffered dismemberment before the war in the face of betrayal by her Western allies, and in which the Soviets had only recently "liberated" these Central European Slavic lands from the brutal Nazi German oppression, the appeal was strong. Especially, as the Soviet government's ultimate power over Prague was manifest in the final sentences of the dispatch:

Therefore, call all the available members of the [Czechoslovak] Government together and inform them of the contents of our discussion with Stalin and Molotov. We [Gottwald, Masaryk, and Drtina] regard it as essential that you should withdraw from participation in Paris and publish it so that we have the announcement here by Thursday [July 11] afternoon. [13]

President Benes, after reading the dispatch, said, "It is absolutely clear that the acceptance of participation must be withdrawn."

The economic consequences of the rejection of the Marshall Plan made it impossible for the postwar governments, whether Communist or not, to restructure the aging Czech capital plant. That did not prevent an even more retrogressive Soviet economy from exploiting it, but it did help turn Czechoslovakia, which had been one of the ten most highly developed industrial countries in the world between the two wars, into a moribund industrial society by the 1970s.

It may never be possible to quantify adequately the benefits to the Soviet economy of the transfers from Czechoslovakia, East Germany, and the other Communist-dominated Central European states during the early postwar period when Moscow dictated the terms of that trade. In part, of course, this is a problem complicated by the vagaries of the international markets. Soviet petroleum exports, for example, were priced arbitrarily until the world petroleum crisis brought on highly inflated prices imposed by the Organization of Petroleum Exporting Countries (OPEC) in 1975. Then, the Soviets raised prices to their Central European customers. Following the collapse of oil prices in 1981, the Soviets promised a scaling back of prices that would follow international markets. By 1989 it appeared to many observers in the West that Soviet prices to the Communist customers in the region were again above world prices. Furthermore, the revelations of *glasnost* on the statistical front indicate that even Soviet officialdom may not be certain about their real price structures.

A Polish revisionist economist, in a book that tries to examine the inadequacies of Soviet-style planning from a econometric point of view, puts it this way:

> After the period of unilateral advantages for the Soviet Union in the Stalinist period came a period where terms of trade (rather than diktat) became important, and the Soviet Union as a commodity exporter, became a loser. With the terms of trade in general and energy resources in particular, the USSR neither took full advantage with respect to price adjustments, nor did it press for immediate trade balancing (which would be impossible anyway). . . . Besides another change is occurring at the time of writing [1988], since world market prices of oil are now lower than intra-COMECON prices, thus reversing the issue of the flow of benefits with respect to price level (but not necessarily that of trade balancing).[14]

Under Soviet initiative, the East Bloc has tried to evolve an international organization that could more effectively coordinate economic relations among the socialist countries. This so-called Council for Mutual Economic Assistance (CEMA) was supposed to put the Soviet Union, bigger than all the other six members combined, together with Mongolia, Cuba, and Vietnam, into a more rational trading relationship. But trade in goods and other financial transactions between these generally noncomplementary countries are not always based on economic incentive and, in fact, often deflect it away from more natural partners.

A former member of the CEMA staff, writing in the West, says that CEMA is . . .

> A foundering and ineffectual bureaucracy not above the influence of independent national interest. . . . CEMA is plagued by a haphazard, redundant, and arbitrary infrastructure. . . . The need to substantiate desired policies and

projects with an ideological underpinning is ever-important to East Bloc leadership, as evidenced by the operation of the International Institute of Economic Problems in the World Socialist System. . . . The situation is such that administrative units can exist and operate virtually without substantive agendas, and meetings are timed to coincide with announcements of inter-governmental agreements to eclipse their lack of action. . . . Without significant hard currency resources of its own, CEMA's role in the financial sphere is reduced to that of a clearing house for transferable rubles, through the International Bank of Economic Cooperation. . . . It is not the influence of the USSR but rather the mutual exclusiveness of economic integration and the socialist economic system that prevents and will continue to prevent CEMA from fulfilling functions sought by Soviet and East Bloc leadership.[15]

Thus, the attempt to imitate integration efforts in Western Europe, whatever the real intent of Soviet policy, has turned out to be just one more embarrassing aspect of the failure of the system. That was admitted publicly in January 1990 when the Central European states sought to abandon the moribund CEMA organization altogether at its Sofia meeting. Western news dispatches, however, as so often in treating economic news from the Communist countries, gave CEMA a respectability it never had. It was primarily an organ of Soviet exploitation, however inefficient.

Whatever deficiencies in Moscow's attempts to milk the satellites in the post-World War II period derive from the general uneconomic nature of the Soviet system, it is clear that, particularly in the early postwar years, Moscow received an important "transfusion" from Central Europe. Like so many aspects of the seventy years of Soviet history, this transfusion was somewhat obscured by the bizarre political occurrences within the Soviet Bloc, including the East German revolt of 1953, the Hungarian Revolution of 1958, and the Prague Spring of 1968.

CHAPTER 5

TWO DREAMS IN THE SAME BED

Détente to the West, Respite for the East

A French journalist, Eric Laurent, has probably described these dreams[1] best:

> Détente is a word sufficiently vague to cover a reality infinitely subtle, fluctuating and ambiguous. From 1972 to 1985, East-West political cooperation and relationships existed [from the point of view of Washington] without fundamental priorities. Peripheral [considerations] dictated certain simple tactical momentary responses, in new ideological dress, leaving final objectives in question.[2]

There is at least the possibility, with 20–20 hindsight, that détente emerged primarily from the American frustrations of the Vietnam War. President Richard Nixon wanted to disentangle the United States from its travail in Southeast Asia. He had seen the conflict turn Lyndon Johnson out of the White House and defeat his ambitions for a second term in office. Nixon was imbued with a wide-ranging knowledge of foreign policy issues founded on an extensive participation in foreign business as well as political affairs, probably more than any president since Woodrow Wilson. His particularly thorough knowledge of the affairs of the multinational corporations was acquired during his enforced exile from politics during the Kennedy-Johnson years after he narrowly lost the presidency to John Kennedy.[3]

73

The immediate priority was Southeast Asia, which fell into the domain of his chief steward of foreign policy, Henry Kissinger. The more cynical Washington foreign policy establishment wits had not too incorrectly characterized Kissinger as a brilliant geopolitician for whom problems more than a thousand miles from Vienna were *terra incognito*. All of the feasible solutions that the American establishment could devise in Vietnam had been attempted (except the maximum use of American force, which it calculated would bring the Chinese Communists directly into the war). There was nothing left, therefore, but to fit into a wider global strategy what became known fashionably in Washington in the late 1960s as "mired down with 80 percent of our resources in three little insignificant countries in Southeast Asia."[4] And if the enemy in Vietnam was Hanoi's Communist regime principally supported by the might of the Soviet superpower, perhaps what was needed was to strike a deal with Moscow to disengage the United States.

These two collaborators in *realpolitik*, perhaps unknowingly, were picking up on an earlier vein of U.S. policy established in the first months of the Kennedy administration. It had been worked in the depths of the State Department by Assistant Secretary of State Averell Harriman, an old Soviet hand who had warned Franklin Roosevelt of the pitfalls of dealing with Stalin (largely to no avail) during the war years when Harriman was Washington's emissary to Moscow. Harriman and his assistant Roger Hilsman, a career diplomat with some Asian experience, had plotted the overthrow of the Vietnamese patriot and embattled leader, Ngo Dinh Diem. Harriman argued that both the United States and the Soviet Union had parallel policy interests in that they wanted to halt the intrusion of what appeared to be the growing influence of Communist China throughout Asia. Therefore U.S. and Soviet interests were congruent in Vietnam and Moscow might help find a Vietnam "solution" for the United States owing to enormous Soviet influence as the principal logistics source for Hanoi. From that commonality, an accommodation could be found in Indochina. And, so the argument ran, a worldwide accommodation might be reached between what appeared to be growing Soviet power and declining U.S. willingness to make good on John Kennedy's pledge "to make any sacrifice" for American world leadership. But the death of Diem probably spelled the end of any possibility of creating a viable Vietnamese resistance to the intrusion into Vietnamese internal politics of Hanoi, Moscow, and Peking. It also eventually meant failure of American policy in Vietnam. A deal with the Soviets turned into a chimera that brought new defeats and tragedy to the West, as Kissinger himself admitted (in a moment of unusual candor) in a famous, if since carefully edited, speech in Brussels.

Meanwhile, in Moscow, it was the Brezhnev era. This is now characterized by "the reformers" around Gorbachev as the years of drift and decline of the Soviet economy. "The Brezhnev trends," according to these latter-day critics, included a declining gross national product, rising inefficiency on every side and corruption everywhere, a widening technological gap with the West, and a deterioration of living standards. Although Brezhnev's original partner in power, Kosygin, had been a strong advocate of reform and reorganization of the Soviet economy, Brezhnev was cautious. There were limited reforms, nevertheless, in 1965, such as an attempt at decentralization and some effort to halt the drain on the treasury of the state enterprises. These reforms were modeled in part on those that Khrushchev earlier had tried and failed to implement.

As Brezhnev became more secure in domestic political policy, however, the Soviet Union tried to substitute Western trade and acquired technologies for the pursuit of major domestic reforms. That does not mean that Brezhnev was oblivious to the need for domestic reforms. "If the Prague Spring showed what could happen if reform went too far, the revolts in Poland which dislodged Gomulka in 1970 revealed the dangers of doing nothing—and almost certainly had a profound effect on Soviet leadership."[5] Brezhnev sought to balance several basic issues with a strategy that included placating both the *apparatchiki* with a minimum of structural reforms and the Soviet consumer with a promise of more resources for consumer goods, while increasing defense spending and moving technology ahead with Western imports.

In fact, although Brezhnev, with his fatherly image and generally placid exterior, may have masked the real developments for the general public in the East as well as in the West, it was already apparent to acute observers both inside and outside the Soviet economy that fundamental problems were destroying the base of the socialist system. Even to a not very perceptive observer so typical of the Sovietological industry in the United States that produced tome after tome on Russian problems in the 1950s and 1960s, largely based on official Soviet statistics and ideological rhetoric, there was a vague understanding of the coming crisis in the

Soviet economic system. In virtually the same terms an advocate of *perestroika* would explain the situation today:

> It would appear, however, that the problems faced by centralized planning at the present stage of development of the Soviet economy are too basic to allow the system of economic planning and control to go unchanged for very long. Much will depend on what happens to the objectives of the political leaders. If the international situation substantially worsens, then the Soviets may again move toward mobilization and centralization. . . . And the economy has reached an impasse, where the planning and control methods of the past are fetters on continued progress.[6]

Andrei Sakharov, the Soviets' most renowned scientist, and Roy Medvedev, a historian who had discussed Stalin in what was under Brezhnev highly provocative criticism of the Soviet past, put it bluntly and crudely in a letter in 1970:

> Comparing our economy to that of the United States we find that we are behind not only on the quantitative plane, but also—and this is much sadder—on the qualitative plane. The gulf between the United States and us is all the greater in the newest and most revolutionary sectors of the economy. We are ahead of America in coal extraction, but behind in oil, gas and electric energy; we are ten years behind in chemistry and infinitely behind in computer technology . . . We simply live in another era.[7]

This kind of statement became commonplace, even in the Soviet press, by the 1980s, but in 1970, only a few years after Nikita Khrushchev's famous "We will bury you" challenge to the Americans and the pyrotechnics of Sputnik, it seemed revolutionary and seemed to present a whole new perspective of the Soviet economy and politicoeconomic thinking in the USSR.

The Soviet leaders' motivation for détente, as a Senate subcommittee reported in 1974, was closely related to, if not dictated by, these problems in their economy. Growth was declining, manpower reserves were becoming exhausted, the balance of payments deficit was growing, agricultural inefficiency was apparent, and the Soviets could not respond to demands for technological development. Having rejected Kosygin's feeble attempts at economic reform through decentralization, the Soviet leadership had opted for massive assistance from the West.

This policy was all the more attractive because while it is expected to bring large amounts of capital into the Soviet Union, the repayment is to be mainly in the very commodities that the Western-financed project would produce. At the same time, the flow of Western technology and know-how is expected by the Soviet leaders to narrow the growing technological gap with the West and to improve Soviet export capacity. The Americans, Japanese, and the Europeans are to build up whole industries for the Soviet Union and develop vast regions there at very little cost to the Soviet Union itself, and with minimal risk to Soviet institutions. Contrary to widespread Western belief, the 'more liberal' economic strategy abroad is quite compatible with conservative policy at home. Indeed, this double-pronged economic strategy is an alternative to domestic economic reform which the Soviet leaders feared might jeopardize the stability of existing Soviet institutions and general political strife.[8]

"Very little homework" had been done in the United States on how Soviet trading worked, how Moscow's government monopolies could be manipulated by the Kremlin against Western competitive enterprise, and how "many Western business leaders have shown themselves to be remarkably eager to take Soviet economic propaganda at face value." The Senate report pointed out how the U.S. company Control Data Corporation and other firms were, by selling $3 million worth of computers in three years to the Soviets, giving them fifteen years' lead time in computer R&D. Lockheed and other aircraft firms were competing to provide the Soviets with the latest in American jetliner technology. The Soviets were negotiating the purchase of the highspeed computer "Cyber." "The economic and technological advantages of détente are thus, somewhat one-sided and in the long run this asymmetry could be dangerous," the article concluded acerbically.

Nevertheless, Nixon and Kissinger saw their tactics as a sophisticated campaign of "linkage." That is, rather than conclude individual agreements with Moscow in different areas, progress toward accommodation would be linked to a quid pro quo (Vietnam was the best example from the American side). Kissinger planned that if the Russians wanted credits, trade, and technology for their modernization drive, they would have to compromise on such items as arms control and cutting back on military expenditures to provide the resources. Nixon had launched a trial balloon with the Export Administration Act of 1969. It cut back the restricted U.S. goods that could be shipped to the Soviet Union, and loosened the restraints on the so-called CoCom (Coordinating Committee for Multilateral Export Controls) controls, the North American Treaty Organization (plus Japan) Western alliance ban on strategic goods for the Soviets. On January 9, 1971, Nixon sent Leonid Brezhnev the first in a series of messages in which he suggested that the United States would help the Soviets to modernize their economy. Brezhnev responded with what appeared to be a historic shift away from Soviet autarchy. And within six months after the Nixon-Brezhnev Summit, Kissinger had what he thought was an agreement to permit the United States to extricate itself from Vietnam.

Solzhenitsyn characterized the negotiations for détente using a chess metaphor:

> This is like two players sitting at a chess board, one of whom has a tremendously high opinion of himself and a rather low opinion of his opponent. He thinks he will, of course, outplay his opponent. He thinks he is so clever, so calculating, so inventive, that he will certainly win. He sits there, he calculates his moves. With these two knights, he will take four rooks. He can hardly wait for his opponent to move. He's squirming on his chair out of happiness. He takes off his glasses, wipes them, and puts them back again. He doesn't even admit the possibility that his opponent may be more clever. He doesn't even see that his pawns are being taken one after another and that his castle is under threat . . . But even if this chess player were able to win the game on the board, carried away by the play, he forgets to raise his eyes; he forgets to look at his opponent and doesn't see that he has the eyes of a killer. And if the opponent cannot win the game on the board, he will take a club from behind his back and shatter the skull of the other chess player, winning the game that way.[9]

An extensive public relations campaign by the Nixon administration to sell détente to the American public and to the business community was initiated by a trip by Commerce Secretary Maurice Stans to Moscow in late 1971. He told *U.S. News & World Report* that the United States would help develop Soviet raw materials with capital repayment and interest paid for by export of such products as natural gas, oil, timber, pulp, and nonferrous metals. Stans emphasized that Moscow was interested in also acquiring machine tools, factory equipment, complete plants, industrial technology, and so on. *Business International* sponsored a roundtable discussion in Moscow with over seventy U.S. corporations participating in conjunction with the Stans trip. Many of the firms reported that the Russians were interested in doing "real business."

In a reversal of long-term policies, on June 3, 1971, Washington approved the export of $50 million worth of equipment for the manufacture of light trucks in the Soviet Union. Mack Trucks made public June 17, 1971, a preliminary agreement to design and supply machine tools and trucks to the Soviet Union's Kama River Heavy Truck Plant. In all the project would entail the shipment to the USSR of $750 million in machine tools and the purchase of $22 million worth of Mack trucks by the Soviet Union. Ford Motor Company, apparently as a result of representations by the U.S. Defense Department, refused to build the plant. But on August 9, two unidentified companies received permission to ship $162 million "worth of foundry equipment for automotive castings." A third license was granted to Swindell-Dressler Company of Pittsburgh to design the plant. In testimony before congressional committees, representatives of the Nixon administration argued that the trucks produced by the plant would be used only for civilian purposes.

The program of linkage rolled along, propelled by private U.S. business that was encouraged informally by the U.S. government. The icing on the cake came with Nixon's trip to Russia in June 1972, which was a far cry from his visit as vice president in 1959 to a Moscow trade fair. Then, he had held his famous no-holds-barred debate in a trade fair mock-up American kitchen with Nikita Khrushchev, which had contributed to the anti-Communist posture that had helped win him the presidency. Within half an hour of his return from the Soviet Union, Nixon called the Congress into extraordinary joint session and told them that a new foundation had been laid "for a new relationship" with the Soviet Union. In a nationally televised speech, Nixon did caution the country that the Soviets remained an ideological adversary and that the United States must maintain a vigorous economy and a confident spirit. But he said that "one of the most extensively discussed subjects on our agenda" in Moscow had been the Vietnam War. He said he could not reveal what had been said or agreed upon because that would jeopardize the results, but he hinted at Moscow's help. In October 1972, a U.S.-USSR Trade Agreement was announced. The United States agreed to extend Most Favored Nation (MFN) trade concessions to the Soviets and to provide long-term credits for American purchases. The Soviets, in turn, agreed to pay $722 million for their World War II and postwar lend-lease debts. And euphoria reigned in the White House and among Kissinger's associates in Foggy Bottom.

The rationale for this policy was presented by the secretary of commerce in a government document on U.S.-Soviet commercial relations in 1972. If we did not sell to the Soviets, other competitors in other allied countries would. This attitude toward more relaxed restrictions on Soviet trade had come as early as the Export Administration Act of 1969. But Nixon and Kissinger did not view this expanded trade as primarily a business or an economic consideration—although it was true that Nixon's long associa- tion with the multinational companies and the highest echelons of U.S. business gave them a receptive ear at the White House. The two geopoli- ticians saw expanded trade as an important bargaining lever that would influence the Soviet political behavior.

When the Congress clipped the wings of what began to be called, sarcastically in some quarters, Kissinger's Grand Design, with credit restrictions, Kissinger replied in his habitual funereal tones:

> We have approached the question of economic relations with deliberation and circumspection and as an act of policy, not primarily of commercial opportunity. As political relations have improved on a broad basis, economic issues have been dealt with on a comparative broad front. A series of interlocking agreements with the USSR has been negotiated side by side with the political progress already noted. The 25-year-old Lend Lease debt was settled; the reciprocal extension of most favored nation (MFN) treatment negotiated, together with safeguards against the possible disruption of our markets and a series of practical arrangements to facilitate the conduct of the business in the USSR by American firms; our government credit facilities were available for trade with the USSR; and a maritime agreement regulating the carriage of goods has been signed. . . . The technology that flows to the USSR as a result of expanded US-Soviet Trade may have a few indirect uses for military production. But with our continuing restrictions on strategic exports, we can maintain adequate controls—and we intend to do so.[10]

Kissinger's grand design rested on a faulty premise. Greater economic interdependency between the West, including the United States, and the Soviets would restrain Moscow's behavior. It was such a weak premise that one of Kissinger's harshest critics, the economist G. Warren Nutter, said that it was an argument that Professor (Historian) Kissinger would never have made to Diplomatist (Negotiator) Kissinger. "He has little backing from history. Economic interdependence is not exactly new." Nutter added that "On the eve of World War I Norman Angell argued in *The Great Illusion* that the intricate network of world commerce had destroyed all possibility of gain from war. Yet the warring nations of Europe in the twentieth century, as in the nineteenth, normally were close trading partners."[11] Had not Germany and France, the two largest trading partners in Europe, gone to war in almost every generation for 200 years!

Nutter argued that precisely because the Soviet weakness was in economic and technological areas, it would have to be the focus of creating any Soviet vested interest in peace. "Over time, trade and investment may soften the autarchic tendencies of the Soviet system, invite gradual association of the Soviet economy with the world economy, and for a degree of interdependence that adds an element of stability to the equation." Nutter's reply was that the Nixon-Kissinger agreements really asked for economic aid to the Soviet Union with no guarantees that autarchy would be abandoned. Would that bring Moscow into dependency on the West? "Hardly," Nutter said. "Historically, tribute has been no more successful than trade in preventing conquest or domination by a foreign power."[12]

Whatever its merits, the Nixon-Kissinger program began to unravel when in December 1974, congressional skeptics limited Export-Import Bank credits to the Soviet Union to a puny $75 million a year over four years with additional severe limits on energy project developments. Moscow had already had to swallow a bitter congressional pill when the (Henry "Scoop") Jackson Amendment tied credits to permission for Jews to leave the Soviet Union. Moscow nullified the 1972 trade agreement, including its promise to pay lend-lease debts, ostensibly in retaliation for the reduced credit facilities. The Nixon administration argued that the Congress had broken "linkage," although as one commentator put it:

> However, in this sense "linkage" carries a rather different meaning—not one of economic for political benefit, but one of exchanging fairly definite and immediate economic benefits for rather uncertain expectations and hopes about future Soviet conduct. To say that such an approach leaves many questions unanswered and doubts unresolved is probably no more than to state the obvious.[13]

Yet "the détente spirit" lingered on. "Regardless of who rules the Kremlin, I do not believe that the Soviet Union will suddenly shelve its ambitious plans to develop Siberia and to improve the lot of the consumer," Samuel Pisar, one of the détente business activists, wrote in *The New York Times*.[14] Pisar argued that world energy and raw materials shortages, and the fall of the Gomulka government in Poland "because it neglected the material needs of the worker and the housewife," dictated the continued general drift of détente. He said the very size of the Soviet proposals (a dozen projects of more than $1 billion) meant that the United States would have to participate because it would be too much for the West Europeans and the Japanese alone. If Congress would back off the limit on credits, Pisar said (and he may have had some insight on Kremlin policy), then the immigration restrictions could stand. Robert Conquest, the scholar of Soviet history, took the other view:

> The recent Soviet rejection of the American trade terms—whether or not partly, or largely, influenced by the later reduction of the economic inducement of loan levels—merely shows that one's general analysis of Soviet motives was correct. The Soviets have, as it were, been flushed out into the open. And they are now in a position, one hopes, where they know they can no longer get something for nothing, and will seriously feel the various pressures which may make them, or some of them, to recognize the dead end of their total policy.[15]

Alas, even that was optimistic! Conquest came closer to the truth—as later events proved—when he said, in the same article, "The true Soviet economic interest does tend in the direction of some limitation of armaments. But only if the Soviet leaders see that the West is not going to bail out their economy as much in the future will that economic interest predominate in the face of the political-ideological drives that now prevail over it."

The Russians continued to talk about specific projects with Exxon, Gulf, IBM, and Tenneco. One reason was that American policy was still equivocal:

> Talks between IBM and the Russians, for instance, elicit different responses from various branches of the US government, depending on their perspective. The Commerce Department might look at the talks in terms of increasing US sales overseas. Justice might look at the negotiations from an antitrust perspective. State might look at them in terms of their effect on détente and Defense might worry about technology transfer. The Congress, in the

meantime, might be more interested in Soviet policy toward emigration. While all seem to have varying degrees of interest in the MNC's [multinational corporations], no one person or agency appears to be focusing on the overall aspect of the problem—or even a major portion of the problem such as national security.[16]

It might well be argued that, although Kissinger had accepted to a considerable extent its failure and some of the responsibility for its going awry, the general drift of détente continued. Kissinger's alibi was that the Watergate Affair and its aftermath had destroyed the ability of the Nixon administration to cope with the subtleties of the détente strategy. Others who had advocated it, or something like it, saw it as a failure of tactics not of strategy. Few asked the fundamental question of whether a scheme so Machiavellian in its formulation and execution could actually be implemented by a democratic government, which inherently required openness, directness, and, above all, an appeal to public opinion for its support. Nutter faulted Kissinger for a fundamentally flawed perspective

> Diplomacy simply assumes a personalized shape in Kissinger's eyes. And so we have the familiar style: personalistic, secretive, mysterious. The public is asked to trust the creative statesman implicitly while he sculpts a new order visible to his mind's eye alone. How can he impart to the masses a comprehension of why and how it will work when it has never existed before? Perhaps he cannot, but then too bad for creative statesmanship, so called: it is something our political system cannot afford, for nothing is more at odds with the tenet of democracy than the principles of truth by authority. It is not in the American style to bet everything on a horse before knowing its track record and what course it is going to run. American foreign policy must rest on consensus, and it can only do so if its grand design is fully revealed and openly discussed. Similarly, American diplomacy must rest on an institutional foundation, even at the risk of being contaminated by bureaucracy. Whatever verdict is rendered on the issue of personalized diplomacy, there remains the question, at least equally important, of whether the substance of détente constitutes the best foreign policy for the United States.[17]

Détente was a mixed strategy that involved an attempt to create interdependency, as Nutter said, as the carrot, deterrence as the stick, and arms control as the rein. So strong was Kissinger's personality and imprint on

American policy and so weak was the foreign policy establishment and its ability to produce alternative strategies, that the essence of détente—even after its dramatic failures—continued to dominate American policy for the next decade.

The drift continued, even when the White House changed occupants, and Jimmy Carter believed he was elected with a mandate to redirect policy, including foreign policy. Yet, there was little basic inclination to return to fundamentals and examine the basis of the détente-drift policy. In fact, the Democratic strategists believed that they were implementing what had been lost in the fires of Watergate. After the disaster that overtook Carter when the Soviets invaded Afghanistan and, as he said, taught him more in twenty-four hours about communism than he had learned in the whole process until then, there was no longer any possibility of restoring détente. And the Carter administration began, as a symbol of that change, a massive reconstruction of U.S. defense forces that was essentially the same buildup that the Reagan administration would continue.

Jerold Schechter, public relations man for Zbigniew Brzezinski, Carter's National Security Adviser, told a French author that the Carter administration was "no more hostile [to the Soviets] than the previous ones to economic cooperation with the East, and businessmen felt as much at ease with us as with Nixon and Ford."[18] Would détente have gone on indefinitely, then, he was asked? "Indefinitely, if we had not had, in 1979, the invasion of Afghanistan which obliged us to act." But didn't that action prove that the Soviets accorded priority to their geopolitical interests even at the risk of economic cooperation with the West? Schechter replied: "That is in effect the whole question, for which no one yet has arrived at an answer."

Yet, in the inner White House struggles of the Carter years, but particularly after the invasion of Afghanistan, the Brzezinski team jokingly called its group "the Brzezinski Raiders," a reference to their hardline attitudes as contrasted with others in the White House and in the Carter administration. Schechter left the White House before the end of the Carter administration, to join the staff of Armand Hammer. A one-time correspondent for *Time* in Moscow who had discovered, among other things, during his stay there official Soviet anti-Semitism, Schechter had written critically of the Communists. That he would leave the White House and join the U.S. businessman with the longest record of collaboration with the Soviets, going back to Hammer's father's day as an intimate of Lenin and a founder of the Communist Party of the United States, was perhaps a minor symbol of the lingering hope for accommodation with Moscow.

How much did the Soviets profit from the erosion of controls and the Western credits they received during the more enthusiastic early years of détente? It is an astonishing, but highly indicative, piece of evidence about U.S. policy-making toward the Soviet Union that no overall evaluation of the economic benefits of détente for the Soviet Union has ever been compiled inside the U.S. government. Nor, in fact, with all the speculation on the Soviet economy among the Sovietologists, has that been done by the scholars, probably because the external component of Soviet economic activity has always been considered a minor element by most Western observers.

Clearly, however, despite the abbreviated Nixon-Kissinger program, cut off by the fears in Congress of what was actually being negotiated, there were huge Soviet economic gains in the period. American exports to the Soviet Union had increased fivefold during the 1970–1973 period. Much of this included extremely valuable high-technology products that the Soviets had previously been unable to purchase, or had had to arrange through industrial espionage and third-party transfer at considerable additional cost and time. For example, the Soviet Union was suffering a desperate shortage of ground transport in the late 1960s and early 1970s. The dimensions of that crisis are shrouded, or perhaps lost, in the incredible statistical morass that current Soviet economists are admitting. But it seems only common sense that the heavy U.S. and German inputs of trucks, and truck and tank-making equipment at this time, helped to relieve some of the transport burden. It has become the cliché of clichés, but all too true, that U.S. military intelligence found that the first Soviet troops moving into the Afghanistan conflict did so on trucks made in the Kama River factory! At the time licenses were granted for U.S. computers and other capital plant equipment for the truck assembly line, State Department representatives had assured the Congress that the product of the plant would go only to Soviet civilian consumption.

But perhaps the most important prize of early détente was what has come to be known as The Great Grain Robbery. The Soviet Union suffered a failure of crops in the summer of 1972. Moscow was faced with what appeared to be a food situation that might have duplicated the famines of the early Soviet period. Washington gave permission for Moscow to buy 700 million tons of grain—the largest sale in the history of the Chicago grain markets. Including 440 million bushels of wheat, it was 25 percent of the total American crop. The Nixon administration publicized the sale as providing markets for the American farmer, reducing tensions with the Soviet Union, and improving the American balance of payments. In fact, the sales depleted U.S. grain reserves, caused higher prices for American food, and cheated the U.S. farmer, in addition to handing the U.S. taxpayer an enormous bill. The incompetence of American management in handling the sale was almost unbelievable and certainly was a measure of the lack of subtlety in pursuing the so-called interdependency track of détente. President Nixon had announced on July 8 that the United States had concluded a $750 million, three-year sales agreement with Moscow. Under the agreement, Moscow would buy the grain from private dealers through the commercial market. But the United States would extend long-term credit facilities from the Department of Agriculture's Commodities Credit Corporation. However, it was not until after the sales were made that the Department of Agriculture (September 22) announced that it was eliminating the export subsidy, which was no longer needed in the face of strong overseas demand. (Months earlier, the USDA Agricultural Attaché in Moscow had reported on February 9 and 18 that the Soviet winter crop had been heavily damaged and that it would have to buy large quantities later in 1972.) The USDA used the subsidy to sell to the Soviets at $1.63–$1.65 per bushel while the U.S. domestic price was climbing to $2.10 per bushel. Meanwhile, the Soviet Union and the United States signed a three-year agreement establishing rates for U.S. vessels carrying the grain to a number of Soviet ports. The huge movement of grain had required that additional ports be opened in both countries. American shipowners would receive a subsidy from the U.S. Maritime Administration covering the difference between the Soviet rate and the cost of shipping.

Total losses to the U.S. taxpayer alone for the purchase of the grain was said to be in the tens of millions of dollars. The General Accounting Office, while stating that nothing illegal had occurred, reported that farmers were not provided with adequate advice. And there is no doubt that farmers, too, lost enormous sums because of the depressed prices paid with the use of subsidies by the government, especially for the wheat that was involved in the sales. Secretary of the Treasury George P. Shultz admitted publicly that the United States had been "burned" on the grain deal. To add insult to injury, there were confirmed reports that part of the grain had been resold by the Soviets at profit to Italy.

Yet, the question, which is apparently constantly debated in the innermost Soviet economic circles, is what happens as a result of massive foreign aid to the Soviet economy? One of the most notorious examples is the huge Togliatti plant on the Volga, which opened in 1970 despite numerous problems after it was designed, built, and initially run by the Fiat firm of Italy. In its day, the Italian plant sold to the Russians was regarded as "state-of-the-art" in world automobile production. By the fall of 1988, however, the plant was described by the Soviet press to be in a "pre-crisis" situation. The plant produces 600,000 cars each year, which is half the total Soviet output, and employs 110,000 workers. Most of the product is still based on the FIAT 124, a 1960s car, marketed in the Soviet Union as the Zhiguli (the Lada overseas). There has been no leapfrogging by the Soviets over the original plant and technology; the plant remains the same one that the Italians delivered to them.

> New hatch back models, also based on Italian designs, are now [mid-1988] under production. All are poor in quality. On any given day, more than 5,000 cars lie in the factory, unfinished for lack of parts; workers routinely cannibalize finished cars for components in order to keep the lines moving. Some 150 parts are made from sub-standard materials, and though the suppliers have recently been subjected to the new State Control Commission, workers at the plant say they are as bad as ever. . . . Alienation is rife; embezzlement, drunkenness and absenteeism are growing. "Who can speak of better quality in these conditions?" asks the [Literary] *Gazette*. . . . Workers at the plant itself should be enabled to buy their own product much more easily. At a price of 9,000 rubles, it would take an assembly line worker on 200 rubles a month nearly four years to get a car if he did not eat or drink.[19]

Is this not just another example of the long tradition of how imported technology goes to pot in Russia?

One can only marvel at the fact that Fiat's Milan headquarters has announced a new agreement to rebuild and expand the facility.

CHAPTER 6

SOCIALISM IN ONE COUNTRY

How It Works, Or Doesn't Work

The origins of the present Soviet crisis lie in the turn of events at the end of the NEP. The reconstruction of parts of the czarist economy by the limited free enterprise of the NEP was followed by a new reversal in the Soviet drama. Although Stalin had earlier been a relatively minor player in the endless ideological disputations of the Bolsheviks, by the end of 1924, he was the rising star of the leadership, and began to preach the view that it was possible to create socialism in Russia by the efforts of its people alone. When the Bolsheviks had grabbed power in Petrograd and asserted that socialism could come in a backward country like czarist Russia as part of a worldwide revolution, Lenin had already twisted the Marxist concept that socialism would develop in the highly industrialized countries of Western Europe and America. Orthodox Marxists had said socialism would come in an inevitable progression of economic historical development, and more backward countries would have to make the same progression (through capitalism and revolution). Stalin now argued— picking up an argument first advanced in Bolshevik circles by Bukharin— that the Soviet Union would not have to wait for the world revolution that would bring socialism to Western Europe. The latter was a fleeting hope as the 1920s progressed and some political stability returned to those countries that had been decimated after World War I. Rather, socialism could be established in the Soviet Union before it developed in the more advanced countries.

Whatever Stalin really believed and knew about economic policy—and there is much to suggest that, similar to his other political views, his economic concerns were part and parcel of his xenophobia, his bitter hatred of Europe and the West in general—his idea of socialism in one country became a weapon in his fight to wrest final control of the Communist Party and the state from his major enemy, Trotsky. Trotsky was vulnerable, for, as an intellectual who had spent much time in the West, at various times he had insisted that socialism in Russia, without the revolution in Western Europe, would be lost. Lenin, too, before his return to Petrograd, had spoken of "an Asiatic despotism" developing under a socialist imprimatur in Russia were it to be installed without being a part of a world revolution.

Furthermore, Stalin introduced into the argument the issue that the Soviets would not only have to build socialism in isolation in their country with only their minority sympathizers abroad, but they also would have to develop the country's potential to defend itself.

> His version of the theory of socialism in one country in no way abandoned the postulate that the Communist revolution would, in time, spread beyond Soviet borders, and would eventually become worldwide. The innovation lay in asserting the autonomy of the Russian national revolutionary process, in making construction of a socialist society at home independent of the international revolution.[1]

Stalin, of course, had already learned, as every Soviet leader after him has had to do, that his advocacy of any policy had to be wrapped in the mantle of Lenin's prestige by proving that it was the course of the dead leader.

Stalin denounced Trotsky and other opposition voices to his "socialism in one country" as a failure of nerve, disloyalty to the Russian masses, and the need to have a "certainty" of purpose and a faith in ultimate success. How Stalin with all his crude rhetoric and primitive logic carried the day against his much more sophisticated opponents will remain one of those psychological and political mysteries that appear so often in politics. One student of Stalin and his times, Robert C. Tucker, has ascribed it to the fact that much of his audience inside and outside the Party consisted of politically unsophisticated men and women who had not participated in many of these same debates before the revolution. A member of that audience, who would later defect to the West, has written:

> Our mood was one of healthy optimism. We were sure of ourselves and the future. We believed that, provided no war came to interrupt the reconstruction of Russian industry, our Socialist country would be able, within a few years, to offer the world an example of a society based on principles of liberty and equality. How could it be otherwise? The old capitalist Europe was moving from crisis to crisis. . . .[2]

Although Stalin had associated himself earlier with those who attacked the idea of exploiting the peasantry and rural "surpluses" for "primitive capital accumulation" that would finance Soviet industrialization, hindsight has given us clues to his opposition to any kind of gradualist approach to this or other economic problems almost from the beginning of his career. By the mid-1920s he was attacking those Bolsheviks (who had joined their earlier Menshevik Social Democratic friends) warning that the road to development might take fifty or even a hundred years.

> War Communism had given way to NEP as a matter of general policy, but its imprint upon the thought and behavior of a great many party members had not been effaced. For Stalin, as for many others of his generation and those younger, the Civil War had been a formative influence. It showed in their style, their approach to people and problems, even their mode of dress. Their very Bolshevism had undergone a certain militarization.[3]

With the victory of Stalin (ironically assisted by Bukharin) in the Fifteenth Congress of the Communist Party of the USSR in 1929, the industrialization at breakneck speed, with priority for heavy industry, and the forcible mass collectivization of the peasantry, would be the hallmarks of Stalinism and would create the new Soviet economy in the 1930s. It is with the results of that process, sometimes called in Marxist circles the Third Russian Revolution (Menshevik = First, Bolshevik = Second), that the Soviet Union lives today.

It is not true, of course, as the Soviets with their local Communist and more naive economic-determinist allies preached in the underdeveloped countries after World War II, that the Communist leadership under Stalin brought their country from a nonindustrial to an industrial state in a half century. On the eve of World War I and the Revolution, the Russian Empire was significantly behind the other major industrial powers, but it had reached a considerable level of industrial development. Even some Soviet scholars have acknowledged this. One Soviet source in the 1960s concluded that in the period from 1860 to 1910, world industrial production grew by a factor of 6, Britain by 2.5, Germany by 6, and Russia by 10.5. Alec Nove, the doyen of Sovietologist economists, concedes that if the industrial and agricultural growth rates of the period from 1890 to 1913 had continued—a very big "if" of course—Russia might have achieved a reasonably healthy economy in fifty years.

Instead, after the brief interval of the NEP, the Communists under Stalin were to turn to forced industrialization and development requiring every human sacrifice. The principal instrument for this development was to be the so-called five-year plans. Historians are somewhat at a loss to explain the origin of the concept; certainly, there is little if anything in the writings of Karl Marx, from whom all Communist dogma is said to derive, to anticipate them. In fact, rather than "provide" for industrialization, Marx had "required" it for a society to move on toward the ultimate paradise of a collectivized, classless society.

The NEP had shown the Soviets a way around their dilemma of a peasantry that refused to contribute its grain and other exportable surpluses to pay for imported machinery and plant. The Communists feared, however, that continuing to supply the peasantry with manufactured goods would absorb all the investment capital, prevent the expansion of heavy industry, and lead to very slow progress in industrialization, if not actual stultification. And socialism was considered synonymous with industrialization. The peasantry had long been seen by many Russian intellectuals, as had the rural sector of the society in general, as an impediment to modernization. Stalin and his cohorts had grasped the concept that rapid collectivization would not only remove the bargaining power of the peasantry in the economy, but also, by squeezing the grain from them at arbitrary prices, could net the capital to invest in industry. It could be argued that he was only repeating, on a much grander and crueller scale, what the czarist finance ministers had been doing during the last decades of the nineteenth and the beginning of the twentieth centuries. These economic aspects of the collectivization were, of course, buttressed by political concerns—collectivization expanded the police powers of the state to control opposition. And various students of Stalin have ascribed enormous importance to the paranoid aspects of his personality.

The earlier ideas of Trotsky and Bukharin of the 1920s on "militarization of labor" were to become acceptable, too, to Stalin. "Armies" of workers and technicians were thrown into the task of fulfilling physical targets set by the central planning bureaucracy, *Gosplan*.

The formulation of the first Five-Year Plan required detail that did not really exist in the confusion of the postrevolutionary scene, compounded by the real reconstruction achieved under the NEP. For example, the first Five-Year Plan called for 14.7 million workers to be employed, but, by 1932, the state claimed that 22.9 million were working at all projects. As political repression produced more and more victims, prison labor was used—such as the half million used in six years of building the Baltic-White Sea canal through Karelian granite without machinery, a project that later proved unnecessary. Although the regime turned to heavier taxation, the gap between official and free market prices grew as inflation spiraled upward. Those who were too critical ended up on trial as "wreckers," so opposition inside the Communist Party and the planning bureaucracy was stilled, regardless of the excesses of the drive for targets, and "sabotage" provided a ready answer to any obvious failures.

It is still not clear exactly what the first Five-Year Plan accomplished, although industrial success in the first two years generally is thought to have been considerable.

> It is the customary belief that in the prewar period the rate of development was exceptionally high. Truly, a multitude of enterprises was built, new sectors appeared and profound changes in the economy occurred. However, progress was confined mainly to heavy industry, construction, and transport. The agrarian sector of the economy, on the other hand, experienced stagnation (as is known, in terms of the grain harvest and head of livestock at the 1928 level was reached and surpassed only in the 1950s). In the period, 1924–1941, national income probably grew by a factor of 1.5. By no means a record pace.[4]

The appalling suffering, miscalculations, and propaganda make it hard to evaluate exactly what the material progress was. However, by 1932, by juggling figures, it was possible for Stalin to claim that the main parts of the Plan had been fulfilled. Gigantic industrial projects had been completed in the Urals, the Kuznetsk Basin, the Volga region, and the Ukraine. Textile mills were built in Central Asia and new factories were built in Leningrad and Moscow. The Turkestan-Siberian Railway was extended to Karaganda—5,500 kilometers of railroad added in all. And Stalin was able to boast at the Seventeenth Party Congress in 1934: "Is this not a miracle?"

> It was then that the government, by stages, imposed upon the economy its own priorities, by ever-tightening control over resource allocation, physical output, credit. The "Stalin" model was created in the process of trying to do the impossible, and therefore facing every day the necessity of assuring supplies to key projects or "shock-constructions" at the expense of others regarded as of lesser importance.[5]

Many of the projects initiated in the first Five-Year Plan were not completed nor even started and were left to subsequent five-year plans. But the pattern of highly centralized physical control of resources, over-expansion of heavy industry, and neglect of consumer demand, even minimal needs, was established, and it has continued to this day.

The systemic excess of demand and shortages plaguing the Soviet economy (and those modeled after it after the conquest of Central Europe by the Red Army in 1945, and the addition of Cuba, Vietnam, and other former colonial areas to the Soviet Empire in the post-World War II period) have existed from the beginning. Scholars attribute this problem to the fact that central planners have only one way to react to perceived needs—either to increase production of goods in short supply—or, failing that, to fake it.[6]

In one of the landmark exposures of the corrupt nature of the Stalinist economic system, two Soviet economists have, tongue in cheek, explained how the system works:

> When fulfilling a plan is difficult or altogether impossible (this is sometimes the case, alas!), making up the shortfall in rubles is conceivable in two ways: simply padding reality (pieces, tons, meters, kilowatt-hours and so forth) or raising the price of each unit product. The first way is dangerous and a criminal offense. The second way is much simpler and safer. But different sectors are in manifestly unequal positions here. Worst off are the steelworkers, power engineers, coal miners, and construction material manufacturers and, partly, chemical workers, in a word, workers of the raw material sectors.

Their product selection is stable, and new types of products appear infrequently. And the wholesale prices of old products have long been established and recorded in price lists, and violating them is just as ill-considered as direct figure-padding. Nor will the customer pay more than what has been established. The situation is different in manufacturing industry—in machine building, for example. Of course, here also a long assimilated product sells at the fixed prices indicated on the price lists. But the product selection here changes rapidly. In the last five-year plan the machine builders assimilated on an annual average the production of approximately 3,000 types of new products (for comparison, all the other sectors of industry together [account for] only 700 types a year). Naturally, there are no prices for these items on the price lists; they have to be determined from scratch. And this is a lengthy business—it sometimes takes years. In order not to impede technical progress, which is slow as it is, one-time and provisional wholesale prices are determined for the new items. What freedom there is here for the devotees of an easy life! There is no difficulty getting any price. And the constant price, which is determined subsequently, is usually little different from the provisional price.[7]

A Polish observer, Jan Winiecki, shows how, incredibly, the planned economic systems have produced layer on layer of falsity:

Thus plans are drawn up, which with respect to aggregate economic growth and the production structure (especially the latter!) cannot be executed due to the shortage of resources. There may be many causes. . . . the resources are not there because *the quantities reported earlier by enterprises were*—to some degree—*fictitious* [author's emphasis]. . . . According to A. Shitov, first deputy chairman of the USSR Committee for National Control, "to a greater or smaller extent additions (to the actual output figures) and other distortions were discovered in every third enterprise."[8]

Winiecki points out that resources also may not be of the proper quality, there at the right time, nor at the correct place. The result of all these inadequacies is increased costs, a decline in quality, and cost overruns that are compensated for at higher levels by subsidies, lower taxes, price increases, and so forth, "with the tacit understanding that it is quantity—always in short supply—that counts most." Winiecki points out that "decades of economic growth under central planning [have] built into the system lasting distortions that aggravate shortages even further and make excess demand much worse and difficult to eliminate." He says that the most interesting feature of all of this process is that the system is not only wasteful but increasingly wasteful:

> The burden of central planning [which] weighs upon the economy becomes heavier over time. Costly projects with obsolete technology need modernization from the start. Thus, a new planning period is again considered as another period of ("obviously" necessary) rapid growth of investments. The long run, in which consumption would increase substantially due to an earlier lengthy period of high investment, never comes. Investment becomes not so much deferred consumptions but *deferred further investments* [author's emphasis].[9]

Once the fate of the economy was put into the hands of the planners in the 1920s, statistics became their handmaiden.

> Prior to 1925 statistics had computed the development of industry roughly as is done to this day in the majority of countries: the data on the production of products in physical terms in the preceding years were compared with the same information for the subsequent year. . . . The situation began to change as the management was centralized. Enterprise came to be given a directive plan, in respect of the total production volume included. . . . The accounting was not being conducted in physical units, as before, but in rubles—the quota for the plant in respect of total production volume could not be expressed other than in terms of cost. In this case the accounts were reliable given two conditions: the wholesale prices were constant, the product list also. But this was not the case—otherwise stagnation would have been observed in the economy.[10]

What is further implied in all this, of course, is that as the sophistication of the economy grows, the problems deepen. Or, as the sophistication of the product concerned rises, the inefficiencies increase. Or, to put it still another way, the inefficiencies of a higher skilled economy—say, those of Central Europe before they were communized, or the Soviet economy as it moved from its more rudimentary state in the 1930s to the post-World War II period—are even worse than those in a more primitive economic era. It may be these factors that explain the decline, perhaps in real terms but certainly in relative terms, of the more sophisticated prewar economies of Central Europe such as those of East Germany and Czechoslovakia.

According to a Soviet émigré economist, Igor Birman:

Although some things may not be so good about the American standard of
living, in spite of our shortcomings, life in the Soviet Union, the Soviet
standard of living, is 4.5 times worse. Many, many decades must pass for the
average Soviet to reach the level of today's American diet, to be able to dress
the same, to have such spacious and comfortable housing equipped with the
same appliances, to spend as much on rest and recreation, to travel as much
and as conveniently, to study in such buildings, be treated in such hospitals,
etc. I remind the reader that according to simple estimates based entirely
upon official Soviet data, the USSR will catch up to America in 1976 in meat
in 57 years, in fruit in 62 (or even in 172), cars in 138, housing in 155,
telephones in 130, and roads in 260 years. They will reach this level if the
rate of growth is at least maintained, for which there is little hope.[11]

Birman was writing (originally in Russian which has only recently been
translated) to criticize what he saw then as Central Intelligence Agency
overestimates of Soviet productive strength and living standards. But the
message was clear then, as it is clear today:

Despite all reservations, limitations, and contradictory examples, the history
of our civilization is the history of development of the economy, of the
current and purposeful growth of production for consumption. And this is
not only "capitalist" ideology. At the basis of Marxism lies the promise of
communism, under which consumption will not be limited and the blades of
my scissors will come together. You can endlessly preach to people that
luxury is harmful, that limitation to some "rational minimum" is a virtue.
Nevertheless, people want more, sooner, better.[12]

In June 1988, *Sotsialisticheskaia Industriia*, in an interview with Marina
Mozhina of the USSR Academy of Sciences, revealed that 20 percent of
the Soviet population, or 57 million people, have a monthly income of
seventy rubles. This means that they live on the brink of what Soviet
official terminology calls "underprovisioning." This official "poverty line"
in the Soviet Union is said by the government to be 200.6 rubles or less
for an urban family of four—a figure established by two Soviet economists
in the 1950s and 1960s and clearly antequated because of the continuing
inflation. According to the *Soviet Statistical Yearbook*, the average pension
in 1986 was seventy-five rubles a month. Mozhina says that many pensioners are "living in poverty" on less than fifty rubles a month. There has
been other confirming evidence offered in the Soviet press and by dissi-

dent economists in recent months. All this refutes the long history of
Soviet propaganda arguing that the society, while offering modest living
conditions, did maintain a more adequate social welfare net than Western
societies, particularly the United States.

Ultimately, that standard of living would have to depend on the aims of
the society, including what part of its product would be used for purely
political (military) ends, and what part would be used for satisfying
human demands. Both would depend on the efficiency of the economy in
producing goods. By the mid-1980s, any index of Soviet economic
efficiency was appalling:

> Soviet steel enterprises used five times as much iron ore as US firms, but they
> only made twice as much steel. With this steel the Soviets produced half as
> many final products, machine tools, and equipment as their US counterparts.
> Of these products, the bulk were heavy, large, crude, low-productivity
> machinery tools. These tools cut metal to produce other tools in such a way
> that 20 percent of the entire Soviet metal output went to scrap. An estimated
> 25 percent of Soviet machinery and other manufacturing was useless or
> unusable output. Soviet firms produced five times as many tractors and eight
> times as many combines as the US, although Soviet farms produced half as
> much grain as American farms. Adding imports and thus roughly as much
> grain feed as the grain-exporting US, Soviet farms produced half as much
> meat as the US.[13]

This is the sad story of the Soviet economy in a nutshell, as reported by
Mikhail S. Bernstam of the Hoover Institution.

But these problems are not new. Nor have they been secret to those
acquainted with the functioning of the Soviet economy, both inside and
outside the country. Repeated attempts have been made since the end of
World War II to get at some measure of reform of the system. And it is in
that context that *perestroika* must be viewed. In 1965, picking up on earlier
attempts by Khrushchev for populist programs that would improve the
life of the average Soviet citizen, a series of reforms was attempted to
revitalize the system. This effort has come to be known as the Kosygin
Reforms (after Brezhnev's original partner in the overthrow of Khrushchev, Prime Minister Alexei Kosygin). Khrushchev's own efforts had
largely gone to naught because they refused to reject the accepted Stalinist
ideological constraints about the nature of the economic system. Direct

taxes were reduced in 1957, but only against a backdrop of higher prices on food and basic consumer durables produced by a new turnover tax. The minimum wage was increased, but adjustments in prices and wages that had been effected by a monetary reform in 1961—essentially a zero was struck from the currency—were soon wiped out by the continuing inflation. A campaign was undertaken to curb speculation, black market activities, alcoholism, and "hooliganism," but it turned into an anti-Semitic campaign that was used against critics of the regime.

When Brezhnev came to power in May 1965, he laid a "new" program before the plenum of the Central Committee. This program was essentially an attempt to implement the reforms initiated earlier by Khrushchev. These reforms were suggested in the writings and lectures of Evsei Liberman, a relatively obscure professor from Kharkov Engineering and Economics Institute. In June 1962, Liberman had presented two lectures at the Economics Institute of Sciences in Moscow, wherein he finally had been able to draw attention of high Party officials to what had reportedly been a long personal campaign. Liberman's program, which has become a milestone in the annals of Soviet-style planning inside and outside the Soviet Union, sought to grant greater authority to "enterprise" (production unit) managers in making decisions about procuring raw materials. Liberman would have reduced the long list of economic indicators for managers. The result of dropping much of the centralized control would lead toward the principle of using "profit" as the main standard for judging production units, which would be put on an individual profit and loss accounting (*khozraschet*).

There is no doubt that Liberman had powerful backing, although his initial lectures were bitterly attacked by Moscow economists and bureaucrats, who considered him something of a country bumpkin. The support, in contrast, appeared to come from the *Gosplan*, the highest level of Soviet planning, apparently precisely because it understood that the whole process of trying to dictate the "norms" of tens of thousands of production operations was simply an impossible task. Liberman was initially bitterly attacked, according to an émigré economist, who attended some of the lectures.[14] His critics argued that if such decentralization were to occur, the state would lose control of economic policy. Ministry of Finance officials were particularly bitter critics, who argued that the changes would result in an irreplaceable loss of revenues. A representative of the State Committee on Prices (*Gosskomsen*) argued that under such a system as

Liberman proposed, his committee would not know how to set prices. Statisticians questioned the accuracy of Liberman's calculations.

Liberman seems to have lost this initial encounter, and was actually badly shaken by the bitterness of the criticism. His proposals took flight, however, when *Pravda*, the official Party newspaper, dolled them up in a famous article published under his name—although perhaps it was written at least in conjunction with another author, under the title of "The Plan, Profits, and Bonuses." This tacit official blessing for Liberman's program won over members of the government bureaucracy. Between 1963 and 1965 reform discussions proceeded apace, in many instances going far beyond Liberman's original proposals. In 1966 the Central Committee ordered *Gosplan* to establish an interbranch commission to examine the reform proposals, and all central planning agencies were ordered by the Council of Ministers to set up special departments to implement the reforms. Although proposals for reform were far from complete, a Decree of Reform was published in September 1965.

> The experimental character of the first five year period, between 1965–1971, reflected the government's indecision as to how radical the economic change should be. Therefore, at the implementation stage, a number of pre-1965 reform proposals, some of them Liberman's, some derived from his ideas, and some completely original, continued to be reevaluated and modified, while on occasion already accepted proposals were suddenly abandoned. Officially, the government decided to "experiment and debate" while the reform was taking root; in reality, the bureaucracy was confused by the new ideas, and it had to improvise. Crucial to Liberman's proposal was the argument that legitimate profit from the state enterprises rather than the turnover tax should be regarded as the chief source of the government's revenue. Liberman had also argued that since data was so difficult to accumulate, that several of the reforms should be postponed until 1971. But the Council of Ministers refused the request in favor of proceeding immediately as advocated by the powerful voices in the government bureaucracy, perhaps a premeditated attempt to derail them. Experimental reforms at a select group of plants had already begun in 1966, in fact.
>
> By 1971, local Soviet governments began to argue privately that the plan was difficult to implement. Decentralized investment was well below the 25 percent of total investment that had been agreed on. The reforming price mechanism was not working, and the Interbranch Commission was arguing that another decade was needed to study the results and try new solutions.

What had happened was that the bureaucracy had jumped on the reform bandwagon but "Liberman's proposals were adopted by the bureaucracy and transformed to represent its institutional interests."[15]

All through the 1970s, the planners backed away from the fundamentals of the Liberman proposals, continuing to "micromanage" the economy. Whatever their merit, the failure of the reforms certainly was owing to the opposition of the vested bureaucracy. There is the fundamental question, however, of whether Liberman's reform proposals went far enough, of whether the introduction of "profit," establishment of a price-market system, direct links between raw materials producers and consuming industries, direct links between exporters and overseas buyers, wage differentials based on work, competition among industries for investment capital, and so forth, can be introduced into a system such as the one in Communist Russia. All these issues are again being restated and debated in speculation over Gorbachev's *perestroika*.

CHAPTER 7

GORBY! GORBY! GORBY!

The Man Behind the Image

"How can we agree that 1917 was a mistake and all the seventy years of our life, work, effort, and battles were also a complete mistake, that we were going in the 'wrong direction'?"[1]

Mikhail Gorbachev asks this rhetorical question in his book explaining his program to remodel the Soviet Union. How indeed! Yet, increasingly, that is what is happening as the "mistakes" of the Soviet past—the bloody blundering of confused ideologues—give way to the criticism of braver souls in a population increasingly aware of how far from reality official propaganda has been. Nowhere in the entire tableau of Soviet history is the problem so difficult to rationalize as in the growing spate of economic problems. There is, after seventy years, an increasing tendency by the experts to find that all of the investment and suffering were expended for totally mistaken goals. Worse still, most of those same experts argue increasingly for a program of reform that stipulates the need to rebuild the Communist system more or less in the image of the Western economies. Essentially, Soviet policy now seeks a way to use the most commonplace instruments of the Western marketplace and private property to restructure and rebuild Soviet society. Yet, somehow, they must be justified in a "socialist" context and without destroying the monopoly of power exercised by the Soviet *nomenclatura,* the elite of the Communist world.

In this drama, the principal player is Mikhail Gorbachev, now general secretary of the Communist Party, which has had a seventy-year monopoly of power in the Soviet Union, and president of the USSR, the second if not the first military power in the world. Were Gorbachev at the highest echelons of political power in a Western democratic state, it would be necessary to ask and answer who he is, where he comes from, what his political ideas are, and how well he can fulfill his functions. But on the Soviet scene, where personal power has been wielded by a series of dictators or near-dictators since the regime was founded, those questions are even weightier. No "great man in history" theories are needed here to justify an attempt to analyze his role, for his personality will dictate much of what happens next in the incredible saga of the Soviet state.

As is true of so much in the Soviet past, there are still large gaps in our knowledge about this leader of the Soviet Union. Although he has been hailed in the West as a reformer, perhaps even a "democrat," and certainly as a consummate politician, we have only a minimum of evidence and speculation to prove or disprove such conjectures. The most ordinary biographical facts available in the West on political leaders are still not available in the Soviet Union. And there is evidence to suggest that there has been manipulation and less than the truth in the official biographies of Gorbachev presented to his own countrymen and the West.

There is no denying, however, that everything points to a remarkable personality. To watch Gorbachev, for example, thrust accidentally into the events of the Chinese Communist crisis in Tiananmen Square in Peking in mid-summer 1989, at a live press conference transmitted around the world, is to watch a professional politician of the highest caliber at work in a moment of crisis. Treading carefully through the most ticklish diplomatic quagmire, his magnetic personality comes across even on television. It is obvious why he has charmed such diverse personalities as Margaret Thatcher, Ronald Reagan, and, apparently, François Mitterand.

Gorbachev's initial success in international circles was as much as anything else a product of the growing anxiety in the West as it watched the gerontocracy of the Soviet Union turn from one old, sick, and dying man to another. The fumbling of Soviet leadership—a USSR armed with the most destructive weapons known to man—was nervewracking. After the eighteen-year reign of Brezhnev, whose last years were dominated by his infirmities, the former secret police chief Yuri Andropov had only fifteen months in the high office, after which he was succeeded by

Konstantin Chernenko for thirteen months. (As the Russian wits had it, when one Muscovite asked another if he had been to one of the funerals, he replied, yes, he had a season ticket.) Gorbachev's visit to Britain in 1984 was a welcome breath of youth and vigor; no more baggy suits, no more wives trailing funeral biers, no more wooden photographic postures.

Gorbachev's role as the first leader of the Soviet Union from the post-World War II generation—the first post-Stalin leader—has been trumpeted in the West. Yet that description, too, begs the question. As far as we know, Gorbachev is the son and grandson of minor Soviet officials, who directed the *kolkhozy,* the government collective farms, in his native north Caucasus area. This is in the famous Russian-Ukrainian "black soil" region, the most fertile in the vast Soviet empire. And college schoolmates have referred to Gorbachev's implied criticism of Stalin's forced collectivization of Russian agriculture, something in which his father and grandfather must have taken part. Furthermore, the adolescent Gorbachev apparently lived in this region, generally referred to as Stavropol Territory after its most important center, during the Nazi occupation of the Caucasus. It is a fact that has been glossed over in his official biography by some questionable arithmetic.

> What Gorbachev so carefully concealed when he was in Moscow [in university] was that for two years he didn't attend school at all. There was no place where he could, because the years in question were 1942 and 1943, when the Stavropol Territory was occupied by Hitler's troops and the German staff was headquartered in his native village of Privolnoe. This had to be concealed because in Stalin's time, all those who lived in occupied zones were automatically regarded as politically unreliable—in the best case; in the worst, they were classified as collaborators and accomplices of the enemy.[2]

Nor did Gorbachev as a young student at Moscow University escape the bitter end of the Stalin era. A classmate says:

> I don't want to accuse Gorbachev of anything. He was influenced in his ways [by the system]. But as secretary of the *Komsomol* [Young Communist League] he would speak out demagogically and require expulsion [and punishment of certain people] as required of him. I heard him several times when he was at [the Krasnaya Presnya Raykom] *Komsomol* organization and his speeches were very dogmatic, very pro-Stalin; he would not deviate from the speeches of First Party Secretary Kirakozov at the time.[3]

In fact, there is circumstantial evidence that Gorbachev—in the privileged position of being an ethnic Russian from a "peasant" background—
was forced to leave Moscow and return to Stavropol after completing the
prestigious Moscow Law School because he had zigged when he should
have zagged relative to the Party line. There are reports that his ultra-
Stalinism and his participation in the agitation surrounding the so-called
Doctors' Plot (Stalin's last attempt, apparently, to begin a new purge,
beginning with the Jews, shortly before his death) cost him allies. Gorbachev was unable to make a transition to the new post-Stalin leadership
in Moscow, although in his last year at Moscow's law school he and Raisa
had lived well, by Russian standards, in a new apartment in what was then
the chic Lenin Hills. There seems to be little doubt that Raisa, the woman
whom he had met and married at the university, and perhaps he as well,
regarded the next twenty-three years of their life that would be spent back
in the north Caucasus as an "exile" from the bright lights of Moscow.

Yet law school in Moscow was a privileged environment for any young,
ambitious Soviet student—then as now. The school was the principal
recruiting ground not only for personnel for the huge Soviet civilian
bureaucracy, but the "the security organs"—the secret police and its
affiliated organizations. In fact, young Gorbachev, something of a hick
"outsider" to the more sophisticated Muscovite students, was believed to
have been an informer for the secret police.

> Gorbachev did his best to justify his [1952] admission to the [Communist]
> Party. He helped attack those students who had concealed certain facts of
> their biographies. I recall several cases. He had a girl expelled from the
> *Komsomol* and from school because she had concealed the fact that her
> grandfather was an enemy of the people. A student, Gorodetskiy, was
> expelled because he had failed to report that his father was in a [gulag] camp
> in the Kolyma.[4]

"He was really the plague of the law school. We feared Mischa like the
devil himself. When he walked by, everybody stopped talking," another
classmate recalls.[5]

Stavropol, the area to which the young Gorbachevs returned, is an
isolated part of the Soviet empire. But its Kuban Cossacks, eighteenth
and nineteenth century settlers whom the Czar placed there as the area
was conquered by the Russians from the Turks, are noted for their

independence and self-esteem. (Solzhenitsyn's "hero" in *August 1914* comes from the area and you get a vignette of that local amour propre in one of its heroes.)

Gorbachev started the long road of rising in the Communist Party apparatus as chairman of the *Komsomol*'s city committee. After a very slow start, that career finally began to blossom from 1960 when Fedor Kulakov was sent from Moscow to become first secretary of the Communist Party in the Stavropol Territory. Kulakov, a self-taught agronomist with outstanding organizational talents and a strong personality, had been sent down from Moscow by Nikita Khrushchev to take charge of the rich agricultural area. Kulakov had worked on a state farm and in sugar processing and knew about the problems of Soviet agriculture from the ground up. After two years of intensive effort to restructure the Stavropol economy according to the attempted Khrushchev reforms, Kulakov recognized that the university-educated Gorbachev, rare among the country bumpkins in the area, was a talent who could accept the new ideas that Kulakov was trying to implement.

Kulakov took him from the routine Party job in the *Komsomol* and made him his personal assistant, sending Gorbachev to all parts of the huge area to check on agricultural projects that had been initiated. Gorbachev, in turn, modeled himself on the aggressive, successful Kulakov. Their career development patterns are startlingly similar; for example, Gorbachev, like Kulakov, who received an agricultural institute's formal degree after he was managing the issue for Khrushchev, got a degree in agriculture from a local Stavropol institute long after he was directing the farm and food affairs of the region. Gorbachev actually learned the problems of backward Soviet agriculture in the province, earning a reputation as an expert in the field. And, perhaps more important, he gained a political reputation as a "reformer" under Kulakov's guidance.

When Khrushchev fell from power in 1964—as a result of a power play by his opponents in which Kulakov perhaps played a minor role—Kulakov returned to the center of power in Moscow to work as the secretary in the Central Committee dealing with agricultural problems, where he ultimately rose to become a member of the Politburo. In the endless rumors that surround the top leadership of the Kremlin, it was speculated in the early 1970s that Kulakov, one of the most dedicated and effective members of the top Communist bosses, would assume the real power under Brezhnev. That was not to be.

Meanwhile for Gorbachev, these events reestablished his connection with Moscow and the center of power. As a result of Kulakov's sponsorship in the Kremlin, Gorbachev moved onto the fast track. In 1970 he became secretary of the Party in the Stavropol Territory, a large, rich agricultural area, whose importance in the economy was great even though it was at the outer geographic fringes of the Russian heartland. During his term as first secretary in Stavropol, Gorbachev won a reputation as being something of an innovator. One woman who knew him well at this time recalled that there was a small *kolkhoz,* or collective farm, in the region near Pyatigorsk where he put into practice some of the ideas he had for improving the Soviet Union's outlook on agriculture. He apparently first set about improving the living standards of the people who worked on the collective farm by arranging for the installation of natural gas and electricity in their dwellings. Then he set aside larger private plots for the collective's members to produce their own food and surplus for sale in the cities. In addition, he persuaded the Party and planning authorities to give the collective's members greater freedom over what they produced, when they produced, and even where and for what they sold it. It was a model collective farm and apparently did very well but only because Gorbachev had worked determinedly to make sure it did.[6]

However, it is at least arguable that at this point Gorbachev not only became the typical Soviet *apparatchik* but the quintessential Communist Party functionary of the Brezhnev era, one of more than 175 provincial Party bosses. A bad harvest in 1975, which some would argue was Gorbachev's responsibility, left him unscathed. There is also anecdotal material that has drifted to the West suggesting that Gorbachev's modus operandi was that of a typical middle-echelon Party official at the time— no hint of his promised democratization of later years.

The critical geography of the area, more than anything else, may explain Gorbachev's rise to prominence. In the Stavropol area are a number of the so-called sanatoriums—watering holes—which served the privileged higher echelons of the Party. Gorbachev saw to it that whenever important Muscovite leaders came to the spas—and they came often as the diseased and the invalided became the norm for the aging leadership—he (with Raisa) was on hand with gifts to arrange whatever was necessary to make himself known. (Raisa, meanwhile, had been able to get the equivalent of a PhD in Marxist-Leninist philosophy.) And it is highly likely that Kulakov introduced his young protégé in Stavropol to both Andropov, a

native of the Stavropol area, and Mikhail Suslov, the ascetic chief ideologue and kingmaker of the Party (who had also once served the Party in
Stavropol).

Both Andropov and his wife were diabetics and visited the Krasnye
Kamni sanatorium every autumn in the 1970s "to take the cure" of the
waters in the European fashion. Andropov, the austere secret police chief,
had few intimates and even fewer confederates in the Party. But he was,
by all accounts, a bitter critic of the drift and corruption of the Brezhnev
era.

Furthermore, one of the anomalies of the Soviet system—particularly
in recent years—is that the KGB and the other security organs are
undoubtedly the most worldly and best informed of the Soviet bureaucracies. Given their wide access to information on both internal and
external problems, their large numbers of cadre who have visited and lived
abroad, the necessity for them to make tough, unsentimental analyses of
the Soviet domestic and international political problems, and their use of
such professionals as Soviet newsmen, KGB officials have long been
considered sophisticates. Despite the incredible disinformation put out by
the KGB as Andropov came to power about his "liberal" tendencies,
embellished with stories that may or may not have been true about his
love of Scotch and Western jazz, there is a general belief among scholars
and those who watch the Soviet scene, that he was among the most
cosmopolitan Soviet leaders since the early Bolsheviks. And it is entirely
conceivable that he did have an understanding of the desperate and
growing need for a program to revitalize the system. That "Andropov
testament" either ended with his early death from longstanding illnesses,
or was deliberately passed on to an acolyte such as Gorbachev. There is
the possibility that a link was forged during this intimacy in the Stavropol
visits between Andropov and Gorbachev that further explains Gorbachev's
later political sophistication in Moscow. Some émigré circles talk of an
Andropov program, something akin to the outline for future policy that
Lenin left behind with his widow before his death and which was later
suppressed by Stalin, or the plea for his eventual vindication that Bukharin
had his young wife memorize and which she has only recently recounted.
Whether such a testament actually exists or not, there is the possibility
that it was Andropov's generally sophisticated view of the crisis in the
system and the need for a radical overhauling that has been passed on to
Gorbachev. For there remains something of a mystery about the way an

archetypal product of the Soviet system, which abhors deviants (especially during the Brezhnev era of conformity, stagnation, and mediocrity), has become the spokesman for the most radical transformation in seventy years.[7]

Kulakov's death in July 1978 provided a new opportunity for Gorbachev. As his major disciple and an agricultural expert, himself, Gorbachev gave the funeral oration for his old mentor from the top of Lenin's mausoleum in Red Square—the site made famous by the periodic gathering of the Soviet leadership at moments of transition or commemoration. Rumors swept Moscow about Kulakov's sudden death, because he had been an unusually vigorous and apparently heathy man, and some of the major figures of the Party did not appear at the funeral.

A few weeks later: "On the evening of September 19, 1978, a special train carrying General Secretary of the Party Leonid Brezhnev, accompanied by Konstantin Chernenko, to Baku, the capital of Azerbaijan, made an unscheduled stop at the resort town of Mineralnye Vodi on the bank of the Kuma River in Stavropol Territory. On the platform of the station they were met by KGB Chairman Yuri Andropov, who was at that time taking his regular course of treatments in nearby Kislovodsk, and Mikhail Gorbachev, Party boss of the Stavropol Territory. Here, during that brief stopover, Gorbachev's destiny was decided: by the end of the year he was in Moscow. And since that meeting was briefly mentioned in the [controlled] Soviet press, it must be regarded as an historic event. On September 19, 1978, four men, each of them an official leader of the Soviet Union when his turn came, met on the platform of a little railroad station in the Caucasus: Brezhnev, Andropov, Chernenko, and Gorbachev."[8]

Two years later, at a remarkably young age by the standards of Soviet politics, Gorbachev, because of the Kremlin infighting and the attrition because of the advancing age of most of its members, had become a full member of the Politburo. Although there was much speculation about his succession when Andropov died, the last of the dinosaurs, Chernenko, was chosen instead to follow Andropov—the last gasp toward the rapidly disappearing past of those who had known the Stalin period.

Who, then, is this Gorbachev? The noted Soviet scholar, diplomatist, and historian George F. Kennan, in answer to the question of how the Soviet system "which has put such a premium on conformity, on safety, could provide a Gorbachev," says:

You know, I really cannot explain it. Numbers of us who have known that country for a long time simply stand without an explanation as to how a man with these qualities could have emerged from a provincial party apparatus in the North Caucasus. I have asked that question of people in the Soviet Union. One thing that they said was that you must remember that he was a student of law at Moscow University and they told me to my surprise, because I had never known it, that the law school had retained certain types of teaching and training, and training also in mannerisms of the law which existed in almost no other place of legal instruction in Russia, and that may have had something to do with it. . . . I think it is rather a miracle.[9]

And that is an opinion reflected in much that appears in the Western media and statements by Western leaders. Yet the reality is quite different. One of those Communist leaders who did have a real conversion at the cost of power and almost his life, Milovan Djilas of Yugoslavia, says:

Nothing is impossible under Soviet rule. . . . But . . . political systems are not in the habit of committing suicide. In any case, Gorbachov [sic] strikes me as a true believer and I cannot see Gorbachov [sic] presiding over the liquidation of Communism. He is a man who has begun to recognize what ails the system and is trying to change an Absolute Monarchy into a Constitutional Monarchy. . . . Perhaps in his heart of hearts Gorbachov [sic] realizes that the Marxist conception of socialism is a museum piece. We don't know. What we do know is that he behaves as though he believes in the basic soundness of the Soviet system and its reformability through technology, renewed dedication, and the introduction of selective freedoms.[10]

It may be as British Prime Minister Margaret Thatcher has said, that "Gorbachev is a man one can do business with."[11] But that business would be successful only if the West recognizes that we are not dealing with a Western reformer nor a reformer in the Russian religious tradition. There is no evidence in Gorbachev's formation to suggest anything but the apotheosis of a party *apparatchik,* and one of the Brezhnev era that he so bitterly criticizes; nor are we dealing with that rare individual who has had a "Saul-on-the-road-to-Damascus" conversion.

In discussing Gorbachev the man . . . It cannot be precluded that he is a type of Soviet "closet liberal," at least in economics and foreign policy. Human history abounds in oddities, and Gorbachev's "closet liberalism" could conceivably be one of them. Still, it would be an oddity indeed: His whole background, entire political socialization, personal (as part of the Communist Party of the Soviet Union) dependence on the legitimizing aspects of the struggle to defeat capitalism and—on top of all this—everything he has done to date argue against the "closet liberalism" hypothesis. It is far more certain that Gorbachev is committed to the Soviet brand of socialism, to maintaining and increasing the relative strength of the Soviet state compared to the West, to the pursuit of the "historic struggle" and to transforming the world in Moscow's image. What we have seen thus far is most probably what we are likely to get in the future. Gorbachev is a problem solver, a tenacious competitor, and, in the Soviet context, a pragmatist.[12]

Gorbachev, after all, belongs to a post-World War II generation. He not only has been exposed to a wider range of experiences in the Soviet Union than the Stalin generation before him, but also visited Western Europe as a tourist several times during the 1970s. There is an unconfirmed report of a six-week trip through Italy and France that he and Raisa took, similar to the pilgrimages of wealthy young Russians in the czarist past. Gorbachev also has had the experience of Kulakov's agricultural innovations in the Stavropol area including the use of incentive workers "brigades." These, combined with the rich soil and other naturally beneficial agricultural endowments of the region, permitted even the wretchedly inefficient *kolkhoz* system to produce at levels well above those of other Soviet regions, suggesting perhaps the possibilities of change to the young *apparatchik*.

But more than anything else, Gorbachev's pragmatism must be the knowledge, shared by perhaps only a minority of the Soviet elite, that if the trends of the Brezhnev years were to continue, certain catastrophe would lie ahead for the regime. For despite whatever political victories the Soviets managed abroad in the two Brezhnev decades, the long-term outlook was grim. Growth was declining. Hidden inflation was rising with a runaway budget. The technological gap with the West was widening. Food production and distribution were worsening. Corruption had become a way of life permeating every level of society, even the highest echelons of the Party. The population was cynical and apathetic. Alcoholism had reached levels unparalleled in the rest of the world. Moscow was having to borrow in the West to cover her growing balance of payments deficit. With little to sell except oil and gold, both commodities were under international price pressure. And, building on the reversal of policy that occurred in the Carter administration as a result of the invasion of Afghanistan, after a decade of allowing the Soviets to catch up, the United States was beginning to rearm with the possibility that it would again get the upper hand with new breakthroughs in military technology. If it was not a crisis situation, as Gorbachev described it publicly, it was a precrisis situation in the traditional Marxist jargon.

The economic root of this crisis is basic. It lies in the growing failure—after decades of success in accomplishing the Communists' purposes—of Moscow's two-compartmental economic system of allocating the bulk of resources for the military and space while starving the civilian sector. Increasingly, the Moscow planners are finding that holes in the Chinese wall, which was supposed to separate these two economies in a Stalinist model, ironically are even more exaggerated in the post-Stalin period. For example, Murray Feshbach's thesis holds that public health facilities have degenerated to a dangerous level—lowering longevity for men and accounting for a higher infant mortality rate.

> Premature mortality of adult males (leading in part to an estimated reduction of life expectancy of males by four full years) occurred in the period 1965–1966 to 1978–79, reflecting deaths in ages 20 to 44 beyond past experience. This is due primarily to alcoholism either directly or in accidents, poisonings and injuries, or from chronic degenerative diseases associated with alcohol abuse (e.g., ischemic heart disease and cirrhosis of the liver) . . . without any assertion that the United States health system is ideal (especially considering rural and inner-city health delivery as well as concerns over cost levels) but . . . [the statistics] indicate that the Soviet male population is at much greater risk of age-specific mortality than that of the United States. . . . [it] implies a life expectancy of only 56 years at birth for the USSR, for the United States, the appropriate "West" tables yield a figure of 66 years. . . . The Soviet level is much below any I have previously estimated, which in turn were below the last published Soviet figure. Even assuming that 56 years is purely a statistical result and the "correct" figure is somewhat higher, the implication of this low level is that the length of the working life of a Soviet male is dramatically short. . . . Even if the life expectancy figure is 60 or 62 (on average), this does not bode well for major improvements unless the overall health situation can be radically upgraded.[13]

Unfortunately for the Soviet leadership, public health affects the whole manpower pool and thus breaks down the theoretical separation between military and civilian even in a totalitarian society.[14]

However successful the Stalinist economic model has been in producing Soviet military equality with the West, it is now proved to be less than what is actually happening in the USSR. All that is self-evident in civilian life—record shortages paralleling the worst years after World War II, a plunging standard of living, increased corruption in every aspect of the society, and growing disparities and frictions among regional/ethnic groupings.

It is not so apparent, however, in the military-space sector where the Soviets have always been remarkably successful at camouflaging failures. The West, for example, knew little about the massive military nuclear catastrophe of the 1950s until a Soviet émigré writer exposed it in detail almost twenty years later.[15] Therefore one can only hypothesize how much the pattern of shortages and technical inadequacies influences the military-industrial economy. But President Reagan's advocacy of an American SDI (Strategic Defense Initiative)[16] and its high step up to new technology, along with the growing possibility of "smart" battlefield weapons compensating for the armored superiority of Soviet conventional warfare, all hint at the threat to the only remaining Soviet strength—its military power.[17]

When I suggested, during a visit to Helsinki in the fall of 1988, that there might be another, specific Soviet military disaster of which we are unaware, which triggered the search for *perestroika,* a Finnish intelligence official told me, "Yes, we think so too, but we don't know what it was." Edward Luttwak, the controversial young strategist, has suggested that the miserable defeat of Soviet fighter aircraft in the 1982 Israeli-Syrian encounter may have been the touchstone, demonstrating in a dramatic single incident how far behind Soviet electronic miniaturization has fallen.

On June 10, 1982, the few hours of air warfare between Israelis and Syrians in Lebanon confirmed [former Chief of the General Staff Marshal Nikolai] Ogarkov's worst fears. That Israelis should defeat the Syrians in jet-fighter combat was not unexpected, but in the past all human and material factors, had resulted in 10–1 or at most, 20–1 ratios in favor of the Israelis. On June 10, however, the addition of a clear electronics advantage in Israel's fighter aircraft, missiles, and airborne early warning resulted in a sensational air-combat ratio of 85 (or 89) to zero. Worse, the Israelis had begun the day by destroying sixteen batteries of Soviet-made anti-aircraft missiles (enough to equip a fairsized NATO army) without losing a single aircraft, by using an array of US and Israeli-made electronic warfare devices (as well as excellent tactics). That was the very kind of absolute technological advantage in electronics that Marshal Nicolai Ogarkov had warned could utterly overcome numbers and devalue generalship, thus negating the entire Soviet strategy of military accumulation. In the aftermath of the Syrian debacle, Ogarkov's complaints became even more vehement, his demand for an acceleration of military research and for institutional reform (e.g., of the Soviet Academy of Sciences) even more outspoken.[18]

An émigré Soviet scientist, reporting a conversation to me that he had (shortly before he left Moscow in 1989) with an old acquaintance who works for one of the secret military-scientific establishments near Moscow, told this story: His colleague explained how it was possible for the security organs working through commercial contacts in the West to ferret out and send to his institute the latest Western computer software in six months despite U.S. and CoCom strategic embargo restrictions. But, he said, no sooner did his colleagues in the institute assemble it and learn how to use it, when they realized they were again at least six months behind the developments in the United States and Japan.

"Although [Marshal Nikolai] Ogarkov may have fallen into relative disfavor, his impassioned 1983 and 1984 criticisms of the capabilities of Soviet industry and economy to meet the needs of the military did not fall on deaf ears; in fact, they have since been frequently reaffirmed by other military spokesmen, although obliquely," write two Soviet analysts.[19]

The object of Soviet disarmament proposals, as I pointed out in an article in 1985, is not disarmament per se, but to identify and channel Western defense efforts into those areas of military strategy and tactics with which Soviet strategy can cope.

The Soviets are confronted with an unprecedented scientific-technological challenge in the development of new generations of weapons. Mr. Ogarkov has emphasized "there are now other purely military preconditions restricting the opportunity for imperialism for unleashing new wars. These preconditions are caused by the rapid scientific and technical revolution in military affairs." President Reagan's espousal of revolutionary new weaponry in the Strategic Defense Initiative proposals has further complicated this aspect of the Soviets' strategic problem. With the beginning of a new Defense Cycle [20-year-periods of armament-building], the Soviets are attempting to identify the long-term military-technological outlines of future weapons systems

. . . to try to minimize the risks and uncertainties in strategic-weapons development through successful [disarmament] negotiations.[20]

The possibility that Moscow might be facing altogether new weapons systems of high-technology calibre against which their decrepit economy could not compete was the consideration, rather than the long lines at every shop in Moscow and the growing shortage of food and civilian consumer goods, which was the real stimulus for, finally, an unprecedented Party debate over "revolutionary" economic changes—the most forthright since the 1920s. Michael Tsypkin, a professor at an American military university, says:

> Gorbachev and his advisers have tried to strengthen the traditionally weak link between basic science and production. Twenty-three Interbranch Scientific and Technological Complexes (MNTK) have been established; these large R&D and production "pyramids" have been consciously modeled on the Soviet A-bomb and ICBM projects of the 1940s and the 1950s. The Interbranch Complexes are to deal with high-priority areas: lasers, fiber optics, micro-computers, machine reliability, genetic engineering, etc. Led by prominent scientific administrators in emulation . . . the Interbranch Complexes are to overcome the compartmentalization within Soviet science and the R&D communities and the gap between science and production. . . . It is perhaps no coincidence that in 1989 the US Department of Defense defined twenty-two top priority areas for scientific research, a number curiously close to that of the Interbranch Complexes. But unless economic deterioration is reversed and established elites are ready to give a slice of the political pie to unorthodox newcomers, the structure of Soviet science and the status of the scientific community in the society are not likely to change drastically.[21]

Gorbachev, and what is probably a minority of the Soviet elite, saw the economic and cultural trends of the Brezhnev Soviet Union leading relentlessly and inevitably toward the ultimate disaster—crack-up of the economy and the society and the end of the regime. One must never minimize the possibilities of shifting ideological ground for personal gain among Soviet leaders, of course. Perhaps the most famous and obvious was the Khrushchev-Malenkov debate on economic policy. After Khrushchev won the power struggle and successfully deported Georgi Malenkov to run a power plant in Siberia, he adopted most of the Malenkov program of ostensible reform, which, of course, largely failed. Gorbachev and his supporters among the *nomenclatura* know intimately the history of attempts by Khrushchev, Kosygin, and others to "reform" that system. Then, can we not hypothesize that Gorbachev and his backers also know that a successful restructuring can only come through tactics that well may put the whole system in jeopardy, yet the only hope of saving the system?[22]

That may be why Gorbachev often talks of returning to "Leninist principles." As a student, a classmate remembers that, after Stalin's death, Gorbachev compared the dead dictator invidiously with Lenin. "He praised Lenin for his ability to be able, for strategic purposes, to retreat when necessary. He cited the example of the Brest-Litovsk peace, which superficially was very detrimental [to the Soviets], however, which did help the Soviets to power at the time. He admired Lenin's policy of two steps forward, one step backward."[23] Of course, there is the obvious problem of legitimacy for all Soviets leaders, as a collective entity and as individuals. Without the iconography of Lenin, the regime is stripped of that legitimacy. It must call on the (still largely) untarnished hero of the October Revolution, despite all the logic which points to Lenin as the author of much of what is now criticized in the Soviet system. In May 1988 during a conversation with a group of American journalists in Moscow, I asked Abel G. Aganbegian, the noted Soviet economist and one of the intellectual stalwarts of *perestroika* (more recently one of its most frequently used Soviet propagandists overseas), a series of questions about the then new "revelations" about the Soviet economy. When he confirmed stagnation, inflation, and unemployment, homelessness, and so forth, and other problems of "the command economy," I asked: "But what is this talk of going back to Leninist principles? Is it not true that all these problems in the economy began with Lenin?" He paused, smiled enigmatically, and then the interpreter translated his answer: "We have a saying among us that when Lenin stands there, in his *shopka* [worker's cap], with his left arm outstretched [the pose of countless statues throughout the Soviet Union], he is blessing all that goes on in front of him." It is true that some braver Soviet analysts, Vasilii Seliunin, for example,[24] have seen and commented on the origins of Stalinism in Lenin's "War Communism." But the myth of Lenin's omnipotence and his "untouchability" in the present debate still permeates the more popular press, and even Seliunin pulls his punches.[25]

Lenin's uniqueness in the Bolshevik firmament has another aspect, however, in that his actions illustrate, more than those of any of the other founding comrades of the Bolshevik regime, a Machiavellian role as the risk-taker, the gambler, the high-roller, the leader who is prepared to bet all on getting power and preserving it. And he represents the ultimate opportunist-pragmatic political tactician, making 180-degree turns, if necessary, to maintain that power. Just as he did in his student days, Gorbachev recently has repeatedly referred to Lenin's advocacy of a separate peace with Imperial Germany in World War I (which was opposed by virtually all the Soviet leadership), "because he was guided by vital, not immediate, interests, the interests of the working class as a whole, of the revolution, and the future of socialism."[26]

CHAPTER 8

PERESTROIKA

Making an Omelet without Breaking Eggs

"The best that can be said of Gorbachev's tenure as CC (Central Committee) Secretary for Agriculture (1978–85) is that he had little influence. . . ."[1] That is the description of Anders Aslund, a Swedish diplomat and scholar, who spent four years in Moscow with direct access to most of the "reformers" group of economists who have been Gorbachev's inspiration and brain trust for *perestroika*. "It is an enigma that a provincial *apparatchik* should turn out to be so reform-minded. One obvious reason is that the state of Soviet society and economy was so bad; another that an intensive review of the country's situation, and a search for solutions, was launched by Andropov, and it was led by Gorbachev."

Again, from Milovan Djilas:

The Soviet leaders' attempt to reform the system is not inspired by some noble realization that the system is universally poorly regarded abroad, but by strict necessity. They have come to realize what other Communists in Yugoslavia, Poland, Hungary, Czechoslovakia, and China realized earlier—namely that Communism doesn't work. It won't work at the economic level nor at the level of satisfying what are human needs and liberties. Put all these factors side by side with the rapid growth of technological advance of the Western and modern worlds and you cannot help realizing that Communism

119

is a 19th century relic and a prescription for disaster. . . . They (the Soviet rulers) realize that Stalinism, the "command economy," and the conservative bureaucracy have made the system a permanent loser vis-à-vis the variously mixed economies of the world.[2]

There is another explanation as well. In the growing realization of the failures of the economy, "reform" became the weapon that Gorbachev has used to defeat his enemies and aggrandize his power in what in many ways has been a typical and traditional Soviet rise to the top.

One very fundamental rationale behind the whole program [of Gorbachev's reforms] has been to provide the new general secretary with a vehicle with which to consolidate his personal position and absolute power. This was particularly and directly applicable to the limited measures undertaken [earlier] . . . [and the fact that later his activities] were marked by a resumption of personnel purges suggests that either Gorbachev has decided that his consolidation of power was incomplete or that other criteria are beginning to play a greater role.[3]

As the leading dissident figure in the Soviet Union and at least a tacit supporter of Gorbachev, the late physicist Andrei Sakharov repeatedly pointed out, inside and outside the country, that Gorbachev's campaign for reform of the system has paralleled his program to accumulate personal power. And it could well be argued, as Sakharov said in a speech in London in early 1989, that no one since Stalin has succeeded in accumulating so much personal power in the Soviet system. This consolidation of power has been justified—particularly by foreign supporters and well-wishers—as necessary for making the reforms that are demanded in the Soviet system against the combined power of the enormous entrenched and coddled bureaucracy, the *nomenclatura*.

Gorbachev, himself, has written, in a defensive aside on his program, that there are elements of a "revolution from above" in his program.

What is meant [by the term "revolution from above"] is profound and essentially revolutionary changes implemented on the initiative of the authorities themselves but necessitated by objective changes in the situation and in social moods. It may seem that our current *perestroika* could be called "revolution from above." True, the *perestroika* drive started on the Communist Party's initiative, and the Party leads it. . . . I spoke frankly about it at the meeting with Party activists in Khabarovsk in the summer of 1986. . . . We began from the top of the pyramid and went down to its base, as it were. Still the concept of "revolution from above" doesn't quite apply to our *perestroika*, at least it requires some qualification. Yes, the Party leadership started it. The highest Party and state bodies elaborated and adopted the program. True, the *perestroika* is not spontaneous but a governed process. . . . *Perestroika* would not have been a truly revolutionary undertaking, it would not have acquired its present scope, nor would it have had any firm chance of success if it had not merged the initiative from "above" with the grass-roots movement.[4]

Yet, the most common reaction of ordinary Soviet citizens one encountered in Moscow and its environs in the spring of 1988 was total skepticism. The standard reply that friends and I elicited in response to questions about what ordinary citizens thought of *perestroika* when we asked taxi drivers, mourners we met in a cemetery on the outskirts of Moscow (where we had gone to pay homage at the grave of Andrei Pasternak), churchgoers on the steps of one of the several churches being refurbished, shoppers in a market where the empty shelves almost seemed to indicate it was out of business, and so forth, was a cynical smile, a shrug of the shoulders, or a blank expression.[5]

In the Soviet Union, one does not have to search far for the reason for any lack of public acceptance or enthusiasm for yet another attempt to "reform" the society. Soviet citizenry has every reason to believe, on the basis of past experience, that modifications of the system are as likely to mean that conditions will get worse rather than better. And the citizen who has accommodated himself to the system (as expressed so aptly in that oldest of Soviet jokes, "They pretend to pay us, and we pretend to work") looks on any change as one that may necessitate new sacrifices and privations.[6]

Perestroika's economic reform aspects are a continuation of the earlier efforts, particularly the Khrushchev and Kosygin reexamination of the economy. But they also represent the views of a particularly vocal and forthright group of economists and social scientists, many of them originally concentrated at the Economic Institute at Novosibirsk in Western Siberia. The leading theoretician of the group was Tatiana Zaslavskaia, whose name was attached to the famous "Novosibirsk Report" of 1984. That document, apparently ordered by Andropov and bureaucratically administered by Gorbachev, was to be the formal start of the process. It may not be an accident, as an old Stalinist cliché has it, that in Siberia the initiators were far from the bureaucratic corridors of Moscow. One of Gorbachev's early collaborators, and now a conservative opponent, Egor Ligachev, has idealized the role of Communist cadre in faraway Siberia. Abel Aganbegian, the most well-known of the group, told our group of visiting American journalists in May 1988 that he was not—as reported, among other places, in a cover story in *Time* magazine—Gorbachev's principal economic adviser. The reporters, like "sharks" smelling the blood of a purge or a demotion, quickly moved in. We asked, then, what he was doing. He replied he was a researcher, a consultant, and that he might not always be "here" [Moscow]. We asked, then, where he would go. And he replied that he might go back to Novosibirsk "Where I lived very happily for 25 years," with what appeared to be a certain nostalgia for other times and other climes.

Yet, it is a vast oversimplification to speak of a Gorbachev economic program for reform. To use a metaphor from American football, although Gorbachev has proceeded along a wandering path of reform with perseverance, he has been a broken-field runner. As one strategic or tactical concept has fallen by the wayside, he has ducked, doubled back, moved laterally, and then struck out again. The game is far from over, and it is not clear how far the ball has actually progressed beyond the original scrimmage line when he first got control of it.

Theoretically, the process began on December 10, 1984, when—three months before he was elected general secretary—he laid out what were to become his famous slogans in a speech on ideological revision before the Central Committee. It was inevitable, given the long history of ideological struggle in the Party, that he should begin with ideological rationalizations for the program. Gorbachev warned of the possibility of economic deterioration and the need to speed up economic progress. He spoke of the need for reinforcing "the human factor in social progress," pointing out the increasing role of higher sophistication and education in the role of the worker in modern industry. He spoke of specific new organizational methods, integrating research with production—historically the weak link not only in Soviet but in Russian science and economic development. He talked of "self-governing" labor relations, of "self-management," and praised a particular new system of worker brigade contracts that had been initiated under Andropov. And he spoke of political reform—"a perfection of the Soviet political system and a further development of socialist democracy." This Gorbachev speech was followed by others after he became general secretary. They also contained threats of new discipline and restrictions on workers and managers who did not measure up—much as Andropov had done when he came to office—with some temporary results in increasing productivity, it appears.

During the next few months, the rhetoric dimmed as he was apparently forced into a tactical retreat by those who have come to be called "conservatives" in the Party and the bureaucracy; in fact, the vested interests of the Soviet elite—the *nomenclatura*. Meanwhile, Gorbachev was moving to build a majority in the Politburo for his own personal control through the appointment of other Andropov protégés and the elimination of Grigorii Romanov, the Leningrad Party leader who had been Andropov's major and his only rival for general secretary. Regional satraps were being replaced at the same time that he chose five new ministers for the central government in July 1985, along with a new prime minister. The key economic planner, State Planning Committee Chairman (*Gosplan*) and deputy chairman of the council of ministers, N. K. Baibakov, was relieved after twenty years. Before the end of 1985, Gorbachev had removed five of the eight deputy chairmen of the council of ministers, and removed twenty-two Soviet ministers or chairmen of state committees. The pace continued into the new year in preparation for the Party Congress. Fleet Admiral Gorshkov, the most prestigious Soviet military figure in the post-World War II period who had presided over the creation of the new Soviet bluewater navy, was unceremoniously relieved of his command after thirty years. There appears also to have been an unusually high turnover of major operation commanders in the army along with two service commanders, and the first deputy minister of defense. (Gorbachev did not get his own minister of defense until 1987.) At the Congress of the Party the Gorbachevization continued. Five new Party secretaries, including A. N. Iakovlev, former ambassador to Ottawa whom Gorbachev had come to know on a trip to Canada (see Chapter 1), were installed. Boris Pomarev, the longtime director of international activities for the Party, was fired, and replaced by an old comrade (and competitor) from Georgia, a KGB cadre, Eduard Shevardnadze. Almost half of the Central Committee was new. As a result of all this, Gorbachev had appointed five of the total of twelve full Politburo members. Therefore, with the Brezhnev "seat-warmers" who would go along with any new policy, one short year after his election to general secretary, Gorbachev had essentially secured his control over the senior echelons of the Party and the state.

On economic matters, Gorbachev at first seemed to be turning his attention to agriculture; naturally enough, that was the one economic subject about which he knew a great deal. The drain of foreign exchange for grain purchases abroad, which was constantly growing, also presented a real economic problem that had to be dealt with sooner or later. Gorbachev did move quickly to reorganize the vast Soviet farm and food bureaucracy into a superministry (*Gosagroprogr*). But it was to be torn apart again in early 1988, still as a part of *perestroika*! He talked of new methods of running the *kolkhozy* based on "a creative utilization of the Leninist idea of taxing, applied to contemporary conditions." That was a reference to the changes made under the NEP after the agricultural deprivations of "war communism." In reality, what it meant was that farms would get a stable procurement plan for each five-year plan period— something that Brezhnev had promised but that had never been implemented. The sale from the farms of surplus potatoes, fruit, and vegetables would be permitted (in effect, legalizing the black market that supplies the greater part of these foods to the large cities). Gorbachev seemed to be calling for a combination of the state-run system and intensification of the attempts to stimulate private entrepreneurship in the rural areas. But at the Congress, the subject went into eclipse—in part because one of Gorbachev's appointees to the politburo, Egor Ligachev, formerly Gorbachev's closest collaborator, had developed into a go-slow critic and the spokesman for more "conservative" elements. In August 1987, Gorbachev took up agricultural reform again, but the issue faded quickly in the plenum session of the Central Committee, after the "conservatives" reacted strongly to Gorbachev's hints that he wanted to go to leaseholds for *kolkhoz* land.

During 1989 there was more talk of movement toward "privatization" of Soviet agriculture. A trial balloon was sent up, cut down, and sent up again, that the government would pay for marketable surpluses in foreign exchange. Yet, in fact, reports from the field indicated that no such thing was occurring; since the farmer realized that additional income was useless with the shortage of consumer goods, he was being paid in special scrip as a new device to get his cooperation.

A private type of farming could develop on rented leased land, if other conditions such as free access to free markets, genuine trade of material inputs instead of factual assignment of their short supplies were given, and most important, if the farmer himself could choose what to produce, in which way, perhaps on the basis of contracts if these were freely negotiated, without a chain of command above him. It may be that a test part of these conditions will be met with family farmers outside the *kholhozes* and *sovho-holzes,* as recent legislation seems to imply. Yet it seems certain that for the foreseeable future such "peasant farms," if they become a reality at all, will account for a tiny fraction of Soviet agricultural production.[7]

An important additional caveat is needed to explain the very wide gap between Soviet promises in agricultural reform and their actual development. The very large production in private plots relative to that obtained from the government collectives is obtained because of the illegal use (the theft) of *kolkhoz* resources (seed, water, fertilizer, insecticides, and so forth) by the owners of the private plots. Therefore, it is not possible to simply say that an expansion of the private holdings would produce an automatic relatively large increase in food production.

In the total chaos of the reform effort, the issue of agriculture may be more important for its overall political meaning than as a specific issue. Gorbachev has been taken to task, particularly by many foreign critics, for not moving on agriculture quickly. The comparison with Deng Tsiao-ping's modernization effort in Communist China is often cited; the very large increases in Chinese agricultural production have surprised many observers. Whatever success the Deng program has had, has been largely attributed to this enormous increase in prosperity in the rural areas owing to releasing the Chinese peasant from Communist agricultural orthodoxy. Gorbachev's lack of emphasis on agriculture may be a result of several considerations. First, of course, is the very difficult political problem any retreat from collectivization poses for a Soviet regime trying to maintain its bona fides as "socialist" while abandoning one after another of the sacred Soviet economic precepts. There are cynics, too, who would say that Gorbachev does not press on with agriculture precisely because after so many years of being acquainted with its problems in Stavropol and again in Moscow, he knows how difficult of solution it is.

There may be an even larger issue, however. A French expert who has visited more than 200 *kolkhozy* over the past five years argues that the problem is now a cultural and sociological, as well as economic, one. The deprivations of the famines of the 1920s and 1930s, Stalin's anti-*kulak* campaign, the Nazi invasion, and Soviet scorched-earth policies and their aftermath, have eliminated those elements in the rural areas that could respond to economic freedom, he told me. "The low level of culture, education, and living standards in Soviet agriculture are beyond the imagination of a Westerner; we have not seen anything like this in Western Europe for centuries. The thread of continuity of peasant agriculture in the Soviet Union has been broken."

It was not only in agriculture that Gorbachev's initiatives appeared to be drowning in the traditional Soviet bureaucratic morass. One of the first campaigns inaugurated by Gorbachev was his May 1985 "Measures to Overcome Drinking and Alcoholism." A vast array of restrictions—limits on when beverages could be sold, the number of shops, drinking places, age limitations, fines, and so forth—were suddenly rigidly enforced. Police began picking up drunkards on the streets. Drinking at the work place was stopped. The campaign was staged with all the paraphernalia of an old Stalinist program; public demonstrations were held against drunkenness, a vast propaganda campaign was initiated, and societies for sobriety were organized. Almost immediately, the results were enormous waiting lines, shortages, and significant price rises in a black market. So much sugar was drawn off into illegal home brew operations that a severe shortage developed throughout the country.

There were results, or claimed results—sales of alcohol fell by 25 percent during the first seven months of 1985, by 37 percent in 1986, and by another 13 percent in 1987. After the initial shock, however, drinking habits were reestablished through the use of illicit alcohol. Arrests for bootlegging reached new records with large numbers in the cities for the first time. It has even been argued that illicit production made up for the whole decline in consumption. And there were warnings that illicit brewing was leading to the growth of a criminal underground, similar to the one that developed in the United States during Prohibition. There were important disastrous economic effects as well. Total revenues from the sale of alcohol with the concomitant turnover tax were reduced by 6.3 percent from 1985 to 1986 according to some economists. (National income reductions were made up by fiddling with the statistics.)

Whatever the exact figures, the campaign against alcohol had aggravated market imbalances severely; a large, but undisclosed, budget deficit had been created; the campaign required the attention of a large police force; and it was likely to be less successful in the long run. Even the most justified administrative campaign had caused such problems that its value was in doubt. The state could not offer any alternative to drinking, neither spiritually nor economically.[8]

The outspoken reform economist Aganbegian put it more succinctly:

We have taken a step backwards. The state has lost its monopoly on wine and spirits; there is a greater gap between supply and demand in the retail trade; there is a shortage of sugar and unprecedentedly high demand for and consumption of sugar all over the country. We have now had to resort to rationing, which has in turn made the sugar shortage worse and increased dissatisfaction.[9]

These faltering first steps in his economic reform apparently demonstrated for Gorbachev that he was slipping into the same pattern as his predecessors in their search for "reform." He looked for causes—and scapegoats—and found them in the resistance of the *nomenclatura* and the bureaucracy to his changes.

By the autumn of 1987, the implementation of economic reform was faltering because of bureaucratic resistance in the central economic bodies and branch ministries. Then, Gorbachev's focus moved back to political issues and to the very role of the Party—a moot point in the reform package. Gorbachev was unequivocal. The role of the Party in running of the economy should be reduced: "the creation of a new management mechanism for the economy allows for the liberation of the Party bodies from, for them, uncharacteristic, purely economic management functions."[10]

What the bureaucrats in the government and the Party fear is that *perestroika* ultimately means writing an end to the principal Soviet myths— that there is no unemployment in the socialist system and therefore, no unemployment in the Soviet Union. D. J. Peterson writes:

While it is still impossible to measure structural unemployment nationwide, it is possible to use some anecdotal evidence to estimate the level of unemployment in selected areas. First Secretary of the Uzbek Communist Party, Rafik Nishakov, has said that in Fergana Oblast one in five youngsters entering the job market cannot find a job. In Novyi Uzen, a town of 56,000 people in Kazakhstan, estimates of *bezrabotitsa* [structural unemployment] range from 600 to 2,000 people, which works out to be between 1.8 and 6 percent of the working-age population in the city.[11]

Repeatedly, in different ethnic and racial disturbances, dissidents have reported that unemployment is part of the problem. Gorbachev has made the elimination of "hidden unemployment"—that is, people who hold down jobs but do little or no work, one of the cornerstones of *perestroika*. In 1988 in Moscow the cliché was that there were fourteen million "bureaucrat-managers" who had to be eliminated to achieve any real economic reform. These people are located in government jobs and also in so-called enterprises. The reform economists have estimated that of the 24,000 enterprises in the country, one in seven currently operates at a loss with these "seat-warmers." It is no wonder, then, that most observers believe—and Gorbachev has periodically pilloried them—that the economic bureaucracy may be the greatest silent enemy to any kind of reform that threatens these jobs, particularly as it is less than clear where job creation will occur in the new system.

Still, the Swedish scholar Anders Aslund argues that there is a large consensus for reform of the economy among the principal politicians and highest bureaucrats, who fall into three groups. There are those he calls the "radicals," headed by Gorbachev, who would turn to market instruments to accomplish a radical restructuring of the whole system. There are "planners" who would make changes on the margin of the present system but not abolish the overwhelming power of the *Gosplan*. Finally, there are "technocrats" who believe that a sufficient amount of technological renovation can be inserted into the system to produce the necessary changes, and who model their program after the Liberman reforms as applied to the German Democratic Republic. Aslund assumes that any program that Gorbachev can effect for reform will have to be a series of compromises among these three groups, as well as from the pressures of the "conservatives" inside the party—and the huge Soviet bureaucracy seeking to prevent any change.

Yet, is that enough? Academician Leonid Abalkin, one of the more vociferous proponents of reform, at the 19th Party Conference in June 1988 pointed out that no radical breakthrough in the economy had taken place and that it was still in a stage of stagnation. The economic growth rate has failed to increase and has probably declined. Qualitative improvements, economic efficiency, product quality, and technical progress are all at dismal levels, according to Abalkin. A few months later, in January 1989, Abalkin warned that no results from the reform effort would be felt by the Soviet people until 1995. "It was clear from the start that our economic inheritance from the past was absolutely grave. There should have been no daydreaming about quick progress toward better living conditions." Abalkin also warned that economic reforms will inevitably lead to closing down more and more unprofitable enterprises, which would mean that, by the year 2000, fifteen million Soviet workers would have to be retrained for jobs in the service industries.

The "command economy" structure that Stalin created still remains in place, but it functions more unsatisfactorily than ever. Although there has been an enormous amount of economic legislation, the results have been confusing because it is deliberately misinterpreted or interpreted for parochial interests by the bureaucracy. Moreover, there are repeated warnings that no important results can be expected in the near term. What this suggests to many observers, both in the Soviet Union and abroad, is that certain fundamentals are not being addressed and, until they are, the tinkering with the system that has occurred so far will not solve basic problems. Meanwhile, as I was told by Finnish government personnel and businessmen—who probably have the most intimate connection of any outsiders with the Soviet bureaucracy and the economic scene inside the country—"everything is getting worse." The Finnish traders said that those parts of the economy that had worked before *perestroika* were now disrupted by the changes that Gorbachev and his adherents had worked. But the "new systems," whether they were for foreign trade or attempts to get more consumer goods into the marketplace, were not working. Thus, conditions, especially those related to retail consumption, were at their lowest ebb since the postwar period after 1945.

While the tinkering continues, as of the spring of 1990, the most basic elements of the problem have not been addressed. These relate to the underlying financial problems that have been building for decades, which are, therefore, the most difficult to remedy. They have been generally described under the rubrics of "price reform," "inflation," "convertibility of the ruble," and "currency reform." They are so intertwined that an attempt to solve one inevitably leads to speculation about another, which, probably more than anything else, explains the difficulty of moving on with any of these aspects of *perestroika*.

Price reform has been the central battleground from the beginning of Gorbachev's campaign. Aganbegian has described the theoretical problem:

> The system of price regulation we have inherited from the old administrative economic system is unsatisfactory. Production was not regulated by the price system because the quantity and choice of product were centrally planned. If the prices did not ensure profitability, central government subsidized the production. If there was a certain, not very high profit, there were subsidies for various other purposes. But if a particular product proved to be highly profitable, most of the profit was taken away for the national budget. So prices were part of the national accounting system and were not seen as decisive economic devices in the producer's development.[12]

From the standpoint of customers, the price system was equally irrelevant. Soviet industries that needed capital goods and plant equipment, for example, were theoretically supplied with these essentials by the planning authority.

But the whole system, as Aganbegian now admits, was based on "incomplete or primitive" notions. No allowance was made for labor, raw materials, or production. These were assumed to be available to the enterprise under allocation from the central planning authority. Investment costs were amortized at rates that were always too low. Reconstruction or expansion of the manufacturing facility costs was not calculated. For most consumer goods, the retail price was made up largely of the purchase tax. In a nutshell, real cost of an individual product was virtually unknown. The waste in such an economy cannot be exaggerated. The most notorious example, widely known and publicized since the 1940s, was that of the price of bread. Set at 1925 prices, the bread price was so low that, although it made it available in abundant quantities for the lowest paid Soviet worker, the price permitted farmers to feed it to their pigs in private plots. When meat was available in the state stores, it was priced in 1989 at one ruble eighty kopecks, but the state subsidy was three rubles fifty kopecks. Aganbegian reckons the total subsidies in the food industry alone amounted to 60 billion rubles a year of a total state budget of 480 billion rubles.

Because there is no way to move quickly from this system to a system in which price would be calculated on cost for both individual items and manufacturing operations without a cataclysmic upheaval in the society, "price reform" has become a major and controversial issue. Huge lists of new wholesale prices for products throughout the Soviet economy were drawn up in the spring of 1989. A fierce battle broke out among the economic reformers, the state planners, and the politicians over implementing them. The principal issue was whether a new system of administered prices was to be announced (the planners' position), or whether a market system of permitting scarcities to dictate prices would become the norm. In the end, the possible effect of a rapid increase in prices that reflected the real shortages was too much for the politicians to risk, so it was postponed. The "conservatives" have called for centralized, fixed prices that would be set administratively so that centralized planning can continue. The "liberals" wanted "market-clearing prices"—that is, prices that would do away with subsidies by raising them to real values. That obviously is social dynamite in Gorbachev's already difficult political situation. There is evidence, for example, that racial and ethnic tensions in several of the regions of the USSR that have claimed the headlines are, at least partly, a reflection of these shortages and price problems.

Much has been discussed and written about the so-called cooperatives set up in the Soviet Union under new legislation supported by Gorbachev and his advisers. One might cynically say that this was an effort to legitimize the already flamboyant Soviet black market, and to harvest its admitted productivity. The cooperatives have become much more of an ideological football than their economic merit or demerit would indicate. The "conservatives" have argued that the willingness to let private entrepreneurs—usually family units—organize cooperatives to service the population is the most outrageous affront to Marxist-Leninist theories of equity and equality. And it has been argued, apparently with some evidence from attacks on some of the cooperatives, that they violate Russian traditional standards of egalitarianism. One might seek more practical reasons that they would be resented by a Soviet population that is faced with shortages and all the injustices of the system. That reason is simply that most of the cooperatives have been located in service industries—fancier restaurants, garages, repair shops of various kinds, software computer sales, imported articles marketing—which are adjuncts of the life-style of the *nomenclatura*, that Soviet elite which already lives well by

Soviet standards. One can imagine the ordinary, beaten-down Soviet citizen seeing the new cooperative ventures as just another addition to the "perks" already accorded the elite.

I. Faminsky, who flourishes under the title of doctor of economics, director of the All-Union Scientific Research Institute of Foreign Economic Relations under the USSR Council of Ministers State Foreign Economic Commission, says:

> Frankly speaking, "uncivilized" cooperative members will flood into the market. I have met such people in the Far East. Some guys sold a carload of timber to Japan. At a price substantially below that charged by the state. They bought motor vehicles. I asked them where they had gotten the wood. Very simply, they said, they had bought it from a timber trade base. The point is not just that the clever guys earned pretty well but that they created a precedent which has effected trade as a whole. For then our partners will demand that we reduce the price. All this in addition to the fact that licensing is necessary. . . .[13]

The campaign in the Soviet media to dramatize the large earnings of some of the cooperative operators has already had its effect. Almost with their initiation, there was a row over the high taxes (as much as 90 percent) imposed on the cooperatives by Moscow City and other local governments. Such high taxes would have removed all motivation for the entrepreneur. By October 1989, amendments to the cooperative laws framed in typical Soviet speak already were clipping the wings of such entrepreneurs. "With a view to ensuring price stability [sic] on the consumer market, Soviets of People's Deputies may set upper limits for prices (tariffs) for basic consumer goods (services) produced and sold by cooperatives, including cooperatives in the consumer cooperative system." And "State monitoring [sic] of prices (tariffs) is carried out in cases where the output (work, services) of a cooperative is sold to enterprises and organizations under contract to fulfil the state order. . . ." And "Cooperatives acquiring goods by means of imports sell these goods to the population at prices no higher than the level of prices laid down for similar goods by the corresponding state organs. . . . M. Gorbachev, chairman of the USSR Supreme Soviet, Moscow, Kremlin, 16 Oct. 1989."[14]

A beginning on price reform has been promised repeatedly, only to be postponed because of the conflicting arguments over what to do. Several spokesmen have now promised that it will begin in 1990 after a "global review" of all prices in the whole system. Obviously, that will be a highly political decision and many Soviet observers have predicted that it could decide not only the fate of *perestroika* but of Gorbachev himself. The dilemma of the reformers was explained very well by Deputy Chairman of the Government Commission on Economic Reform of the USSR Council of Ministers V. Golovachev:

> We are dismantling administrative methods and the economic ones are just barely beginning to function. They do not run with full force, partly because the essential deep foundation in the form of reconstructed property relations has not been created. . . . Look, the market is not developed: there is a strangulation taking on ugly forms. Prices are disorderly and not adjusted to market conditions. Currency circulation is significantly disordered; inflation has taken on dangerous forms . . . Add to it strikes and interethnic conflicts, which cost the country very much. When he is asked why the reforms were initiated without proper preparation ("Why did we, as it is said, enter the water without knowing where the ford is?") [Golovachev replies:] How can you create a normal consumption market, not having created the means of production? To completely escape a transitional period is impossible. But who could have predicted such an intensification of interethnic relations and explosion of strikes? Who could have foreseen that the social conscience would have been insufficiently prepared for self-government and to take on new economic relationships? At this point, I would like to remind you of a very important thought of Lenin about the necessity of a sharp rise in the level of culture in the broadest sense of the word.[15]

Underlying Golovachev's remarks is the Sword of Damocles in the Soviet economy, which is a conundrum—one of the many "secrets" of the Soviet economy for decades—for which there are myriad answers by Soviet and foreign economists, but none without its price. The problem is the Soviet's classic budget deficit—classic in the sense that it resembles in character budget deficits in the West. In the past, however, Soviet propagandists had been able to obscure its real significance as something that either did not exist or had a different meaning in a "command economy." Igor Birman, an émigré Soviet economist, a decade ago exploded the myth of the claimed Soviet budget surpluses.[16] Birman estimated that the total annual deficit of the Soviet budget was about 10 percent of the gross national product. That compares with the U.S. deficit of about 3 percent of GNP. The problem, however, has only recently been acknowledged in Soviet economic debate, and then, according to most outside experts, it has been presented in less stark terms than actually exist. Leonid Abalkin told reporters in Moscow in January 1989 that the official estimate of the budget was off by three times when, in the fall of 1988, Finance Minister V. Gostev acknowledged a deficit of 35 billion rubles in the 1989 budget.

Bringing the budget deficit under control, however, although admittedly difficult, is only a part of the problem. According to statistics released by Moscow in early 1989, Soviet citizens were said to hold almost 300 billion in savings accounts. This "monetary overhang" threatens an already inflationary economy with hyperinflation and has stymied any attempt at price reform and a real turn to markets. An equivalent of about a third of the gross national product, these monetary surpluses would wreak havoc if they suddenly flowed into the market.

Inflation in 1989 was already running at a minimum of 15 percent. In the budget announced in late September, Finance Minister Valentin Pavlov promised not only to halve the state budget deficit ($188 billion at the official exchange rates) but also to introduce new bonds that would absorb this surplus liquidity. How he would accomplish that was not clear, but it was obvious that to entice buyers, he would have to offer interest rates on fifteen to twenty-year bonds of at least 2 to 3 percent above the inflation rate. The extent of the problem, however, was marked by the government's official estimate that individual ruble income would rise by as much as 9 percent in 1990, and that it had been rising at an average of 5.6 percent over the past three years. A commentator for *Pravda* has probably put it as succinctly and as accurately as any outsider might:

> We have lived, borrowing from the future, and now the time has come to pay off our old debts. The economy is now improving, but readers complain that this is not in evidence if you judge by what is available in the stores. The problem is that the commodity supply is growing far slower than the monetary supply. There is no point in blaming restructuring [*perestroika*]. . . . We have lost Rubles 40 billion in revenue because of the fall in world oil prices. True, another Rubles 34 billion is the result of the reduced revenue from alcohol. An extra 18 billion has been "procured" for urgent social programs. Then, of course, there was Chernobyl, Armenia, Afghanistan.[17]

Nothing demonstrated this overall problem of too much money chasing too few goods more than the miners' strike that broke out July 10, 1989, in the Siberian town of Mezhdurechensk and soon spread to all the major mining districts. Altogether a half million miners went out with another 160,000 workers in ten towns supporting their cause. The miners called off their strike when Prime Minister Ryzhkov flew from Moscow to see their leaders and promised to satisfy their principal demands. Soviet leadership, furthermore, had to eat crow. Egor Klochkov, the secretary of the AUCCTU (All-Union Coordinating Council of Trade Unions), said in a statement broadcast over the Moscow Home Service Sept. 5, 1989:

> The [official Soviet] trade unions have accumulated many and varied functions over the decades and have in the process become removed from the basic one: the protective function. The recent mass strikes in the country's coal-mining regions and in other sectors of the national economy showed that the working class, the working people, are not satisfied with the trade union stance; and they are dissatisfied with how they are performing their protective functions. It is not coincidence that in a number of places this protest was not expressed through strike committees. Serious lessons have to be learnt from all this.[18]

Gorbachev characterized the strike and the strikers' demands as "intolerable," and then said he would not meet the workers' demands. Although among the workers' demands were increases in wages and changes in work rules, their chief complaint—for their salaries were far above those earned by most Soviet workers, including white collar workers in Moscow—was the shortages of consumer goods. When a group of sociologists made an inquiry after the strike was "settled" (for it dragged on, erratically through the late summer and fall of 1989), the miners complained most bitterly that they did not have soap. O. Novikova, one of the researchers, states:

> In theory, miners' wages are relatively high, averaging 346 rubles per month, and the vacation time is twenty-four days but can be extended up to thirty-six days for various reasons. Miners obtain pensions at the age of 50; hence, here also, there should be no cause for complaint. When measured in terms of income per family member, however, the miners' wages are shown to be inadequate. . . . almost 60 percent receive less than 130 rubles monthly per

family member, and this, at a time of rising prices, hidden inflation, and blackmarket speculation for needed goods, is woefully insufficient.[19]

These shortages in the mining towns of Western Siberia were not unique.

The extent of the shortages may only be guessed at from the limited details in the Soviet media. However, the demands of the striking miners this summer have made it impossible to conceal the fact that the situation is very serious. Meat and sugar were already being rationed in Volgograd [a not atypical provincial industrial city] when it was announced that from Feb. 1, 1989, detergents would also be rationed throughout the country. (A major Japanese soap company has been engaged with a Soviet partner in a joint venture to build a detergent plant and announced in September 1989 that it would recommence the project which is now 10 years old!) Volgograd also suffers from shortages of other goods. One correspondent reported that "only 75 percent of the sewing machines ordered by the shops were being produced; of detergents, 68 percent; wool fabrics, 35 percent; and furs, eight percent." . . . The fact that increases in wages have not corresponded with an increase in the production of goods is having very serious repercussions. First, the failure to produce sufficient goods to meet domestic demand or be exported, has resulted in a budget deficit, currently estimated at Rubles 100 billion. To solve this problem a situation of 'robbing Peter to pay Paul' has arisen, as may be seen from the letters [printed in *Moskovskaya Pravda*] from Moscow trade unionists complaining about workers not being paid on time.[20]

Nikolai Shmelev, a radical economist among the reformers, said that at the summer of 1989 inflation rate the "budget deficit is enough to ruin the market completely and bring about a 100 percent rationing system some time next year [1990]."

By fall 1989 there was already a flight from money. A journalist writing in a Moscow newspaper reported that long lines were forming in front of jewelry stores where people were willing to buy anything—the more expensive the item the better.

According to Tatayana Konstantinovna Ivanova, deputy director of the Rosyuvelirtorg Central Retail Enterprise, the demand for jewelry rose appreciably last July [1988]. By January it had stabilized and maintained a comparatively high but nonetheless tolerable level until this August [1989]. Suddenly, the dam burst. As usually happens in such cases, rumors of an alleged impending increase in the price of gold triggered the explosion. "Lines grew drastically outside the jewelry stores and they have recently [reached] their highest point today [October 6, 1989]. Some people wait overnight in order to reach the entrance in the morning."[21]

Yet academician O. Bogomolov, one of the more outspoken of the reform economists, wrote in September 1989 that:

> In order to balance the supply of goods and services on the consumer market it would be necessary to raise people's quality of life by approximately 50 percent—even if monetary incomes remained at the same level. According to some estimates, it is necessary to remove at least Rubles 150 billion of *cash in circulation* [added emphasis]. The government will only be able to pay off its debt for this sum if, in addition to increasing the production, and supply of consumer goods, it brings into commodity circulation some of the assets which have been turned into "property of the people"—unused or poorly used land, houses, apartments, and certain enterprises (especially small and medium-sized enterprises), fixed capital, individual types of machinery and equipment and construction materials.[22]

Martin Feldstein, former chairman of the Council of Economic Advisers to the president of the United States, after a series of talks with Soviet economists in the Soviet Union in the spring of 1989, saw this "monetary overhang" as the principal problem of *perestroika*.

> There are only two ways to reduce the "overhang of excess rubles" without a price rise. The government could, in principle, run a budget surplus, thereby taking more money from the public in taxes than it passes out in government purchases, subsidies, and transfers. In fact, however, the Soviet government is now running very large budget deficits, adding to the public's stock of money, and it will take major changes just to bring the budget back into balance. The alternative and easier way of eliminating the "ruble overhang" is to get the Soviet public to hold its financial wealth in government bonds or other liquid financial forms like pensions and life insurance.[23]

Feldstein argues that the liquidity is not as great as in the United States. The problem is that the Soviet consumer has no incentive to hold onto the financial wealth rather than try to spend it for goods and services as soon as those are available. Feldstein concludes, however, that such credit arrangements would require that Soviet investors believe in the contractual arrangements that their government would make. What seems more likely is that the Soviets will be reduced to wiping out this outstanding credit by a "monetary reform"—that is, simply reducing the value of the ruble. No wonder that the new Soviet finance minister, Valentin Pavlov, putting the total of Soviet debt at 330 billion rubles in his first statement after taking office in August 1989, said, "We are under the control of the debt and the deficit."

The problem of the value of the ruble, itself, is fundamental to any such discussion, of course. Officially valued at $1.60, in 1989 it brought as little as twenty cents on the black market in Moscow—even less in some exchanges in Central Europe. One economist, toting up the various administered prices for commodities and goods inside and outside the Soviet Union, counted 9,000 different values of the ruble. In late 1988, a flurry of speculation was started with a report from Moscow that the ruble would be devalued by 50 percent in international transactions. Even that figure excited little interest in the West, however, and ultimately was denied in Moscow. In the fall of 1989, the Soviets announced a massive devaluation of the ruble for tourists and for Soviet citizens buying foreign exchange for foreign travel, cutting it to one-tenth of the official exchange. But the "devaluation" had little meaning for anyone except the black marketers who hang out in front of the Moscow tourist hotels.

Aganbegian has said there are two ways to create convertibility. The first would be to saturate the domestic market with goods, permitting bonds and securities at market prices, or the creation of an internal money market.

> The second road lies through introduction in the near future of a second currency—a special Soviet ruble for foreign economic activity. This ruble must be backed up by the USSR's export potential and by its currency and gold reserves. This ruble could be, for instance, within the boundaries of special economic zones now being set up in Soviet territory.[24]

Abel Aganbegian reminded his audience that such a special currency—the "gold cheronets" (ten rubles)—did exist in the USSR until 1925. Again, a return to NEP—but how different is the situation between an exhausted but still postczarist economy in those years and the grand wreck of the Stalinist economy that Aganbegian and his fellow reformers have now inherited. He calls this dual currency proposal only a temporary solution. But one must ask how, given the corruption and administrative chaos of the *perestroika* era, the two currencies could be separated and their value enforced with less than a return to Stalinist methods of political control.

Federal Reserve governor Wayne Angell, another American financial authority who had extended talks with Soviet economists and bureaucrats during a visit to Russia, told *Izvestia* in September 1989 that the fundamental problem for the Soviet economy was the lack of a viable currency. Ironically, from a central bank that long ago abandoned the gold standard, that was where he wanted to put the Soviets.

> Your *perestroika* reforms face many difficult adjustment problems as you move toward market-oriented socialism. These become impossible problems without a monetary standard of value that is recognized as having predictable value throughout the Soviet Union—and the rest of the world—now and in the future. . . . Some believe it might succeed with a mark, yen, or dollar convertible ruble. But they realize that it would take many years for the *Gosbank* to obtain central-bank powers and credibility to enable the ruble to trade as a hard currency. Yes, it is my belief that without an honest money, Soviet citizens cannot be expected to respond to the reforms—as they do not have a meaningful incentive.[25]

Angell's "solution" is that the ruble should go to a gold standard, apparently using the reported $35 billion gold hoard of the Soviets, as a reserve for a transferable currency. Without some new way to make the ruble a real currency with a relatively stable value, Angell, warns ". . . the reforms run a very high risk of being set back by a general collapse of confidence in the ruble—an inflationary disintegration."

Increasingly, however, the failure to get on with *perestroika* has taken a toll and become a part of the whole process. *The Economist* of London wrote in the spring of 1989:

> Each change of course makes it that much harder for Mr. Gorbachev to persuade Russians to take his policies seriously. It also becomes harder to detect a coherent set of ideas behind the economic reforms, let alone know quite where they are heading. . . . It is turning out to be a far longer, more straggly process than expected. A serious assault on the industrial heart of

the economy is having to wait. Russians are having to wait for a visible improvement in living standards.

By the fall of 1989, the same publication was even more pessimistic:

. . . The Gorbachev team has taken most of four years to work out what it wants to replace the old system with. While the reformers dithered, party hacks in the provinces managed to put the brakes on early economic reforms. . . . Gorbachev the great disperser of power has started gathering power back to the center. In principle, Mr. Gorbachev believes, rightly, that if the Soviet Union is to mend its economy, heal its national divisions, and learn to govern itself better, powers of decision have to be devolved from ministry to manager, from center to republic and region, from party to people. Yet, economic crisis, on the heels of nationalist explosion, has forced Mr. Gorbachev to forget his principles.[26]

Assuming that those principles existed in Gorbachev's new thinking— that is, a firm economic doctrine with which he was approaching the problems of restructuring a huge, if dilapidated, economy—they seem to have changed. By May 30, 1989, Gorbachev no longer talked of moving toward market mechanisms but, rather:

We consider that as the reform intensified, a system of economic relations will take shape that could be described as a law-governed economy. It will be founded not on administrative commands or orders, but on relations regulated by the law. There will be a clear-cut division between state direction of the economy and economic managements [sic]. Enterprises, concerns, joint-stock societies and cooperatives should become the main actors in the economy. To tackle common tasks and coordinate their efforts, they will, I guess, make moves to set up, on a voluntary basis, combines, unions, and associations, to which economic management functions currently performed by the ministries will pass. Both our experience and worldwide economic development trends convince us that this is the right approach.[27]

Perhaps *The Soviet Labour Review* is correct in identifying this statement as a description closely approximating that of a corporatist system.[28] And, although one must acknowledge that a non-European society like Japan successfully built a different model for successful economic development, they followed a blueprint that was much more practical and concrete than anything that has appeared in the confusion emanating from Moscow during the past five years.[29]

CHAPTER 9

DRANG NACH OSTEN

The German Connection

The old thinking was based on the premise that every problem had to be approached from the position of class. From the class point of view, the West's businessmen were exploiters. This being so, we had to avoid dealing with them except when there was no alternative. And so we used international trade only for special one-offer purposes or to help in speeding up our development or improve efficiency. We used trade, quite frankly, to mend holes in our national economy, to deal with certain imbalances, to overcome backwardness in particular spheres, and so on. If we had trouble with agriculture, we imported food; if our own pipe-making industry could not produce enough pipes, we imported them on a massive scale; if our chemical technology and chemical engineering were falling behind, we would buy whole chemical plants from the West, complete with technology.[1]

That is how a Soviet economist and reformer, as well as one of Moscow's most skillful propagandists, Abel Aganbegian, acknowledges that in the past foreign trade played a crucial role in the Soviet economy, which constituted dependence on the West. Nevertheless, the fashionable view has been that external trade, perhaps as little as 4 percent of the Soviet GNP (although increasingly there is evidence that the overall size of the Soviet national product has been exaggerated), was a minimal influence on what took place in the Soviet economy. Aganbegian goes on:

143

Our new political thinking has changed our attitude to the world. . . . When we look at an external political problem now, we do not try to look unilaterally to our own interests, we do not simply try to get what we want and never mind everyone else. . . . From this we have drawn the inevitable conclusion that we must become more involved in the international division of labor, in the system of world economic relations.

Basic, however, to Aganbegian's argument—if it can be taken as Gorbachev and his reformers' view—is how the Soviets are to trade with the West. Increasingly, the problem is acknowledged by all those interested in promoting Soviet-West trade as the Russians' inability to produce goods for which there are markets in the West. Approximately 60 percent of all Soviet exports are petroleum and gas. Much of the remainder is gold and arms. Not only is the near-term outlook for petroleum relatively bleak—with long-term stable real prices if not a relatively lower price—but there are also serious doubts about whether present levels of Soviet exports can be maintained. That certainly seems to be the case, unless there is heavy new investment in the development of new fields and infrastructure. New gold production coming on the world market from a number of relatively small producers around the world has tended to restrain, if not stabilize, gold prices.

Finland's experience with the Soviet Union is described in Chapter 4. It may provide a lesson for other Europeans—and some Americans—who are rushing optimistically toward deals with Moscow in the supposed new era that Aganbegian has described.

Perestroika may have completely changed the traditional view of Soviet relations with the world economy as seen from Moscow as Aganbegian argues. It has also changed the view of the Soviets from the West, at least in some financial quarters, and that view is not necessarily always optimistic. Lawrence Brainard, chief international economist for Bankers Trust Company in New York, a longtime student of the Soviet economy and a participant on behalf of his bank in Polish debt rescheduling, points out that in the past the Soviets have enjoyed a high level of creditworthiness because they were able and willing to place tight controls on imports.[2]

For example, after an episode of external borrowing and rising debt in the mid-70s, a radical change in financing policies in 1976 introduced sharp cutbacks in orders for Western machinery and equipment in subsequent years. While other countries in East Europe and the developing countries were increasing foreign borrowing, the Soviet Union reduced its imports to balance its international payments.

Moscow was able to pursue this policy, in part, precisely because world oil prices were rising. But even after 1981, when the oil price fell dramatically, the Soviets continued to maintain their international borrowing to cover their trade deficit at about $10 to $12 billion annually, about the same as in 1977. Now, Brainard points out, *perestroika* introduces a new element in any Western banker's attempt to measure Moscow's creditworthiness. *Perestroika* apparently will now place the Soviets in a position of relying on their success in global competition and economic interdependence, as Aganbegian has suggested, promoting their closer association with the world trading and financial system. Brainard says this does not necessarily mean that the Soviets' credit rating is impaired by *perestroika*. But it does "imply a transition from a secure, familiar tradition (albeit an inefficient one in certain respects) to an unknown future model of the economy."

Nikolai P. Shmelyov, a member of the prestigious Soviet think tank, the Institute for the USA and Canada, in what appears to be one of the most candid views of the new relationship that the Soviet "reformers" want with the West, told *The New York Times* ". . . What I am interested in is a stable, serious importation of capital—without surprises. Maybe, in the future, we can even have 100 percent foreign ownership of companies in our country. But for the next 10 to 15 years we will have to import capital."

The Soviets pursued rather limited short-term borrowing in the international markets to finance exports and imports during the 1950s. It expanded in the 1960s, largely through the activities of two wholly owned banks—Eurobank in Paris and Moscow Narodny Bank in London. These banks provided Soviet access to the interbank credits in the Eurodollar markets for trade transactions. In the 1970s, the Soviets moved into long-term borrowing from Western governmental agencies. In fact, although it generally went unrecognized, by the end of 1977, the Soviets were the recipients of 50 percent of an estimated $18 billion in foreign debt in official government-to-goverment credits—the largest single borrower. This was a higher proportion, for example, than either Mexico or Brazil. The Soviets preferred these official credits because they were at fixed interest rates and were generally tied to compensatory trade deals—for example, to the bitterly debated Soviet natural gas deal with German companies.

These borrowings often required implied partial cartelization of Western markets which was in keeping with Moscow's own domestic economic designs. Brainard also points out that it fit in with the Soviet propensity for huge natural resource development projects that it had been arranging with Western finance and technology since the 1920s. With hindsight, it is now obvious that such projects contributed to the growing difficulties of the Soviet economy because smaller, short-term payout projects were neglected in their favor. Then, beginning in 1975, two events occurred. The United States passed the Jackson-Vanik Amendment, which required permission for the emigration of Soviet Jews as a quid pro quo for Soviet access to U.S. credits, and Congress imposed restrictions on official (subsidized) Export-Import Bank lending, which also affected U.S.-Soviet economic relations. Meanwhile, the Soviet economy was beginning to stagnate. "The priority [in Moscow] now was to balance payments flows with the West and to prevent an increase in the country's indebtedness. . . . Soviet policy . . . chose austerity in the form of import cutbacks to achieve balance in international payments."[3] Brainard believes that the Soviet leadership was fortunate to have adopted that policy because they did not fall into the difficulties that beset Poland and other East Bloc countries who borrowed heavily in this period. Brainard concludes:

> More importantly, perhaps, Soviet leaders were successful in blunting the efforts of the Reagan Administration to apply economic leverage during the early 1980s in matters relating to grain sales, official Western credits, and the 1981 gas pipeline deal. . . . At the same time, however, Soviet leaders must also realize that the austerity policies have imposed significant costs on the Soviet economy in terms of benefits forgone. The economy has been denied Western technology on a broadly diffused basis.[4]

There is considerable circumstantial evidence that just such a debate over heavy foreign borrowing along the lines Brainard has laid out here continues in the Soviet Union today. One example is the case of the huge West German credit arranged in 1988 by F. Wilhelm Christians, former head of the Deutsche Bank, Germany's largest commercial bank with an old history of dealing with the czars as well as the Soviets. Christians, himself, served in Poland during World War II, and his fellow bankers believe that he has an emotional commitment to expiation for Nazi atrocities in Eastern Europe during World War II. In April 1988, Christians returned from a trip to Moscow where, as the head of a German syndicate, he had agreed to a Deutschemark 1.6 billion line of credit to the Soviets. Rumor has it that on his return to Dusseldorf, he was upbraided by other members of the syndicate for the lack of specificity in the loan negotiations. As something of a postscript, the credit was now described as being only for capital equipment for export to the Soviet Union for the production of consumer goods. But then negotiations dragged on for almost a year before the bulk of the credits were drawn down. In the fall of 1988, six months after the credit had been signed, a West German Ministry of Foreign Affairs source complained bitterly that the Soviets were asking for "buy back" provisions in repaying the credit— that is, that the West Germans should accept at least partial payment in goods to cover interest on the loan. All through 1988 and 1989, West Germans—official and nonofficial spokesmen—were urging credits from the West on the Soviets as an answer to the problems of *perestroika*.

At a seminar on Soviet developments sponsored by the British Foreign Office in Sussex in midsummer 1989, I heard a semipublic reprise of this argument. Another official of Deutsche Bank, their "Soviet expert," sat across the table at a conference of Western, Soviet, Polish, Czechoslovak, and Hungarian participants. He was pleading with the former head of the Narodny Bank in London, by then economic adviser to Soviet Foreign Minister Shevardnadze, to accept Western credits as a way out of the dilemmas presented by the lack of progress in *perestroika*, because of what the Western participants at the conference assumed was the Soviet need to speed up the process.

By the fall of 1988, as a result of what *The Wall Street Journal* called Gorbachev's "three-year charm offensive in Western Europe," West German, British, Italian, and French banks were all offering or planning to offer new credit lines to the Soviet Union. That was so despite some reservations, particularly among British bankers, that the new "pluralization" of Soviet foreign trade (including creating new banking facilities for dealing with foreign lenders as well as permitting some Soviet enterprises to deal directly with foreign buyers instead of through the former monopoly of the ministry of foreign trade) might have cast doubt upon the old concept that any loan from the old Soviet monopoly bank dealing with foreign institutions was "sovereign lending." That is, any debts incurred by a Soviet entity were considered to be debts of the Soviet government.

Meanwhile, Austria had agreed to buy more Soviet oil, West Germany had offered to train thousands of young Soviet managers,

> . . . and Italy agreed to guarantee a loan that Italian banks hadn't yet offered. European politicians, diplomats, and businessmen vigorously contest suggestions that all their activity amounts to a European Marshall Plan to bail out the faltering Soviet economy. The contracts rest on solid commercial foundation, they say, and the credits are trade-related. But most agree that the current flood of contracts and loans clearly is designed to signal Western Europe's willingness to help Mr. Gorbachev both politically and economically as he struggles to push through his program of *perestroika*. . . .[5]

By June 1989, Soviet Prime Minister Nikolai Ryzhkov, revealing Soviet figures on borrowing in the West, said that the total Soviet borrowing had reached $50 billion. That was a $10 billion increase over the total of $40 billion that the International Bank for Settlements in Basel had recorded at the end of 1988. And Ryzhkov reported that it would be necessary to borrow another $14 billion in 1989 just to service the debt. Among other things, he gave this as a reason that Moscow could not buy significant new amounts of consumer goods to satisfy collapsing internal retail consumption and distribution. Ryzhkov was apparently answering the more radical reformist spokesmen within the Gorbachev following, as well as a growing chorus of questions from outside the country, asking why there was not more evidence of progress in *perestroika*. Ryzhkov, an archetypal Soviet technocrat-bureaucrat, who comes from the metalworking industry and is regarded as an excellent Soviet-style manager, is one of the more reluctant members of the Gorbachev team, a defender of centralized planning and a stalwart supporter of maximum power for *Gosplan*. Ryzhkov warned his colleagues, "Can we allow ourselves to fall deeper and deeper into debt?" Ryzhkov shocked Western observers by arguing that debt servicing would absorb 60 percent of Soviet export earnings in 1989, leaving a minimum for food and machinery imports.

"That was news to Western European bankers," Peter Passell wrote in *The New York Times*, "who are lending money to the Soviet Union at lower interest rates than those offered to blue-chip multinational corporations like the Royal Dutch-Shell Group and the International Business Machines

Corporation. And it was a puzzle to Jan Vanous whose widely respected PlanEcon consulting firm keeps a close watch on Soviet borrowing." Vanous argued that total Soviet foreign debt was about $43 billion at the end of 1988, a little more than the Organization for Economic Cooperation and Development in Geneva claimed. But there were critics, including Roger W. Robinson, a former member of the National Security Council, who argued that there are difficulties in the proper accounting of Soviet debt, which is severely underestimated by the major government and intragovernmental organizations that are supposed to monitor it. Robinson says:

> One of the clearest indications of an unwise trend in current Western lending to the Soviet Union and Eastern Europe is the easy availability of untied, general purpose money. Since the early 1980s, the majority of new credits which have gone to the Soviet Bloc have been in the form of so-called balance of payments or general purpose loans with no questions asked by the lender.[6]

Robinson points out that these loans are being made by the same financial institutions, and, in many instances, the same bankers, who lent huge sums of untied monies to the Latin American and Central European governments in the 1970s, which produced the world debt crisis.

Ryzhkov may have been playing a complicated game. For, at the same time that he was bemoaning the debt-service problem, Ryzhkov defended plans for a huge, new multibillion ruble petrochemical development in Western Siberia, which is slated to involve several foreign partners in a joint venture that would, presumably, be partly financed by overseas borrowing. The petrochemical complex project, originally masterminded by Armand Hammer, the longtime friend and confidant of Soviet leaders, is the bête noire for the more outspoken reformers like Aganbegian. They consider it typical of the Stalinist economic dinosaurs that are believed to be responsible for the long-term crippling of the economy.[7] The petrochemical project was a principal target of attack, along with a grandiose project to turn Siberian rivers from their northward direction toward the irrigated cotton fields of central Asia, which critics would say have turned into an ecological disaster. That Siberian project, which became a totem for antiregime dissidents and ecologists, as well as the reformer economists, has been canceled—apparently without the possibility of a reprieve—primarily because the sums for its construction would have been astronomical.

Padma Desai, a Columbia University professor sympathetic to Gorbachev's campaign and relatively optimistic about his possibilities for success, puts the case for heavy borrowing abroad simply:

> Suppose Gorbachev's planners are able to borrow $1 billion from the West because of renewed détente. This money can be used for importing sophisticated machines, or consumer goods that are in short supply. There are thus fairly immediate benefits to the economy. The alternative for the planners is to earn $1 billion by first producing something at home and then exporting it to the United States or another hard-currency country. From this perspective, the strategy of borrowing rather than exporting has a distinct attractiveness. And it is, indeed, succeeding. According to a report (*The New York Times*, October 21, 1988) European banks have signaled their intention to lend more than $9 billion to the Soviet Union in the coming months. With this approach, the planners face the problem of soft oil prices in export markets and current Soviet inability to export manufactured goods to Western markets.[8]

Finance Minister V. Gostev was asked about all this in an unusually frank exchange in *Argumenty I Fakty* (about the same time that Gorbachev publicly asked that newspaper's editor to retire because of its biting criticism of some aspects of *perestroika*):

> In the international market nobody needs our rubles. Bills without value are the same as people without honor. When will our ruble become a convertible currency? Gostev replied: "This depends on economic development . . . For as long as we do not have high-quality goods we have practically nothing to offer to a foreign partner."[9]

Professor Desai neglects to show how what she calls ". . . Gorbachev's reforms . . . limited and even inadequately conceived on the economic front, and guarded on the political front. . . ." will provide the means to repay, or even service these borrowings. Judy Shelton, having studied the problem of the Soviet budget, the "overhang," and the hidden possibility of hyperinflation, has more than doubts:

> The correlation between Gorbachev's reign in the Kremlin and the escalation of Soviet borrowing activities in Western financial markets is striking. Within

two years after Gorbachev took over in March 1985, Soviet debt to the West shot up from about $25 billion to over $37 billion, an increase of 50 percent. During this same period, Gorbachev launched a campaign at improving trade relations with Western Europe and Japan. . . . Under Gorbachev, the Soviets are moving so quickly to pick up Western credits that it is difficult for Western analysts to keep up with them. . . . Western governments so far seem dazzled by all the fancy Soviet footwork in financial markets. . . . The Soviets have discovered a much easier way to get imports they need from the West. They buy them on credit. . . . In general, it is now apparent that Gorbachev is prepared to maximize Soviet indebtedness to the West as part of the price of *perestroika* . . . . At all times we need to guard against losing our basic understanding of the Soviet Union's economic circumstances that shape its need to deal with the West and limit its political actions. . . . The United States needs to convince its allies that making capital available to the Soviet Union constitutes a strategic Western asset.[10]

Yet Washington finds that role increasingly difficult, and not only because of powerful forces inside the American polity that welcome Gorbachev's initiatives as a genuine move toward peace and stability after the long years of the Cold War and all its attendant problems. As the decade of the 1990s begins, the United States and its allies in Europe are face to face with an old European problem—*der deutsche Fragge*—the German question. It is the role that a powerful German society, divided as a nation and with a long history for disturbing the European scene for a hundred years with wars and threats of war, must play in European politics.

Two strong historical currents have dogged relations between the German-speaking world and the Russian-Slavic world from time immemorial. One has been a highly intellectualized and passionate belief (held in both West and East) that an alliance between these two ethos could dominate the world. It has to be remembered, for example, that the whole concept of German (and thence to the world) geopolitics and modern politico-strategic thinking owes much to those who advocated "unity of the Eurasian world island." Another view has been a visceral enmity, a belief (in the West) that there were only barbarians east of the Vistula to be civilized by a superior German culture. And (in the East) there has existed a messianic belief in the Third Rome, a peculiar note for Orthodoxy and "the Russian soul" as the epitome of righteousness in the face of Western frivolity. Even now in the utter intellectual bankruptcy of the Soviet system we see a tacit alliance between the so-called Soviet Communist conservatives and their Pamyat populist-traditionalists for preserving the essence of Mother Russia.

The signing, and then the breakdown, of the eighteen-month Hitler-Stalin alliance was a kaleidoscopic replay of both these themes in a very short period of time—the final act bringing on World War II. While a tradition-bound German bureaucracy was building skillfully on a century of close Berlin-Moscow diplomatic cooperation against other European powers (World War I notwithstanding), Hitler suddenly reversed course and sought to destroy his blood-brother dictator, Stalin, from whom he had learned so much. Stalin, meanwhile, was convinced of the "logic" of the alliance with his fellow butcher for whom he had considerable admiration. (Khrushchev said Stalin thought the Night of the Long Knives when Hitler eliminated the SA storm troopers was a stroke of genius!) To the very end of the flirtation, the Moscow tyrant could not accept Hitler's intention to destroy him.

The existence, since the end of World War II, of two Germanies—one in the East under the domination of the Soviet Union, the other a member of the West European-Atlantic community—has injected a new element in the always difficult German drama in Europe. The possibility—Stalin alluded to it seductively in a letter to the confirmed "European" West German Chancellor Konrad Adenauer in 1952—of reunification of the two Germanies, presumably only possible with Moscow's blessing, has given the Soviets a potential for blackmail against any West German regime. Gorbachev has added further appeal to this theme by creating the slogan of "A Common European House," and his seeming willingness to permit the Soviet Union's Central European satellites to go their own way—at least in terms of economic organization—has added to this new appeal from Moscow.

Viola Drath, Washington diplomatic correspondent for the West German financial daily *Hadelsblatt*, writes:

> . . . It is no coincidence that the old idea of a Middle Europe as an entity has resurfaced as a political alternative [to the current division of Europe into Communist and Western Blocs]. The concept of Middle Europe was formulated as a vision of a cultural, economic, and political Central European network under German leadership after the collapse of Bismarck's empire at the end of World War I. The rationale behind its present reincarnation is the

amelioration of hardships caused by the continuation of the East-West conflict. Designed to function as a bridge between the two ideologies, it is characterized as an "emergency partnership" composed of those Middle European countries that would constitute a battlefield in the event of a contemporary armed conflict.[11]

Edward Mortimer, writing tongue in cheek, says:

In the late 1980s, "Central Europe" has become fashionable while "Eastern Europe" is rapidly disappearing, rather as "Negroes" were suddenly replaced by "Blacks" in polite conversation 20 years ago. Eastern Europe is that benighted region which, supposedly, Churchill and Roosevelt, signed away into Stalin's clutches at the Yalta Conference. Now, courtesy of Mikhail Gorbachev, Yalta is consigned to the dustbin. Goodbye miserable, grey, eastern Europe, you who weighed so uneasily on our western consciences. Hail, reborn central Europe, land of congenial, talkative intellectuals, you who are so flatteringly eager to join our liberal, pluralist, market-driven western society.[12]

But another German commentator, a believer in Gorbachev's bona fides, defines more accurately what is really at risk:

The outer walls of the "common European home" must be in place before the Eastern wing collapses. That requires recruiting the West Europeans as tacit allies in stability vis-à-vis Eastern Europe. The prize for the West Europeans, and especially the West Germans, would be the falling barriers of partition, but the price is no less evident: deference toward Soviet imperial sensitivities. If Gorbachev can pull this off, the rewards will be handsome: maximal Soviet influence in all of Europe which will more than compensate for partial loss of control over the Eastern half.[13]

That concept took on new validity when the hardline East German regime collapsed in 1989 under the dual blows of an eroding economy and Gorbachev's new political line. The danger posed for Western Europe and the United States by this Middle Europe concept has never been spelled out better than by Henry Kissinger, who is in many ways a quintessential product of the Central European cultural heritage:

Finally, it is important to remember that Germany is the last country which should be encouraged to be "flexible." Germany's attempt to pursue an isolated policy in the center of the Continent has brought disaster to Europe twice in a generation. If it is once more placed in the position to make arrangements with both sides—the political expression of neutrality—it will also be capable of menacing both sides, if only by the threat of a change of front. Such a Germany would hardly be conducive to peace and stability in Europe. Western policy must seek to retain Germany as a willing member of the European political and economic institutions, whatever the ultimate security arrangements.[14]

Moscow has played cat and mouse with the issue of reunification of the two Germanies, and the possibility of a concomitant that Western diplomats have long feared, a united, neutral Germany. It may continue to do so, as so many Western observers have so often said with total assurance, because of Moscow's fear of a reunited Germany. But with the growing feeling of an "inevitable" German reunification after the collapse of the Communist state in the Eastern (Soviet) zone, Moscow's influence will increase, not decrease. Gorbachev's message of a unified Europe with the barriers of 45 years gone is a siren song to the West Germans, founded on a traditional and historical appeal today as it has so often been in the past by the *drang nach Osten*—that atavistic fascination with Russia that over the centuries has pulled the Germans into so many misadventures in Eastern Europe. It tugs hard at the Federal Republic today. Seen from Bonn, the German Federal Republic, West Europe's strongest economy with its most powerful army (although without nuclear arms), now faces a crisis-ridden Soviet Union that appears to be withdrawing from the Slavic states of Central and Eastern Europe—long a major market for German goods with long and intimate relations with German culture.[15] Caught in the vise of a growing European hope that a new and permanently peaceful relationship can be built with the East and doubts about the ability of the United States to continue to lead the alliance, Bonn is trying to build a new relationship with the East. At stake is the delicate balance of the Western alliance including the European Community as a barrier to new wars.

In the summer of 1989 the Austrians, after four decades of nervous and very strict adherence to the neutrality provisions of the 1955 Austrian State Treaty, began to debate the possibility of entry into the European

Common Market.[16] It is generally accepted in Vienna that Austrian politicians, with their extremely difficult political impasse brought on by the Waldheim scandal and their longstanding economic ties to the East Bloc, would not have ventured into such deep waters without at least tacit Soviet permission.[17] Meanwhile, everything but gypsies and violins are being brought out to fan the embers of the centuries-long Vienna-Budapest relationship. Hungary has had more than a decade of its own goulash communism, a premature *perestroika*. And although half of its trade was oriented to the West and it was able to borrow heavily from Western banks, Budapest had failed to arrive at an economic takeoff into a non-Communist economy. It desperately needs Austria (and Western financial resources through Vienna) to underwrite projects such as a new joint hydroelectric project on the Danube (which has become a target for environmentalist dissidents), an international joint world's fair in 1995, and the seven million Austrian tourists (and more than $100 million of goods they purchase each year), to keep intact its relatively higher living standards in the Bloc. An Austria inside the European Community (EC) would give the Hungarians a back door to Western Europe's markets. It would also insert a more strongly neutral voice to block any future attempt to reinforce Europe's defenses using common EC economic policies, a basic concept of the original European reunification movement of the 1940s and 1950s. It would be, in effect, a minor repetition of the role that East Germany now plays vis-à-vis the EC through West Germany.

The tenuous 1989 agreements between Solidarity and the Polish Communist government provide another avenue for the Soviets to use Central and Eastern Europe to enhance *perestroika* and fool the West. Those very Polish shipyards where *Solidarnosc* arose were used in the past to build Soviet shipping. Although the period of Soviet primitive exploitation of Poland and the Central European satellites for economic gain may long be over, a Poland refinanced by Western capital—and that is exactly what the Bush administration appears to be considering—could become an important asset in the bilateral trading that still dominates the Council for Mutual Economic Assistance (CEMA) bloc.[18]

Although it is true that East Germany apparently held out against Gorbachev's *glasnost* reforms until his visit there in the fall of 1989, the ousted hardline East German Communist Party chieftains could well have made the argument that they have already incorporated the best elements of *perestroika* in the relatively efficient East German vertical monopolies *(combinats).* Furthermore, they already have advantages that exist in no other Communist state. East German-West German *interhandel* trade is considered technically intra-German trade. It provided not only an opportunity for the East Germans to get West German financing even before the Berlin Wall came down but also a back door for sales to the Common Market. Furthermore, West German payments and subsidies—everything from buying the exit of elderly East German pensioners to "ecological subsidies" to financing and building a new autobahn from Hamburg and possibly a new rail line from Hannover to Berlin—gave the Pankow regime an enormous foreign exchange cushion, even as its economy was collapsing.

The irony is that despite all this the technological gap between the East Germans and their West German neighbor widened and their terms of trade with the West worsened.[19] The biggest splash East German managers could arrange for the 1988 Leipzig fair, the showplace for East German achievements, was a new four-wheel-powered vehicle, based largely on West German Volkswagen technology, that would not match any of a half dozen recent new Japanese and Western vehicles that come out almost monthly. A Munich observer pointed out that while it is true that the East Germans have produced a 65K electronic chip, their low-quality standards indicate that only a minimum actually work. All this to indicate why for Honecker's "reform" successors, an even greater transfer of Western technology, capital, and trade is the sine qua non of their success. Yet, conversely, it was this declining East German economy that provided one-quarter of all Soviet capital imports—even more when its indirect sales of high-tech gear to other satellite economies exporting to the Soviet Union were counted.

There are certainly already voices in West Germany that would attempt to pay tribute in the form of economic aid for Gorbachev's *perestroika,* as noted earlier, in order to buy reunification of the two Germanies and a purported new stability and neutrality in Central Europe. The West German SPD (Social Democratic Party) and its allies in the East are plumping for a united, neutral Germany, a new unitary state constitution, and some form of "socialism." But the fundamental question of East Germany's economic relation to the Soviets—long its chief source of high-tech imports—has yet to be addressed in the euphoria of Germany without the Berlin Wall. West Germany's Chancellor Helmut Kohl is said to have promised additional aid to Moscow during his visit there in January 1990. But no details have been released.

Horst Empke, *fraktionfuhrer* of the Social Democratic Party in the *Bundestag* in Bonn, told me in October 1988 during a conversation about his party's position on the Soviet problem, "Yes, you can say there is an alliance between some of the enterprise heads in the private sector and our party's policy on aid to the Soviets. They would like to see government subsidies as a way to renovate and convert to other product lines. We would like to see them [as an instrument of government policy] to help Gorbachev and *perestroika*."[20] The West has already had the remarkable spectacle in 1987 of Franz Josef Strauss, the late ultra-anti-Communist Bavarian conservative leader, leading a negotiation for a major loan to the East German regime to finance West German exports, ostensibly with a quid pro quo for an amelioration of the border situation and liberalized movement of Germans between the two Germanies. By March 1989, the visit of three West German ministers to East Germany to talk about expanding trade was canceled because of a spate of killings on the Wall in Berlin—by the hated East German Vopos, apparently under new orders to shoot to kill even though Strauss thought he had negotiated an end to that kind of terror!

This strategy of creating a Central Europe which, while with a still strong Communist component, and with still many ties to Moscow, might remain a part of the Soviet system but get resuscitation from the West is being met halfway, willy-nilly, by many Western advocates. An activist mood has overtaken even the most aggressively anti-Communist strategists and observers in an effort to help promote Gorbachev's ostensible goals in Eastern and Central Europe as well as in the Soviet Union. A Czech émigré writes:

> The West must successfully address the new divide in Central Europe and help reformers prove that democracy and a free market are preconditions for a functioning economy and productive relations with the West. This will make traditional communism virtually irrelevant. Otherwise, it is reformers, opposition forces and the West who will suffer a loss of prestige and influence, while conservative Communists regroup and fight back with vigor.[21]

But how can the wreck of once consumer-oriented if underdeveloped economies in Central Europe, demoralized by a half century of Communist economies and ecological disaster, produce under the constant sabotage of a still strong coterie of "conservative" Communists? Their problems will only be slightly less than those encountered by *perestroika* in the Soviet Union as Hungary has already demonstrated. And what is to happen to Soviet and Warsaw Pact troops during this interim period of economic rebulding? They remain, as do thirty Soviet divisions in Germany, not only for Soviet strategic concerns, but as a praetorian guard for the hated remnants of the Communist regimes, reformed or not.

When I traveled extensively in Germany, Switzerland, and Scandinavia, including Finland, in the fall of 1988, trying to appraise this search for a new German-Soviet relationship turning on the resurrection of Central Europe, I found a curious phenomenon all over West Germany and in West Berlin. At the working echelons of both the government and the private sector, there was great skepticism about Soviet Communist Party boss Mikhail S. Gorbachev's motivations, pessimism about his chances of success, and great caution about any Western initiatives toward the Soviet Union. But as one mounted in the bureaucracy or toward the boardrooms of the corporations, optimism grew, flowering into euphoria. That was, of course, also reflected in the near adulation that was given Gorbachev personally when he visited Germany in early 1989, and in public opinion polls showing the Soviet leader more popular than other Western leaders including the political elite of West Germany. It was an index, of course, to how completely Soviet propaganda, spurred on by the Western celebrity syndrome, had been able to present a quintessential Soviet *apparatchik* as a savior of European peace and stability.

Typical of the responses to Soviet commercial and financial initiatives were comments of F. Wilhelm Christians, former cochairman of the Deutsche Bank in Dusseldorf: "We have lost our markets in Latin America. We must and can develop new markets in the Soviet Union." A prominent Swiss bank economist stated: "I do not believe my bank should lend to the Soviets for tactical and strategic reasons. But we will. We are a small country, and when the German banks begin to twist our arm, what can we do?" In a think tank in Munich, closely affiliated to West German intelligence, an economic analyst who has worked on the Soviet Union for most of his career, painted a grim picture of the Soviet political economy but ended the conversation on an optimistic note about possible German-Soviet collaboration. In the Ministry of Defense, a longtime observer acknowledged that, despite little evidence that the Soviets have made major cutbacks or changes in military strategy, his new minister was shortly going to Moscow with Chancellor Helmut Kohl ready to make unilateral concessions in disarmament negotiations. A well-informed newsman of Baltic German origin shook his head after detailing all the reasons that there could be no major movement on German-Soviet economic and political problems, "But you never know . . . something is moving."

By the summer of 1989, West German businessmen had signed a series of deals with the Soviets—fifty of the joint venture arrangements of the approximately 150 signed by the Soviets with all Western firms. Many of these were service contracts with little significance beyond their propaganda value. But the German agreements were substantial: A Baden-Württemberg firm will build new car engine works outside Moscow. A firm from West Germany's high-tech center, Stuttgart, will deliver a state-of-the art navigational system for Aeroflot's operations in Siberia. German companies are providing whole plants for making equipment for producing shoes, biscuits, and other consumer goods. The Deutsche Bank syndicate credit was boosted to Deutschemarks 3 billion during Chancellor Helmut Kohl's visit to Moscow in early 1989. One of the most significant deals under this agreement was an agreement by Siemens and the Swiss-Swedish German firm of ASEA Brown Boveri to "improve nuclear safety after the Chernobyl disaster of 1986," in effect, a Western technological transfer to remedy the enormous problem created by faulty design in the huge Soviet atomic electrical program. Siemens was also involved in a deal to reequip Soviet hospitals with the newest electronic equipment from the West. West Germany, historically the Soviet's biggest trading partner in the West, is now doing more trade with the Soviet Union than the United States, France, and Great Britain combined. The rush of German firms into East Germany with its still-to-be-determined trade relationship with the Soviets was enormous.

During Gorbachev's visit to Bonn in June 1989, the two countries signed two government-to-government agreements that would protect West German investment in the Soviet Union and provide a training program for Russian managers in West Germany. But it was the "atmospherics" perhaps more than what actually occurred during the visit that astonished Bonn's Western allies and marked the direction of possible future relations. Manfred Rowold, in what used to be considered the ultra-anti-Communist *Die Welt*, wrote that Gorbachev was welcomed in "an atmosphere of hopeful thankfulness, of facing a man who had fundamentally corrected the image of the dark and ill-wishing Russian." Lothar Spath, minister president of the state of Baden-Württemberg, and a candidate for chancellor at some future date, said: "The building site for the 'common European house' is not yet complete. There is still barbed wire and the [Berlin] Wall. But in spite of this we have to begin. We Baden-Württembergers are not the kind of people to stand by and watch as things are being bult. We lend a hand." Gorbachev was met by enthusiastic crowds, many of them middle-class professionals, chanting "Gorby! Gorby! Gorby!" Gorbachev was careful not to miss a trick; in the Ruhr, he reminded Social Democratic steelworkers, whose jobs have dwindled as the German steel industry has shrunk, that their fathers had helped build Soviet industry in the 1920s.

Gorbachev was, of course, speaking to a receptive audience. By removing the U.S. Pershing and cruise missiles from Europe, Washington gave increased weight to the Soviet Union's overwhelming conventional military superiority in Central Europe. That could only be offset by the short-range, nuclear-capable missiles. Because the short-range missiles are largely based in the two Germanies, it gave new credence to the claim that the Germans, West and East, would be the new victims, the *schlagenfeld* (fighting ground) of any Soviet-U.S. confrontation; "the shorter the range, the deader the Germans." But to the Americans, the short-range missiles are the only means of defending their troops stationed in Germany, faced with Soviet conventional superiority.

The idea of a German-Soviet partnership, however repugnant to the rest of Western Europe, is surfacing again. Patrick Glynn, summing up the long historical background, concludes:

> It should not surprise us . . . that the Soviet Union, now in another economic crisis, should once again look to Germany for help in recovery. During Gorbachev's recent visit to Bonn, the economic relationship received even more attention than arms control. That relationship is growing. . . . Once again, too, as in the 1920s, the Soviet Union is playing on German resentment and vulnerability, though resentment and vulnerability of a different kind. As an economic superpower—its GNP is two-thirds of France and England combined—and in a condition of total military dependence upon the United States, West Germany today is moved by both fear and wounded pride. The fear is linked to the evident undependability of the American

security guarantee, as shown by the INF treaty and America's behavior regarding Pershing Is. The pride is a natural expression of West Germany's national character and a natural outgrowth of its economic success. Both forces—fear and pride—are leading West Germany to attempt to use its massive economic wealth to solve its security dilemma (which in the wake of the INF treaty no longer seems solvable by military means) through economic appeasement. At the root of this policy is the hope that economic power alone can be deployed to democratize Hungary and Poland, and perhaps eventually the other nations in Central Europe, and to tame the Soviet Union.[22]

Hans Dietrich Genscher, West Germany's foreign minister, a veteran of the Social Democrat-Free Democrat Party coalition of Chancellor Willy Brandt's 1969–72, the subsequent administration of Chancellor Helmut Schmidt, and now the Christian Democratic Union-Christian Social Union-Free Democrat coalition of Chancellor Helmut Kohl, is the personification of these policies. An intrepid traveler, Genscher has been selling the idea of a compromise with the East, a policy that he personally tries to implement through annual visits to his home in Halle, located in East Germany. In early 1989, he risked the wrath of Germany's NATO allies by flying to Washington to propose that President Bush immediately take up with Moscow the possibility of removing all short-range missiles in Europe—the last nuclear defense against the Soviet's overwhelming conventional superiority in Central Europe. In an emotional speech in the *Bundestag* in April 1989, Genscher pictured the Germans as "the main bridge of trust" between East and West. He warned that NATO's insistence on maintaining the short-range missiles during a period of extended negotiations with the Soviets was actually a threat to the Czech and Polish peoples, who had suffered so much in World War II.

> It is also a question of nuclear weapons which can reach the other part of our fatherland. . . . The members of the government swear an oath to dedicate their forces to the good of the German people. The obligation from this oath does not end at the border through the middle of Germany. The national responsibility does not exclude my homeland, the town in which I was born and the people who live in the Democratic Republic; no, this responsibility includes these people.[23]

Genscher vexed his already uncomfortable chancellor, Kohl, much closer to a "European" position and the Americans, even more by calling the missiles question a test of "how serious we are over the [question of] the German nation."

Genscher was expressing more than his own personal attitudes, or even those of the group around him in his own Free Democrat Party, whose constituency draws heavily on professionals and former citizens of East Germany now in the Federal Republic. Even Kohl had to remind Prime Minister Margaret Thatcher that the Basic Law, the Federal Republic's constitution, binds him to serve all the German people, East and West. It was for this reason that the West Germans felt obliged to receive their East German brethren in the fall of 1989 when they fled the growing impossible economic and political conditions in East Germany, not only on moral grounds but also because of the legal position that all Germans are citizens of the Federal Republic. And it was, of course, this flight of young German workers that tipped the scales of reunification. *Bundesrepublik* President Richard von Weizsacher, a respected West German politician and the democratic son of a prominent member of the Nazi era, expressed the new German nationalism in a speech on the fortieth anniversary of the Federal Republic in late spring 1989.

> Just as we do not have or seek to have our own way, so would we be wrong to conceal our interests. Otherwise we would not be a reliable and predictable ally. . . . We in the Federal Republic are irrevocably embedded in the European Community and the Atlantic alliance. We are not a great power. But we are also not a plaything for others. It is to our great benefit to have found friends and partners. But for their part, the alliance, Western Europe and the whole continent are decisively dependent on our contribution. Our political weight derives from our central location, the special situation of Berlin, the size of our population, and our productivity and stability.[24]

The rabble-rousing, left-of-center weekly photo magazine *Stern* put it more bluntly when it wrote "You [Americans] should make a trip through this Germany, instead of resurrecting the judgements of the past as the prejudices of today. The uniting patriotism of the cold war is no longer ours. We'd rather live in this fatherland than die for it, even when that doesn't fit into the American war games."[25]

Karl Kaiser, director of the German Council of Foreign Relations and never far from the West German establishment political line, said, "Inevitably, Germany is shifted into a new position with reform in East Europe and the end of the Cold War." Kaiser went on to add, "But the thought that the future of Germany's economy lies in the East makes the German businessman smile. Germany's choice between East and West was made 40 years ago." Perhaps. It is certainly true that all trade with the entire East Bloc accounts for a very small part of Germany's export-led economy. It is, for example, less than West Germany's trade with Austria or Switzerland. But an official of the German Embassy in Washington, replying to criticism of the West German economic policy toward Latin American debtors after the economic summit meeting in Paris in mid-summer 1989, said: "A certain division of labor has developed over time, where we assume particular burdens with respect to Eastern Europe—Poland in particular."[26]

In the first five months of 1989, West German exports to the Communist world rose by an average of 16 percent monthly (10 percent when adjusted for prices), continuing a modest rise in 1988 over 1986 and 1987. Imports climbed by 18 percent—falling in value (because of the fall in world oil and gas prices) but growing by 30 percent in volume. Altogether, the Soviet Union does 10 percent of its foreign trade with West Germany, 20 percent if only its trade with the West is counted. And the East accounts for 8 percent of total German overseas investment. The growing current account deficit between West Germany and the East Bloc was near Deutschemarks 18 billion over a four-year period (1984–1988). That deficit was financed by Deutschemarks 6 billion in capital exports (loans, and so forth) and trade credits. The West German Bundesbank, the central bank, reporting all this in mid-1989 warned that "Most Communist countries had to watch out that their current account deficits with West Germany did not widen too much, because they had either reached their credit limits or were trying hard—like Romania—to reduce their borrowing in Western currencies."[27]

U.S. banks played a significant role in lending to the Soviet Union and Central Europe in the 1970s. In mid-April 1987, congressional observers were startled and angered by a $200 million syndicated loan headed by the First National Bank of Chicago, not tied to U.S. exports, and at the incredibly low rate of only one-third of a percent over LIBOR (the London interbank lending rate). The loan was apparently a flamboyant attempt by the Chicago bank to get a favored position among lenders for what looked like a rapidly heating up campaign of Moscow borrowing. But by the fall of 1989, over half of the claims of Western banks on Soviet debt were accounted for by the banks of West Germany, Japan, and France. The United States accounted for only 3.4 percent of the total, 1.7 percent if Yugoslavia is removed. American banks got out because the profits were too small and because American trade with the area was limited. Lawrence Brainard, chief international economist for Bankers Trust in New York, says that European banks, too, are unlikely to continue lending to the Communist Bloc on a purely commercial basis.

> Although European banks have been active in these markets, there are reasons why their future lending will be more limited than heretofore. Many European banks perceive rising risks in such lending and exposure are already relatively high. A second reason for waiting is the eagerness of EC governments to see lending go forward. Why take risks on your own account when governments stand ready to underwrite the loans? European banks are telling their governments they will have to step in with guarantees, subsidies, and directed official credits. The EC has already begun to act, approving loans recently to Poland and Hungary through the EC's European Investment Bank. These loans form part of the $325 million aid package approved as part of the 1990 EC budget (including additional contributions from member states out of their own budgets). Twelve other non-EC countries were challenged to match the EC initiative. As modest as these first initiatives appear, there are reasons why similar programs could lead to conflicts between the United States and the Community.[28]

When I drew this whole situation to the attention of a group of German and American participants at a Konrad Adenauer Stiftung meeting in Los Angeles in the late summer of 1989, celebrating with a seminar the fortieth anniversary of the founding of the Federal Republic, the silence was deafening. I asked the members of the audience how they viewed the problem—considering the political propensity to push trade and investment in the Communist Bloc for all the political reasons that Genscher had outlined. I asked what mechanism would limit German official credits with subsidies for exports that surely would be the result if the Russians and others in the East Bloc were not able to pay? And, I asked, with West Germany running a surplus with the United States, how could the latter exercise any restraint on West German efforts to expand economic relations with the Soviet Union under *perestroika*? I am still waiting for an answer. All this, or course, preceded the euphoria induced by the coming down of the Wall and the changes in government in Czechoslovakia, Poland, Romania, as well as East Germany.

The inevitable conclusion is that Bonn—contrary to the economic logic of the Soviet internal economic prospects and its inability to trade with the West—is moving toward a massive new aid program to Moscow for political reasons. The urge to do so exists in all political parties—on the left and the right. The inclination might be given different rationalizations, but it exists, despite the horrendous Soviet economic problems that make any major expansion of normal trade with the West impossible, as well as the intensely enigmatic politics of the Russian Communist state that defy any attempt "to help Gorbachev" with what are essentially internal political problems.

What then is left of the hopes that a Federal Republic could be tied to a new unified West European state that would await indefinitely the settlement of the East German question and German reunification completely on Western terms? By October 1989, *The Economist* of London had concluded, probably correctly:

> It is a mistake . . . to believe that the way to keep Germany western is Euro-federalism. The federalists would like to use the 1992 project to prod the EC's 12 members towards something like the United States of Europe. The *drang nach Osten* rules this out. West Germany is now almost certain to reject any deepening of the EC into a political union that shuts out East Germany—not to mention Austria, Hungary, Poland, Czechoslovakia. Euro-federalists should take note: Germany's new interests are compatible with a great EC-wide market after 1992, but not with EC-wide defence or with a 12-member government of Europe. Expect Germany to push the Community towards widening as well as deepening. Yet trying to push both ways at the same time is bound to cause trouble."[29]

CHAPTER 10

BEG, BORROW, OR STEAL

Soviet Trade with the West

In May 1989, only four days after President Bush had talked of relaxation of trade restrictions with the Soviet Union, Secretary of Commerce Robert A. Mosbacher told an audience, including numerous Soviet trade officials, that Moscow should stop stealing high-technology secrets. Perhaps nothing so illustrates the dilemma of commercial dealings with the Soviet Union. All through the summer of 1989, Gorbachev more and more plainly had demanded that political reform inside the Soviet Union must be "rewarded" with—as he told Norway's foreign minister after a meeting with European ministers at Strasbourg—"economic cooperation from the West," which specifically meant "scientific goods including high-definition television and fast computers and chips."[1]

Against protests from Secretary of Defense Richard Cheney, Mosbacher had already approved removing the restrictions from selling the Soviets desk-top computers. The White House, obviously, believed it had little choice; Bonn had already gone ahead with approval for a joint venture for Siemens for the sale of 300,000 computers to the Soviet Union. (A new plant would be built in Germany for their production.) In a gesture that amounted to closing the barn door after the horse was stolen, Bush went to the Coordinating Committee on Multilateral Export Controls (CoCom) in Paris, the 17-nation Western military alliance's sentry for policing the transfer of technology to the Communists, to obtain approval for NATO-allied countries and the Japanese to sell the desk-top computers to the East. American computer companies had sold about six million personal computers in 1988, almost half of these outside the United States. The Commerce Department and the computer community had argued that equivalent models were already being exported by many non-CoCom producers—Taiwan, India, China, and Brazil. The computer companies argued that the move had come too late, that sales had already been lost to American firms. And Mosbacher chimed in, arguing that ". . . if you listened to some people, you would think they (an early model of the IBM-compatible portable computers) were state-of-the-art machines, but they are not."[2]

Yet personal computers and "lap-top" (small cybernetic machines) computers have become an integral part of modern warfare, a part that the Soviets have found they lag far behind in developing or utilizing. As long ago as 1981, the U.S. military had developed TAP,

> a microcomputer-based system which uses commercially available, desk-top equipment to enhance the capabilities to Tactical Operations Centers. . . . Using TAP, an operator can quickly call up full-color map displays on a video monitor, enlarge or reduce the area displayed, add or delete troop movements, forests, bridges, towns, roads, hills, etc. Newer versions substitute conventional map images for the computer-generated map displays (the map images being stored on videodiscs). Terrain and other features can be superimposed on the map images and at will. The system enables TAP users to: . . . identify and characterize targeting opportunities by correlating intelligence data, doctrinal norms and terrain data. Promote analysis to assist in ground forces control, maneuver, fire support and in air strike planning. Assist in the management and complementary, integrated, employment of all sensor systems, i.e. solve the weaponeering problem for nuclear and conventional weapons.[3]

The proof of this conjecture was seen in the guerrilla successes against Soviet forces in Afghanistan where, under the Reagan Doctrine of giving military aid to anti-Soviet guerrillas, some of the latest in these kinds of weapons—some of them so miniaturized that they could be handheld—played an enormous role in neutralizing heavier Soviet battlefield and aerial equipment, especially the helicopter gun-ships.

The Siemens episode illustrates the whole complex issue of U.S. government attempts to deny the Soviet Union all technology that would enhance its military advantage, not only in strategic and tactical terms, but also in saving the moribund Soviet economy enormous research and development costs. Although Siemens theoretically is making the computers for Soviet schools, the West has repeatedly found that "dual-use" technology—technology that might be used in civilian life but that also has military applications—drifts into the maw of the Soviet military-industrial complex. Whether or not the technology is state-of-the-art in the United States or the West is not always relevant in the Soviet Union, for its technological gap with the West is growing all the time. The possibility that such equipment often is available from other suppliers does not satisfy the Soviet need and desire to import these machines with Western credits (in this case German) and from a more reliable and efficient producer. Perhaps most important of all, it neglects the argument that, although technological transfer among the major industrial powers of the world—including the USSR and the Communist Bloc—is probably inevitable in the age of advanced communications, slowing that transfer and making it more expensive for the Soviets seeking military advantage may be of crucial consequence.

Here is how Richard Perle, a former Pentagon official and advocate of denying Moscow U.S. technology, put it:

> The chief criterion for assessing the impact of a technology transfer is not whether it is obsolete by American standards, but rather the degree to which it will advance the Soviet Union's capabilities. . . . each technology has a time dependency to its singular value to American weapons systems. . . . critical products should be controlled on the basis of their intrinsic utility, and not on commercial specifications or end-use statements. From time to time, commercial firms criticize the United States control list for containing items that are not on the CoCom list, which means that CoCom countries can trade in those items but American firms cannot. Consequently, it is argued that the United States should not have a unilateral list, but rather that its list should conform to the CoCom list. This argument overlooks the purpose of strategic controls. Their purpose is to protect the strategic lead time of United States military forces, while minimizing the impact on commercial trade. The objective cannot be reversed; i.e., to encourage commercial trade with the Soviet Union while minimizing the impact on strategic lead time. Since advanced weapon systems and their supporting technology are usually concentrated in the United States and not in CoCom countries, it is to be expected that the American list will lead the CoCom list in control items.[4]

Even in a world where the United States has lost a great part of its vast technological lead at the end of World War II, these arguments still hold true. The majority of United States research and development is now conducted in high-technology industry. High technology provides two-thirds of all Defense Department hardware purchases for the military forces. Furthermore, it can be argued that defense research and production depend increasingly on parallel commercial developments, such as the development of high-speed integrated circuits in computers. That means that the whole question of high-technology exports—particularly those with dual civilian and military uses—has become more than ever a difficult problem for the government.

Part and parcel of the new relationship between Moscow and Washington has been an effort to arrange exchanges of professional citizens of both countries, particularly scientists, in what seems a laudable and innocuous way to further understanding and the possibility of peace. As détente revived in the later years of the Reagan administration, new government-to-government agreements were negotiated on cooperation in science. On January 12, 1988, an agreement was signed in Moscow that Guri I. Marchuk, chairman of the Soviet National Academy of Sciences, called "a tremendous advance in our scientific relationship."[5] Yet neither the issue of emigration of Jewish scientists who were refused exit visas because they supposedly knew "state secrets," nor the troubling issue of scientists and others being consigned to psychiatric hospitals because of political dissidence was settled. Of course, Soviet propagandists have claimed that the exchanges are a rewarding two-way process. At a Boston meeting of senior Soviet scientists with Americans, Dr. Andrei A. Koko-shin, deputy director of the politically powerful Soviet think tank, the Soviet Institute for the USA and Canada, told newsmen that

> Washington's assertion that we had to buy foreign equipment to make quiet submarine propellers is merely a red herring . . . We see these assertions as excuses to avoid cooperating with us in technical matters, and I doubt that most American scientists agree with that point of view. There are important areas of computer science in which American and Soviet experts could collaborate. Americans make fine computers, but Soviet mathematicians are the best in the world. A marriage of these two areas of expertise would benefit both of us. Moreover, Soviet software development is already very advanced in many areas—significantly ahead of the West.[6]

A few months later, however, a leading Soviet scientist blasted Soviet science, saying researchers "resemble soldiers attempting to fight a modern war with crossbows. . . . Although the Soviet Union has one of the largest scientific work forces, it has only a modest record of achievements and is contributing little to the world's scientific knowledge." Roald Sagdeev, director of the Soviet Space Research Institute and a key adviser to Gorbachev, writing on the subject in several places in the Soviet press, said, "Soviet science can be justly proud of its contribution to the discovery of the laser, and Soviet technology exhibited its prowess with the launching of Sputnik and with subsequent space achievements. But such flashes of brilliance are rare."[7]

Yakov M. Rabkin, professor of the history of science at the University of Montreal, writes:

> For the Soviet government, gaining access to American science and technology, important though it is, is secondary to the prospect of a diminution of its controls over Soviet and Soviet satellite populations. Long-term concerns about Soviet technological performance are less important than the constant apprehension about challenges to their power by Soviet leadership. The USSR needs the exchanges as a remedy for the Soviet system's industrial inefficiency. Even though the *nomenclatura* does not mind inefficiency as such—inefficiency concerns them only to the extent that it may be weakening their control of Soviet society—Gorbachev is attempting to reduce inefficiency by reducing the centralized controls typical of Soviet society.[8]

By February 23, 1989, Moscow had the temerity to suggest that it was a neutral ground in the battle among the United States, Japan, and the Europeans for definition standards for the proposed new high-definition television (HDTV), not only a hot commercial issue in the international electronics industry but also a technical issue with important armaments spinoff. Sensing an opportunity to make a mark, Soviet officials in the fall of 1988 offered to sponsor an unofficial comparison-testing of the competing systems in Moscow. "We don't care which standard will be. I proposed premises in our institute, and please come and let's make objective tests," Henrikas Yushkiavitshus, Soviet vice chairman of radio and television, told HDTV Newsletter."[9] A few weeks later, the real level of Soviet science, despite its claims, was revealed when scientists all over the world were informed that some of their attempts at recording data from satellites had been wiped out by nuclear power "leaks" from orbiting Soviet spy satellites. "The problem is caused by the Radar Ocean Reconnaissance Satellites used by the Soviets to observe US naval operations. . . . The Soviet Union has put up an estimated 35 spy satellites powered by nuclear reactors in the past two decades, and the US has launched one."[10]

The United States has attempted to control the transfer of technology to the Soviets at the level of pure scientific research and applied technology from the beginning of the Cold War, after experiencing the wholesale robbery of American proprietary technological secrets during the cobelligerency of World War II. The history of this effort is one of mixed strategies and tactics, uncertain resolve, and mixed results. The first efforts were through administrative procedures beginning in 1947. Determined, however, that national security required an embargo on high technology to the Soviet Union and its satellites that would contribute toward their military potential, the Congress passed the U.S. Export Control Act of 1949 to ensure this strategy. The Export Control Act was replaced in 1979 by the Export Administration Act, which continued the relaxation of controls that had begun with the warming of the Cold War and subsequently were continued by the Nixon-Kissinger détente and the pressures of our trading allies in Western Europe. Because of renewed concern about what the Soviets were doing, the process was reversed in the early 1970s with the passage of legislation giving the Department of Defense a greater role in determining policy. Richard F. Staar, a former U.S. disarmament negotiator, comments:

A senior official of the U.S. Department of State has admitted serious mistakes committed during the 1970s in legal sales of high technology to the USSR. He cited three U.S. decisions, each one of which was approved after Soviet assurances had been received that the transfers involved would be used only for nonmilitary purposes: The Kama River Truck plant received $1.5 billion in US and Western technology. The vehicles produced by the plant were used in the invasion of Afghanistan; others continue to support Soviet troops facing NATO in Central Europe. American precision-grinding machines, sold to the USSR in the 1970s, produce small ball bearings which have been integral to development of the massive force of Soviet missiles that threaten the United States today. Two large floating docks, sold by the United States to the USSR for ostensibly civilian use, were diverted for repair of Soviet naval vessels. By late 1979 and the Soviet invasion of Afghanistan, it had to be abundantly clear that legally imported technology from the West was enhancing and improving USSR military capabilities. The belated answer was a tightening of US export controls.[11]

Richard Perle claimed moderate success with the revised policy:

> Our latest initiatives to improve the multilateral CoCom and unilateral license validating systems for West-to-East trade have proven successful. We feel it has forced the Soviets to resort to less dependable and more costly methods of covert diversion through Free World and neutral countries in order to acquire the high technology equipment required to upgrade their military capabilities. For example, Richard Mueller, the mastermind of many diversion cases, established more than sixty front companies in a number of Free World countries to obtain critical commodities. While we cannot gauge how many people are resorting to the same tactics, increasing evidence leads us to believe that the magnitude of the Free World diversion problem is highly significant.[12]

In theory, the Department of Defense reviews applications for export of high-tech goods, and would recommend that the president disapprove the issuance of an export license if it disapproves. The crunch had come, of course, when the Carter administration in January 1980 cut back grain shipments to the Soviet Union and suspended several licenses for high-tech exports in retaliation for the Soviet invasion of Afghanistan. President Reagan, largely for domestic political reasons, lifted the partial grain embargo in April 1981, arguing that although it was an immediate prop for Soviet foreign exchange, it did not contribute toward the long-term solution of the Soviet agricultural morass. That argument may have been economically sound, but in June 1982, when Reagan extended the strategic controls by banning the sale of energy-related equipment to the Soviet Union by U.S. companies and their overseas affiliates, there was an outcry in Europe. The action, which was bitterly debated within the administration, was aimed at halting or slowing down the construction of pipelines that would make the West Europeans, through a series of interlocking agreements, increasingly dependent on deliveries of Soviet natural gas. Western European allies were particularly critical of the extension of American controls to U.S.-affiliated companies abroad. Reagan removed the controls in 1982.

The entire episode has become a major center for debate in the whole question of the use of export controls. There is a substantial case to be made that the U.S. action did further inhibit the Soviet Union's capacity to earn foreign exchange, and therefore, force the movement toward economic reform; by slowing the gas project, it permitted Norwegian, Dutch, and other producers of natural gas to make dècisions and to solve technological problems that eliminated what Washington considered the spectre of Soviet political leverage over West European energy supplies. The Reagan administration effort to amend the law again in 1983 was caught in the battle over advocates of trade expansion and those arguing inside the administration for security constraints. The administration's recommendations were not accepted by the Congress.

The battle continues. In September 1985, a Defense Department-Central Intelligence Agency White Paper stated that:

> Virtually every Soviet military research project—well over 4,000 each year in the late 1970s and over 5,000 annually in the early 1980s—benefits from [legally and illegally acquired Western] technical documents and hardware. . . . technological equipment and information collected by the Soviets in the West during the late 1970s through the mid-1980s has enabled the Soviet military-industrial complex to . . . redirect the USSR technical approaches in about 100 projects each year for weapons systems and key military equipment . . . to initiate several hundred new short-and-long-term projects per annum in technical areas hitherto not considered . . . to raise technical levels of several thousand developmental projects every year for military equipment, manufacturing and design . . . to eliminate the need for or shorten more than 1,000 military research projects per annum, thereby reducing—up to three-years—the lead-time required to produce more advanced weapons and equipment.[13]

David G. Wigg, a former deputy assistant secretary of defense for policy analysis, has argued that the West Europeans who push for trade with the Communist Bloc are making a crucial economic miscalculation. He estimates:

> The annual dollar cost to NATO of technology loss (exclusive of national security loss for which no measure exists except the outcome of war) to range from $15 billion to $40 billion, depending on the technologies and weapons systems compromised in any particular year. . . . In 1987, NATO's exports to the world totaled $1.32 trillion. That same year NATO exports to the

USSR totaled $12.9 billion or 0.9 percent of total NATO exports—a sufficiently small number that it could be considered statistically insignificant. . . . If we assume that the overall net profitability resulting from exporting to Moscow averages a reasonable 12 percent of sales of all of the NATO commercial interests concerned, it amounts to around $1.5 billion or one-tenth of my low estimate for the annual cost of technology loss and one one-hundredth of the high estimate—hardly an impressive cost/benefit outcome for the national interest.[14]

Over all the history of the attempt since 1949 to coordinate the denial of technology by all the NATO allies and Japan to the Soviets and the East Bloc through the CoCom organization has been a half-hearted battle.

The secretariat of CoCom in Paris was housed in a few thousand square feet of space in an obscure, rundown annex to the U.S. Embassy in Paris. Its "professional" staff consisted of a few full and part-time translators and several typists. There were no modern office or word processing equipment (a hand-operated mimeograph machine was used to copy thousands of documents). The U.S.G. (U.S. government) contributes the Secretariat's quarters as a payment in kind and the other countries contribute about three hundred thousand dollars to maintain the basic operation.[15]

The Japanese government had refused to contribute more than $40,000 toward CoCom's operations "because of budgetary restraints." The European delegates, usually career bureaucrats with little technical competence, had, as their advisers on highly controversial issues, the representatives of their national firms involved in the proposed transactions. The Reagan administration made an effort to remedy some of this as it tried in its own idiosyncratic way, to tighten the implementation of restrictions on high-tech transfer as part of its whole program of rebuilding U.S. defenses after the collapse of détente with the invasion of Afghanistan in the Carter administration.

There was considerable confusion within the administration over the issue, however, and it produced one of the first major crises within the new administration. Reagan tried to lay down what some of his advisers called "clear markers" for U.S. policy at the first economic summit in Ottawa in 1981. Under-Secretary of State Meyer Rashish argued for the necessity for maintaining energy and financial security for the Europeans. The administration, however, reluctantly went along with the approval to sell two pipelayers for the first of two giant pipelines that the Soviets were building, which eventually would have terminals in Central Europe to supply German and, therefore, the West European natural gas networks. The United States laid down sanctions on an embargo when martial law was declared in Poland for additional equipment that would have increased Soviet costs of the construction for Moscow. A mission was sent to Europe in 1982 to try to persuade the Europeans to join the embargo, or at least not to undercut it. It failed, and Reagan interceded personally at the Versailles Economic Summit in June 1982. The argument was that, not only would sales of natural gas to Western Europe provide the Soviets with additional fungible funds they could use for their continuing arma- ments race, but that Western European dependency on Soviet sources of energy supply would be an enormous strategic asset for the Soviets. The Europeans, of course, were reluctant to see that American sales of grain— restarted by the Reagan administration because of domestic pressures— while helping Moscow through its food crisis, would not contribute to the long-term solution of its basic agricultural problem, nor, in fact, reduce its dependence on the West. The Europeans equated their gas deal with U.S. sales of grain. And Reagan's pleas were rejected at the summit. But the deepening crisis in Poland led the administration to intensify its position, extending its sanctions to subsidiaries and licensees of American companies in Western Europe. This provided a new area of controversy with the Allies, who charged that Washington was exercising illegal extraterritoriality under international law.

The barrage of diplomatic outrage unleashed by this action brought to a head a crisis within the Reagan administration. Retired General Alexan- der Haig, Reagan's first secretary of state, despite the fact that he had sat at the helm of NATO in Brussels as its commander and recognized the strategic considerations of the argument, opposed the White House policy, arguing that it endangered the intimate and complicated relations within the NATO alliance at a time of crisis when other aspects of the functioning of Western European defenses were also in jeopardy. National Security Adviser William Clark, who considered the issue vital to Ameri- can security, prevailed, backed by hardliners in the economic section of the National Security Council (NSC). To a considerable extent, it was that issue that caused Haig's dismissal as "vicar of the President's foreign policy."

Norman A. Bailey, Judge Clark's economic adviser on the NSC, gives this account of the next round:

> To our allies' credit, these talks (Allied negotiations at the ministers' level in La Sapinière, Canada, in October 1982) led to agreements that provided a framework for the coordinated actions taken over the next nine months in the areas of energy, security, and export controls. On the basis of the La Sapinière agreements—which were implemented by the Williamsburg Summit in May 1983—the President lifted our Poland-related pipeline sanctions. The effort then turned to negotiations within the International Energy Agency (IEA) designed to block the second parallel strand of the Siberian gas pipeline from becoming an export pipeline to Western Europe.[16]

During the next few months, several technological, business, and political decisions occurred that had the effect of diminishing significantly the economic attractiveness of the Soviet offer of gas for Western Europe. Huge Norwegian gas deposits, which had appeared to be difficult to reach because they uncharacteristically lay under rather than over oil deposits in the North Sea, turned out to be exploitable with new deep-drilling technologies. It resulted in a long-term contract for $64 billion, which assured Western Europe of adequate supplies of gas into the twenty-first century. The outlook for overall demand for energy, including gas, in Western Europe began to drop, thus making new sources less urgent than before. The Dutch had been holding a considerable portion of their gas in reserve because they assumed that it was an appreciating asset. After examining the situation with the prospect of radical change in the long-term energy price outlook, they decided to open their gas reserves to exploitation. As the months passed, the Soviets had difficulty maintaining supplies. They had promised the Europeans that under no circumstances would there be any cutoffs, but the situation changed radically as bad weather and Russian shortages forced cutoffs. As with so many victories for U.S. strategic policy, even if this one did come about as much by luck as by design, it has been overlooked in the continuing debate in which opponents of the strategic embargo against the Soviets argue whether embargoes ever work or whether they are not actually counterproductive because they create tensions and frictions with our NATO allies.

In early June 1989, the explosion of a four-year-old Soviet gas pipeline, which caused the death of more than 500 passengers traveling in two passing trains, confirmed the predictions of those who had opposed the West European gas deals. *The Economist* of London interpreted the accident as evidence that the Soviets, desperately trying to compensate for the falling price of their energy exports by driving for larger volumes, were losing the battle.

> Even shaky Russian statistics suggest that oil and gas investment will have to rise by 50 percent every five years in real terms simply to keep output at its present level. Worse, a growing proportion of Russian oil is becoming more expensive to produce and sell. And gas, apparently still cheap to exploit (although some Soviet economists have questioned the simplistic way its extraction cost is calculated), will become ever costlier as Russia struggles to meet the ambitious export targets with marginal reserves. . . . *Soyugazexport* plans to lift exports to Western Europe by 40% by 1995, which would leave the Soviet Union with a third of the market. . . . This may revive American worries about Western Europe's dependence on Russian gas.[17]

Those worries had already been mothballed by the second half of the Reagan administration by a combination of American business pressures and the erosion of "The Evil Empire" ethos by Reagan himself. Soviet proposals to welcome joint ventures between Western investors and Soviet enterprises, with the Western partners bringing technology as well as capital to the partnership, constituted a new siren song. Reagan's startling and unexpected appointment of C. William Verity as Secretary of Commerce in October 1987 surprised even the closest inner circle, and apparently was one of the aberrations in Reagan's policy brought on through the influence of Mrs. Nancy Reagan and her closest collaborator, presidential adviser Michael Deaver. It was a devastating blow for those in the Pentagon and elsewhere in the administration who favored a tough line on the strategic embargo.

Verity was known as a prominent exponent of trade with the Soviet Union. His background not only included service as the chief executive officer of Inland Steel, an old 1930s partner in Stalin's industrialization, but he had been Lieutenant General Pitovranov's American counterpart on the U.S.-USSR Trade and Economic Council. Five American firms— Combustion Engineering, Management Partnerships, Honeywell, Inc., Armand Hammer's Occidental Petroleum, and IDG Communications— all high-tech companies, had already indicated that they were interested in such Soviet partnerships. The companies had problems in getting organized in the Soviet Union because of Russian difficulties and their own investment problems.

The legal sale and export of U.S. and Western manufactures and technologies to the Soviet Union is only the tip of the iceberg. Since the 1920s, Moscow has directed an elaborate campaign of industrial espionage in the West—often intertwined and indistinguishable from the general campaign to secure military and political intelligence. All through the 1930s and 1940s, the Soviet embassies' trade representatives were commonly the head NKVD [predecessor to the KGB] officers in the local security and espionage operations. A reserve KGB lieutenant general, Evgenii Petrovich Pitovranov, an officer of the USSR Chamber of Commerce since 1966, has been the chief Soviet liaison officer for the U.S.-USSR Trade and Economic Council in New York, an organization of the chief American lobbyists for and participants in U.S.-Soviet trade. Pitovranov was so deeply involved in Soviet "security organs" (secret police) that he served eighteen months in prison when Lavrentii Beria, Stalin's last secret police chief, was apparently foiled in a coup to take power and killed. The Soviet body collects economic information and performs most of the functions of a similar Western organization but

> Some of the chamber's functions involved deception. In the USSR, it helps inspect Western equipment, some sold legally to civilian industries but destined from the first for defense-related organizations. . . . The exact number of chamber employees is unknown. Of the approximately 140 officials who have been identified, about a third are known or suspected intelligence officers, of whom a few are GRU (military intelligence) and the rest KGB. Analysis of the career patterns and activities of the remaining officials suggests that the actual number of KGB and GRU officers is higher.[18]

Operatives for the Chamber have been caught in France, West Germany, Japan, and the United States in industrial intelligence activities. All overt and covert industrial intelligence operations such as the Chamber of Commerce of the USSR and other organizations lead into two Soviet organizations—the Military and Industrial Commission or VPK (*Voenno-promyshlennaia Komissiia*), attached to the presidium of the Soviet council of ministers, and another program under the Soviet Ministry of Foreign Affairs. Both are considered highly skilled screening networks for passing information on to the dozen "customer agencies" in Soviet industry. These twelve ministries and enterprises provide the two organizations with detailed requirements of foreign technologies or machinery they wish to obtain.

During the Tenth Five-Year Plan (1976–1980), for example, more than 3,500 requirements from these twelve ministries could be met successfully. About half of the 30,000 pieces of hardware and one-fifth of the 400,000 documents collected throughout the world were used to improve the Soviet military equipment and weapons systems. However, only one-third of the VPK requirements were fulfilled, completely or in part, each year, suggesting that Western efforts to prevent this legal and mostly illegal high-tech transfer do have some effect.[19]

These operations are extremely elaborate and unique in each country. In Sweden, for example,

Industrial espionage is handled [in the KGB station] by Line X. The GRU organization in Sweden has a special division for science and technology. Since 1983, the chief of Line X has been Technology Attaché Evgeny Belyayev. He was born in 1932, and formerly worked on the State Committee for Science and Technology, GKNT. He has subordinate to him some 15 KGB officers, with cover positions especially at the Embassy, the Soviet trade delegation at Lidingo and at Matreco Handels AB at Sodertalje. The GRU has some half dozen officers specialized in technology espionage. The cover positions are most often to be found in the Embassy and the 45-man strong trade delegation. Among these is, for example, Second Secretary Gennady Bachtin, who earlier had a cover position in the Soviet trade section in Denmark. From what can now be judged, the Soviet intelligence services are trying to hand their industrial espionage increasingly over to their colleagues in some of the East European sister states. This especially applies to the GDR, Czechoslovakia, but also to Poland and Hungary. The fact that both of Czechoslovakia's intelligence services were acting as Soviet proxies is witnessed by, among other examples, the spy disclosures [in Sweden] of last spring and summer [1987] . . . there are still some ten Swedish firms involved in the continuing traffic of embargo-covered high-technology. The increased resources of the [Swedish] customs service may, however, be expected to limit the continued activity of precisely these firms.[20]

The illegal activities of Soviet agents and their collaborators seeking either transfer of embargoed Western high-tech goods or of technologies to make them is legion. In August 1986, the Royal Canadian Mounties captured the "technobandit" Charles J. McVey II, a fugitive from a U.S. indictment that, as an exporter in Orange County, California, he had shipped embargoed computers to the Soviet Union. Another "technobandit," a West German businessman, was convicted in Los Angeles in February 1987 of shipping computers and other electronic equipment to the Soviet Union after evading arrest for five years. In November 1987, Greek, Cypriot, and NATO security agencies uncovered a Bulgarian network to ship computers and software useful in research on ballistic missiles to the Bloc. Earlier in 1987, a Greek agent had passed to the Soviets technical information that made it possible for Moscow to reproduce a version of the Stinger missile, the hand-held rocket with electronic targeting that had been so effectively used by Afghan guerrillas against Soviet aircraft. Four French businessmen were arrested in April 1988 for illegally exporting machine tools that could produce turbine blades for jet engines and power-generating equipment. Earlier, France's third largest bank, Société Générale, was embargoed as an agent for any U.S. exports by the Commerce Department for its role in financing the export to the Soviet Union of equipment to make semiconductors. A Scottish subsidiary of a New Jersey firm was caught exporting to the Soviet Union specialized furnaces and presses for making a woven carbon product called carbon-carbon, used to increase the accuracy of missile warheads. A row broke out between the Commerce and Defense departments in September 1987 over permission granted to IBM and a Japanese company to ship a powerful computer to a Soviet-owned company in Hamburg, West Germany, which had bought American computers earlier, designed to keep up with shipping and inventories. "Australian firms have already been caught out exporting to the Soviet Union computers whose hardware originally came from the US," an Australian publication reported during Prime Minister R. J. Hawke's December 1987 trip to Moscow.[21] In December 1988, Miami police arrested a Dutch citizen who was believed to be a part of a dozen companies operating in the United States to smuggle $100 million worth of computers to the Soviet Bloc. An internal report of the Federal Republic says that by 1988 Soviet industrial espionage in West Germany had reached staggering proportions—with sixty espionage operations, 37 of which were run directly by Moscow. In March 1988, the West German discovery of four Soviet emigrants and a native West German engineer in a plot to steal the plans of the "Eurofighter" aircraft was "the biggest blow to the Soviet secret service since the establishment of the Federal Republic in 1949."²² In June 1988, Canada expelled four Soviet officials and banned nine others, who had served there during the past sixteen years, for trying to infiltrate an electronics contractor with access to radar, sonar, and computer-driven equipment that controls shipboard weapons. A few months earlier, President Reagan had overruled a Pentagon decision not to transfer naval technology to Canada. In December 1988 Japanese police raided the offices of a chemical company accused of selling to the Soviet Union a specialized gas, which was commonly used as an ingredient in fire extinguishers but which also could be used in manufacturing missile guidance systems. In July 1989, a widening investigation found that Japanese computer chip manufacturing machinery had been sold through a former South Korean military attaché to the East Germans. Depending upon how it was used, this machinery could produce electronic chips for personal computers or spy satellites and nuclear devices. In August 1989 Finnish courts indicted two business-men for shipping eighteen personal computers, a graphics workstation, and other technology to the Soviet Union.

The most highly publicized and perhaps the most important violation of the West's agreement to restrict strategic technologies to the Soviets and their allies, however, came in the summer of 1987. It was then learned, generally, that a Japanese company, with the help of a Norwegian state-owned corporation, had made a major sale to the Soviets of critical engineering equipment. The businessmen sold eight giant computer-operated milling machines to the Soviets for installation in a Leningrad shipyard. The machines were provided by Toshiba Machine, a subsidiary of the giant electronics and heavy electrical manufacturing entity, Toshiba. Before World War II, a substantial interest in Toshiba was owned by General Electric of the United States; it had close and enormously profitable ties to American manufacturers and U.S. markets. The machines are industrial robots—each weighs over 250 metric tons, stands three stories tall, and can grind in nine different directions to produce such complex shapes as turbine propeller blades. "The machines combine the complexity of the human hand with the computer's ability to repeat the operation over and over again."²³ The violation of the embargo involved falsely identifying what was to be shipped, shipping it to a different Soviet customer through a giant Japanese trading company, C. Itoh, with a smaller Japanese trading company, Wako Koeki, running interference with its old connections to the KGB buyers. The Norwegian government-owned company, Kongsberg Vaapenfabrik, supplied the computerized electronic controls for the machinery. Although Richard Perle said Toshiba and C. Itoh, two of Japan's largest concerns, and Kongsberg Vaapenfabrik, a state-run company in Norway, "were not victims of a clever KGB scheme," officials of the Japanese trading company that headed the group making the sale signed their contract with two well-known KGB trade operators. Toshiba Machine had a history of questionable dealings with the Soviets, having sold other equipment to the Baltic Naval Shipyard in 1974. In fact, a Japanese engineer, who worked in Leningrad on the installation of the equipment, reported sighting a wide variety of other Western equipment there.

The sale, while above world market prices, was relatively small—$17 million. But U.S. intelligence and Pentagon spokesmen have argued that the future cost of repairing the damage to the American antisubmarine warfare strategy will run in the billions of dollars, perhaps as much as $8 billion over the next ten years. Until the 1970s, quietness in design was not a major priority of the Soviets, who preferred to rely on speed and deep diving as defensive techniques. In reconstructing the whole scheme much later, it appears likely that the Soviets had moved to acquire the equipment because the Walker family spy group (a minor U.S. naval petty officer who with members of his family had supplied the Soviets with a vast array of intercepts, finally uncovered in 1988) had warned Moscow of the importance of noise from propeller blades in the water as part of U.S. advanced antisubmarine warfare surveillance and interception techniques. The sound of the propulsion through the water of the propeller is 90 percent of the total noise emitted by a submarine traveling underwater. To meet sound reduction goals, manufacturing tolerances must be less than one-tenth of a millimeter. Although propeller blades can be shaped by hand to meet these requirements, automation is necessary to produce the critical tolerances at a reasonable construction speed. It was this missing ingredient that Toshiba and Kongsberg supplied the Soviet shipyard. *The Economist* of London (June 27, 1987) reckons that the difference in technical perspicacity is that Western sources could hear a Soviet submarine 200 miles away before the addition of the new more finely ground propellers, but now that recognition difference has fallen to only ten miles.

News of the Japanese-Norwegian sale first surfaced in December 1985, when a former manager of the Wako Moscow office, Hitori Kumagai, wrote a letter complete with exhaustive documentation to CoCom describing the sale in all its details. CoCom referred the letter to the Japanese government's Ministry of International Trade and Industry (MITI), since the member states of the alliance are supposed to police the embargo themselves. But no Japanese government action resulted. In 1986, U.S. officials interviewed Kumagai, and MITI issued a denial of his report. In March 1987 a demarche from the State Department again solicited a denial. It was not until Secretary of Defense Weinberger made a personal appeal to his Japanese counterpart in April 1987—timed to arrive on the eve of Prime Minister Yasuhiro Nakasone's visit to the United States—and the story was subsequently published in *The Detroit News* that the matter was taken into hand. Japanese police raided Toshiba Machine, C. Itoh, and Wako Koeki in locations across Japan in April.

At the news of the sale, a firestorm erupted on Capitol Hill, where the argument over the sale immediately became entwined with the continuing discussion of Japanese trade policies and the increasing pressure in the U.S. business community to sell military techologies for the continuing Japanese defense buildup. A Senate Republican-Democratic-Conservative-Liberal coalition demanded blood and sought to insert amendments in trade legislation that would impose secondary boycotts on Toshiba Machine and even on its parent, Toshiba Electric. The latter firm had been charged with earlier violations of shipping microelectronics assemblies to the Soviets in the 1970s. These allegations have been repeatedly denied. But Toshiba Corporation Chairman Soichi Saba, with the possible loss of millions of dollars in the U.S. market, assumed responsibility for the mistake in the Japanese fashion, apologized in full-age advertisements in the major American newspapers, and resigned. The penalties meted out by a Tokyo court, however, were light—Toshiba Machine was fined the yen equivalent of only $15,750; two former employees were given suspended sentences.

Spurred on by a press campaign, the Norwegian government, a loyal NATO partner, moved quickly to investigate the accusations. Three Kongsberg officials were indicted, and seized documents showed that Japanese, French, German, and Italian firms had been conspiring with the Norwegian firm to violate the strategic embargo on numerically controlled machine tools in a wide range of locations that included the satellite states as well as the Soviet Union.

Kumagai, in an article in a Japanese magazine, speculated that the

Soviets' inordinate security at the Leningrad shipyard and questions they asked him when he was in Moscow, suggest that the Soviets are working on a revolutionary type of propulsion for submarines that would be even less detectable.[24] He also suggested that other machinery from other Western producers was being used to boost Soviet submarine-building efficiency to leapfrog over Western developments. Kumagai, in defense of his fellow engineers, wrote:

> Even if field engineers are aware that "machines for the production of bolts" conflict with the CoCom rules, they will do their best to complete the manufacturing of best-quality products, if the go-sign is given. This is the same thought as that with which British officers and men, who were prisoners-of-war, constructed the bridge over the "River Kwai", giving full play to their capability, for the benefit of the Japanese forces, under their orders. Toshiba and Kongsberg engineers probably did not at all think, in the process of work at the actual scene, that the propeller-milling machines will be used only for the screws of tankers and freighters. However, at that time, it would have been practically impossible for them to resort to such action as to walk off their job or to carry out a go-slow strike, even if they had realized that the machines may be used in regard to combat ships. Therefore, they only did their best as technicians.[25]

No wonder that Kumagai, in a private interview in Tokyo, responded to the question of where Western authorities should look for violations of the strategic embargo, "Any enterprise which comes to Moscow to deal with the Soviet Union."[26]

Ironically, this outrageous and expensive violation of the strategic embargo gave Washington an opportunity to get Japanese (and Norwegian) government compliance as it had never been available before implementing the CoCom restrictions. Under Secretary of Commerce for Export Administration, Paul Freedenberg, serving under Verity, said that because of fallout from the Kongsberg case

> The Japanese have come farther in the last six months [on export controls] than they have in the last 30 years in terms of changing and improving their overall export control system. They have not only changed their juridical structure—that is to say, raised penalties for offenders, lengthened the statute of limitations, and so forth—but they have also devoted considerably more resources toward administering the program.[27]

Japanese police and intelligence officials, however, had been reporting to their American counterparts for several years that the Soviet effort to exploit Japan's growing technological base, as an alternative to getting at U.S. and European sources, had greatly increased. Japan—with its huge, modern traffic facilities and the continuous flow of visiting businessmen and engineers—was experiencing difficulty in policing what were the increasing numbers of KGB trade officials arriving and touring the country. When the United States and Japan signed a new bilateral agreement for guarding military secrets in June 1988, a Japan Defense Agency spokesman said the problem had become increasingly difficult. He said that secret Japanese defense documents had totaled 147,000—more than one and a half times their number ten years earlier. A London newsletter that circulates among a select world audience of high government officials said early in 1989:

> Happily, Japan is a member of CoCom, and now a conscientious one. Whether Japan will remain a conscientious CoCom member will determine whether or not NATO can maintain a technological edge over the Warsaw Pact. If not, the main pillar of NATO's strategy will crumble. In turn, Japan's role in CoCom will, to a large extent, be determined by Western Europe's ability to give Tokyo a sense of global responsibility and partnership. Washington alone can do this. The conditions for a common European-Japanese-U.S. approach to technology transfer are still favorable. [Soviet Foreign Minister Eduard] Shevardnadze's visit to Tokyo in December [1988] was not a success since Moscow remains unwilling (for how much longer?) to budge on the issue of Japan's Northern Territories.[28]

The Toshiba case did open up a new if highly contentious strategy for U.S. strategic trade policy. Congress had banned Toshiba Machine from doing business in the United States for three years, and had come just short of cutting off its parent company's billion-dollar market in the United States after American businessmen waged a campaign to halt action against it. The whole episode showed how vulnerable huge foreign multinationals, doing a large business in the American market with only marginal activities in the Communist Bloc, could be made in competing against each other in marketing strategies. For example, after a brief encounter with American authorities over the possibility that it had violated strategic concerns, officials of the huge Sweden-based but multinational L. M. Erickson telephone and electronics combine canceled all their sales efforts in the East Bloc. According to Swedish trade and government sources in the fall of 1989, Erickson not only did not want to jeopardize sales in the United States but, more important, it did not want to invite the possibility of U.S. government action in cutting the company off from important technological exchange arrangements with American companies. Toshiba promised to set up a model screening process inside its company, such as most big U.S. concerns have, to avoid the possibility that it might inadvertently violate the strategic embargo rules. Toshiba also hired the U.S. accounting firm Price Waterhouse and two U.S. law firms to investigate and plead its case that it had not known of the violations of CoCom restrictions by its subsidiary, Toshiba Machine. The law firm's fee alone was said to have been $4.3 million. Toshiba Machine argued that a French firm, Forest Line, had earlier received a Soviet contract for similar machinery, squeezing Toshiba Machine out, but the French firm denied it. Still, only a year later, a move to halt the $500 million sale to Japan of RCA's Aegis computerized antimissile defense system for warships was defeated in the Congress. The Pentagon, endorsing the sale for the Reagan administration, argued it was part and parcel of getting the Japanese Naval Self-Defense Forces to patrol the major East Asia sea routes, up to 1,000 miles off Japanese waters.

Does that mean that Japan, probably the second most important source of internationally transferable technology after the United States, will not become a source for Soviet "borrowing"? It probably depends on the larger issues in Japan's political life. Can the U.S.-Japan alliance that has existed since 1950 and that has permitted Japan to prosper under the American nuclear shield, with access to American markets and technology, be maintained in the new heavy seas of competition and misunderstanding that have overtaken both parties?

In terms of business and economics, Moscow has little to offer Japan. When a semiofficial Japanese business delegation returned home from an encounter with its Soviet counterparts in early September 1989 with not even a face-saving announcement, it seemed to confirm an observation made to me in the fall of 1988 in Moscow. I asked a prominent Soviet economist in one of Moscow's leading think tanks about the prospects of Japanese joint development in Siberia—one of the many scenarios that absorbed so much time and study beginning in the 1950s whenever the West's relations with Moscow improved. He answered me, glumly: "I believe that is a bus that has already left." The meaning was clear. Tokyo was no longer interested in investing in the huge, difficult, and somewhat dubious raw materials projects that await development in Siberia. A year later in Tokyo, I confirmed the possibility that what he had said was neither disinformation nor Soviet false modesty when I talked with Japanese businessmen.

Japanese traders have found the same problems as Western businessmen in trying to do business with the Russians. The Soviets have little to sell, and, without a convertible currency, there is little prospect of selling to them—although initially the market appears to be insatiable. Japan has consistently run a heavy surplus in its balance-of-trade with the Russians. Throughout the post-World War II period, however, there has been a dream of the vast Siberian raw materials trove for the Japanese industrial base. Some quarters in Japan had even seen it as an alternative to the longtime Japanese fascination with China.

The principal obstacle to any movement during the 1950s and 1960s was Washington's opposition. The line of the *Gaimushō*, Japan's foreign ministry, was that Siberian development would have to include U.S. political acquiescence and joint American capitalization. That never came. Meanwhile, all during the late 1950s, 1960s, and 1970s, the Japanese moved around the world securing aluminum in Indonesia; timber in the Philippines; iron ore in Brazil and India; oil and petrochemical chemicals in Iran, the Persian Gulf, Indonesia, Thailand, and Singapore; copper in Chile, and so forth. Enormous infrastructure investments and long-term trading arrangements were made, often with great difficulty.

Siberia no longer looks so attactive to a Japan that is moving away from being the major consumer of crude raw materials toward more sophisticated manufacturing and service industries. Like other Western businessmen, the Japanese complain of the difficulties of doing business in the Soviet Union; they have never had, for example, the kind of endless statistical information needed by the Japanese production research. There is Soviet bureaucratic inertia exemplified by a Japanese soap company's announcement, again in midsummer 1989, that it is completing its detergent plant in the Soviet Union after ten years of constuction.

All this is compounded, of course, by the political impasse between Tokyo and Moscow. Japan's line over the years has hardened in her demands for return of the Southern Kurile Islands, seized by the Soviets just after the Japanese surrender in World War II. These "Northern

Territories" appear to be the sine qua non for any peace treaty between the two countries, or for a successful visit by President Mikhail Gorbachev, should that prospect materialize after the 1990 parliamentary elections as has been tentatively scheduled. Subliminally, too, among older Japanese politicians and bureaucrats, is the memory of Soviet duplicity at the end of World War II, when the Japanese tried to use Moscow as a conduit for a negotiated peace with the United States. Instead, they found in August 1945 the Russians attacking on the China mainland and in Korea after the Nazi defeat in Europe.

Does that mean that the Japanese will not join any Western effort, should it get underway, to help *perestroika*, Gorbachev, and Moscow out of the present difficulties? Many younger Japanese, such as the head of one of the most prestigious research organizations I talked with in Tokyo, say, "We must help Gorbachev." A high Ministry of Finance official was slightly contemptuous of "Japanese politicians" for creating what he considers a blind alley with the nonnegotiable demand for the return of the Northern Territories. Some Japanese and Western military personnel believe that the tiny islands play such an important strategic role in Soviet submarine missile deployment, aimed at Japan and U.S. bases in Japan, that Moscow will never yield on their return.

Some Japanese industry association spokesmen, realistic about Soviet prospects but still hopeful, say that Japan could play another role. They believe that Japanese banks and trading companies might finance and organize Southeast Asian deals with the Soviets. Taiwan discussed these possibilities with an unofficial mission in the Soviet Union in 1989. Before the massacre at Tiananmen Square, some Tokyo sources even speculated that—with warmer Moscow-Peking relations—Japan might "help" the Chinese join Vietnamese and North Korean contract laborers in Siberia. And the Russians have talked of Japanese setting up "consumer industries" in the Maritime Territories to produce the goods that would help keep Russian labor in Siberia, and avoid the enormous and costly turnover that is one of the chief problems of Siberian development.

As the chief source of world liquidity, Japan was in 1989 already picking up, willy nilly, a third of Soviet syndicated borrowing in alliance with Western banks—up from less than half that amount only three or four years earlier. But that old dream of Japanese dynamism tied to Siberian resources seems as frozen today as the tundra in the Soviet's Far East.

CHAPTER 11

U.S. POLICY

What Is to Be Done?

If Gorbachev's predetermined strategy is primarily to shore up the system by obtaining a massive transfer of resources from the West, and if his tactics are shifting constantly as his actions thus far suggest, then there might be less danger of his losing power than some Western commentators have speculated. "Unlike the capricious and reckless Nikita Khrushchev, Mr. Gorbachev has loyal allies in the Politburo, military and security services."[1] In fact, it seems clear that the most concrete result inside the Soviet Union, perhaps the only tangible result, of Gorbachev's *perestroika* has been to consolidate his personal power—for example, through the anticorruption campaign, which has also been a pretext for eliminating opponents and installing loyalists, and by steering a "middle course" toward "reform" that permits opponents on the right and the left to be sloughed off. A typical example is the case of Boris Yeltsin, former Moscow Communist boss who lost his high-profile position when he began to criticize Gorbachev from the left, but who remains an important proof for some Western observers of *glasnost* and the new openness of Soviet society.

In the long process toward any kind of permanent political reform, it is still much too early to interpret the ultimate results of 1988 and 1989 elections for the new Soviet parliament and regional assemblies. Certainly, however, one result of the first elections appears to be that Gorbachev has

191

been given one more weapon to use against personal enemies within the Party. For example, when the Leningrad Party leaders were defeated, Gorbachev publicly interpreted it as a warning but not necessarily as the end of their tenure as Party leaders, which, he said, would depend on their future performance—effectively placing them at his mercy in the intra-Party struggles.

This ultrapragmatic (opportunistic) approach, which takes into account all the forces that maintain the leadership in power in the Soviet Union along with Gorbachev's capture of seats of power throughout the bureaucracy for his loyalists, may serve Gorbachev well. There is certainly a well-founded suspicion among seasoned observers of the Soviet political scene that Gorbachev's efforts to build a new structure of power of the Soviets—isolating his ideological opposition of the power of the Soviets—isolating his ideological opposition in the Party and his bureaucratic opposition in the government power structure—is simply another route toward the traditional Russian dictators' autocracy.

That possibility is certainly increased by the powers which Gorbachev has written into the new office of president which he has established. It is ludicrous to talk of it as "a Western-style presidency" as some Western news commentators have done. In the Soviet historical context, it could well become a new dictatorship—outside the Communist Party, or within a new Communist Party purged of its anti-Gorbachev forces.

In any case, if our basic assumption has been correct—that is, that an informed sector of the elite acknowledges that the Brezhnev trends were leading toward ultimate disaster—then even an immediate Gorbachev successor would not have any short-term option but to try to implement his predecessor's helter-skelter attempt to prop up the system.

It is impossible to minimize the seriousness of the difficulties through which the USSR is passing. Yet as the highest defector to leave the Soviet Union in the postwar period writes:

> But it has overcome worse troubles in the past. It has both tremendous natural wealth and vast human resources. In their ability to withstand centuries—not decades—of hardship and privation and yet persevere, the Soviet people are unmatched by any nation on earth, with the possible exception of the Chinese. The West, therefore, should not delude itself by focusing its attention exclusively on Soviet flaws and shortcomings. . . . The Soviet Union neither will reshape itself into a free-enterprise society nor will it soon disintegrate.[2]

There is, however, the real danger that Gorbachev, as proved by his changing goals and tactics in resolving the issues of the economy, may have underestimated what could be done with reform of the system—just as his predecessor Khrushchev did. "The indications are that Mr. Gorbachev, struggling to balance factions in the party, to mollify and disarm opponents, to consolidated his support, is in danger of becoming as vague, ambiguous, inconsistent and unpredictable as Khrushchev and Brezhnev before him," writes one British observer.[3] "Alas, the new gloom about Mr. Gorbachev goes further," wrote *The Economist*.[4]

> Russia's economic mess may be too deep to scramble out of. The sorts of reforms that are needed are unacceptable, if not yet to Mr. Gorbachev and his narrow circle of close supporters, then increasingly to the sceptical near-majority in the Communist Party's Politburo and a (probably overwhelming) majority in the party as a whole . . . the deeper he gets into reform, the stiffer the opposition and the greater chance that he will wake up one morning out of a job—or else throw up his hands and resign.

If such an awakening should come in a few years, or a few months, what would then be the real options that the Soviet leadership would face? And what would be the meaning for U.S. policymakers and other Western leaders?

There would appear to be two poles toward which Soviet policy would be attracted. The Soviet Union could abandon its position as a superpower and the cost of "the Soviet Empire," which one estimate puts at increasing from $13.6 to $21.8 billion in 1971 to between $35.9 billion and $46.5 billion in 1980 in constant 1981 dollars for an annual increase of 8.7 percent, radically curtail its military commitments, retreat to a defensive posture, and become "a developing country"—putting the welfare of its population first.[5] Or, utilizing its continuing enormous military power, the Soviets could turn toward their West European neighbors for "Tatar tribute" searching for a relationship that guaranteed them at least a substantial part of the growing benefits of West European prosperity and economic integration.

Despite speculation, mostly in the West, and hints from Soviet spokesmen, there is as yet no evidence that the Soviet military has suffered from any significant shift of resources toward the civilian sector under *perestroika*. Unconfirmed reports in the late summer of 1985, in fact, said that

Gorbachev had promised the military a 3 percent growth rate in defense expenditures.[6] Perhaps more important, investment in retooling and modernization of heavy industry that is critical to the military continues to have a high priority, as exemplified by the enormous export of ultrasophisticated machine tools from West Germany to the Soviet Union and to East Germany in late 1988 and 1989. This investment could, theoretically, be devoted to pursuing new civilian-oriented production. Given Soviet history, however, one must make the opposite assumption, especially because of the extreme difficulties of transferring theoretical productive capacity in the military-industrial sector to civilian production purposes in any economy. These difficulties are especially acute under Soviet conditions—and it is precisely that inflexibility that *perestroika* seeks to ameliorate.

The Central Intelligence Agency and the Defense Intelligence Agency jointly reported in the spring of 1989 that for a year and a half Gorbachev had been calling on the military-industrial complex to step up its support of the civilian sector. In March 1988 he gave it responsibility for reequipping most of the 260 plants of a disbanded civilian industry that manufactured equipment for food and consumer goods. In September the council of ministers in an effort to reinforce any such structural change passed a decree that permits defense industries to retain profits from over-plan production of consumer goods. Ryzhkov warned bureaucrats against not supporting the consumer goods program.

But the CIA-DIA report goes on to say:

> In the past, attempts to prompt the defense industry to support consumers goods and the modernization program have been relatively unsuccessful because the leadership did not apply substantial pressure and was unwilling to pare back military demands. Last year was no exception. We estimate that Soviet defense spending, as measured in constant 1982 rubles, grew by roughly three percent—in line with the growth rates of the past several years. Procurement of weapons systems was again a major contributor to growth. Expenditures on ship procurement rose sharply, caused primarily by an increase in spending on both strategic and general purpose submarines. Missile procurement—particularly for ICBMs and strategic surface-to-air missles—also displayed strong growth.[7]

Acknowledging Gorbachev's December 7, 1988 pledge to the United Nations for major unilateral armament cuts, the report says:

Some crucial points about Gorbachev's pledge remain unclear. Moscow has not . . . indicated whether the defense budget is to be reduced in real or only nominal terms—i.e., whether the cuts will be made after or before the budget is corrected for inflation. . . . In view of the problems inherent in measuring Soviet defense expenditures, moreover, confirming the implementation of the promised spending cuts will require substantial evidence of reductions in Soviet forces and the flow of weapons and equipment to them. . . . By our estimates, only about a third to a half of the 14.2 percent reduction can be accounted for by savings associated with withdrawing from Afghanistan, complying with the INF Treaty, and carrying out the reductions promised the U.N. . . . Taken together, these criticisms suggest that future Soviet RDT&E may be concentrated on a smaller number of projects, but that those projects funded may be more technologically ambitious than was typical in the past . . . cutbacks in military RDT&E would be especially difficult to confirm.[8]

Referring to the epidemic of new discoveries of Soviet espionage in the West in 1988 and 1989, a longtime student of Kremlin policy at the Hoover Institution says:

This picture of unremitting Soviet military production and concentration of developmental efforts may be correlated with the documented fact that, since the accession of power by Gorbachev in March 1985, the United States has uncovered more efforts than ever before by the Soviet Bloc agents to penetrate its defense activities. The correlation yields a (literally) dark side to the "Gorbachev detente"—one that should give US and Western policymakers pause in assessing the meaning and objectives of his *perestroika*, and its implications for Western security.[9]

Robert M. Gates, then deputy director of the CIA, reported in the fall of 1988:

Soviet research on new, exotic weapons continues apace. Virtually all of their principal strategic weapons will be replaced with new, more sophisticated systems by the mid-1990s, and a new strategic bomber is being added to their arsenal for the first time in decades. Their defenses against US weapons are being steadily improved, as are their capabilities for war-fighting. As the rate of growth of our defense budget declines again, theirs continues to grow.[10]

Although the Soviets have talked about adopting a defensive strategy since mid-1988, NATO commanders are not yet convinced. Nor, indeed, is it all that clear what "adopting a defensive strategy" would mean in the new era of fast-moving, fluid warfare. Warsaw Pact maneuvers, for example, conducted at least annually at Magdeburg in East Germany, only twenty-five miles from the West German border, could easily be the stage for a surprise attack on Western Europe. With its two to one superiority in tanks, tank production was still going full blast in the Soviet Union in the fall of 1989. Furthermore, there is at least the possibility that any Soviet military cutbacks will release resources to accomplish new tactics. Soviet military literature has reflected a concern with the possibility that the growing technology gap with the West would play a major role in any new war. Just as superior German mobility slaughtered Czar Nicholas II's huge armies in East Prussia in 1914, American and NATO electronics directed at huge Warsaw Pact formations might play a similar role in any new conflict. A reporter covering Warsaw Pact maneuvers in the fall of 1988 reported that such, at least, was the line coming from Warsaw Pact commanders there:

> Using technologies like satellites, remotely piloted vehicles, stealth, electronics and thermal imaging, targets ranging from tanks to command posts can be observed deep within the Warsaw Pact territory. New precision guided missiles, target-seeking warheads, and new types of air-delivered mines and fuel-air explosives can attack those targets before they are anywhere near the front. Soviet and other Warsaw Pact officers acknowledge those major advances in conventional military technology and refer to them as a "revolution in military affairs." They also maintain that the United States and its allies are increasing their lead in developing new systems and are concerned that they will continue to do so for the foreseeable future.[11]

The most persistent military critic of the Soviet economy is Marshal of the Soviet Union N. Ogarkov, former Chief of the General Staff of the Soviet Armed Forces and Commander of the Soviet Forces in the European Theater.

> One must also, no less responsibly and seriously, view the practical actions of the US and NATO which seek to implement their planned program of weapons development, of noticeable buildup of their military power. One cannot fail to see that, on the basis of a high scientific-technological potential,

they are rapidly creating a qualitatively new material base for the so-called conventional war, while at the same time constantly maintaining in a high state of readiness their strategic deterrence forces. These are by no means speculations. Many hundreds of billions of dollars are spent by them each year not for the fun of it. These are the real military programs of the US and NATO intended to gain qualitative military superiority in the 1990s already, which in itself cannot fail to pose a threat to the world.[12]

A noted Soviet military scholar, Leon Gouré, says:

Thus somewhat indirectly, Ogarkov is persisting in his earlier calls for a greater effort to provide the Soviet Armed Forces with advanced-technology weaponry. It is noteworthy that all the senior military leaders and service chiefs now seem united in portraying a persistent threat from the West and the need to provide the Soviet Armed Forces with "qualitatively" more advanced weapons and equipment to compensate for numerical reductions of Soviet military forces.[13]

Gorbachev's highly publicized unilateral arms reductions are, then, less than meets the eye. "A ten percent cut in manpower is substantial, but just what manpower will be cut, and will Soviet forces be weaker as a result?" writes James T. Hackett, a politicomilitary expert who has watched Soviet military affairs for decades.

Total Soviet military manpower is now about 5,100,000 so a cut of half a million would still leave the USSR with 4,600,000 men under arms, more than twice the US total of 2,163,000. . . . Another question is whether Moscow will merely remove and retire some of the excess, obsolete equipment it has in forward positions. Gorbachev promises that 5,300 will be the most advanced variety of Soviet tanks. [But even] after the reductions promised by Gorbachev, the USSR would still have an advantage of two to one in tanks, 2.5 to one in artillery, and three to one in combat aircraft. The reductions could actually be a trimming of Red Army fat, redundant forces and obsolete weapons, leaving a leaner and more modern force, better prepared than ever to engage in combat. This could be especially true if the Soviets continue to build and field modern weapons at a rate far exceeding that of the West. . . .[14]

Despite all of Gorbachev's rhetoric, that remains the case. U.S. intelligence indicates that in 1988, the Soviets produced 3,500 tanks (up 200 from 1986); the other Warsaw powers produced 700 tanks. The United States produced 775 tanks; other NATO powers produced 150. The Soviets produced 900 self-propelled artillery pieces; the United States produced 175. The Soviets produced 45 bombers; the United States produced 22. The Soviets produced 700 fighter planes; the United States produced 550. The Soviets produced 400 helicopters; the United States produced 375. The Soviets produced 700 fighter-bombers; the United States produced 525. The Soviets produced 9 submarines; the United States produced 5. The Soviets produced 9 major surface ships; the United States produced 3 only.

In other words, Gorbachev's reductions—to the extent that they actually exist, which is problematical—are quantitative reductions to make qualitative improvements. It has been a generally acknowledged Western intelligence appraisal for several decades that a general debate has gone on within Soviet military and paramilitary circles about the continued presence of antiquated and largely outdated weaponry in the Soviet arsenal. For example, a nuclear-powered submarine that ran aground accidentally in Swedish territorial waters in the early 1980s was considered by nuclear engineers, who had access to data about it, as a "floating atomic time bomb," because its power plant and navigational equipment were so outmoded. The enormous tank inventories in Central and Eastern Europe of the Soviet forces, containing many World War II vintage models, have become strategically outmoded because of the increasing U.S. and NATO use of computerized "smart" battlefield weaponry. Taking such equipment out of service in the USSR would be advantageous to strategic and tactical conventional superiority in the region.

Pentagon strategists deduce that there may be much less to the whole argument about whether, as announced, Moscow has now abandoned its earlier pose and withdrawn to defensive strategies in the European theater.

> At the operational and tactical levels, the Soviets foresee a fluid battlefield in which highly mobile forces on both sides will strive to seize the initiative. Complementary offensive and defensive operations and maneuvers will be required at different times and places on the battlefield. A greater emphasis on defensive operations is the Soviet military planners' response to what they see as the Soviet conditions of current and future warfare. This does not represent any abandonment of capabilities for offensive operations, but rather reflects the view that they will have to defend against enemy attacks as well as stage offensive operations of their own.[15]

Nor is it likely that Moscow's conventional forces' superiority in Europe at any time in the foreseeable future will not be vastly greater than that of the NATO allies given the geographical advantage of the Western Soviet position on the great Eurasian plain, especially after all boundaries of the Russian Empire were moved west after the end of World War II. It is theoretically conceivable, although presumably still highly unlikely, that those forces could be used for a lightning strike against Western Europe. There is evidence that the Soviets have worked for years at plans, including the use of special *spetsnatz* sabotage teams to take out West European communications and other strong points, for such a strategy against Western Europe.[16] Certainly realistic Western defensive strategists must keep in mind that alternative in a deepening Soviet economic and political crisis. Washington policymakers might face a terrible nexus in the future: There could be a need in Moscow to shift gears quickly, a force majeure withdrawal of United States forces in Western Europe because of the removal of their nuclear shield (which now compensates to some degree for conventional warfare inferiority), heightened pressure in the United States for a reduction of military expenditures, and mounting strategic obligations from growing Latin American tensions—all coupled with a general disillusionment by Washington and the U.S. public with its European allies and their policymakers. In that situation, the Soviet conventional strategic threat would grow even if it were held at current or lower levels of growth.

In a world, however, in which opinion polls of Western European populations, particularly the Germans, repeatedly show Gorbachev with more credibility than U.S. and other Western leaders, and those same polls show a euphoria in which they no longer believe in a Soviet threat to Western European freedom, peace, and prosperity, a more enlightened Soviet leadership (in its exacerbated economic and political crisis) appears to be flirting with more sophisticated and subtle strategems. The Soviets are attempting to use their own refurbished image as led by moderate and peaceful leadership, reformist and contrite, a weakened victim of long years of tyranny and economic mismanagement, to enlist Western sympathetic aid to "stabilize" conditions in Central Europe.

Flattered by the constant calls from Soviet economists and bureaucrat-managers for help, American academic and government economists have been trooping to Moscow since early 1988 to give advice to their Soviet counterparts. By the fall of 1989, the Bush administration's resolve to carefully evaluate the Gorbachev regime and Soviet policy changes had moved toward publicly accepting the Soviet leader in his professed role. Secretary of State James J. Baker in a formal speech to a foreign policy group in New York on October 16, 1989, reckoned that *"perestroika* is different from earlier, failed attempts at reforming the state Lenin founded and Stalin built. . . . It promises Soviet actions advantageous to our interests."[17] *The New York Times* reported that officials at the Commerce and the Labor departments had begun discussions with Soviet officials about how to collect data. Janet L. Norwood, the Commissioner for Labor Statistics, Robert P. Parker, associate director of the Commerce Department's Bureau of Economic Analysis, and Barbara Boyle Torrey, chief of the Census Bureau's Center for International Research, all said they had recent discussions with Soviet officials. Federal Reserve Chairman Alan Greenspan had already been in Moscow to give the Soviets his ultraconservative economic strategy (at the same time he was having a hard time selling it to the Treasury in Washington). And more than one Sovietologist, who only a few years ago was willing to accept the most outrageous propaganda about the strength of the Soviet economy, was now willing to accept the mea culpas and professions of weakness of their Soviet colleagues.

U.S. help is aimed not only at assisting the Soviets to solve their internal economic and strategic problems, but also at rearranging the chess pieces on the board of Central Europe in an attempt to relieve the growing strains on the Soviet empire and to provide a mechanism for enlisting Western aid that would not otherwise be forthcoming. Again, we need to put Gorbachev's initiatives in the framework of his Leninist professions, his willingness to take great gambles to save the system. An example is Gorbachev policy in the three Baltic states of Estonia, Latvia, and Lithuania. Gorbachev has permitted the local Communist organizations to go far to satisfy local nationalist tendencies. Needless to say, repression still would be a distinct option in the Baltic states with their fifteen million people—if Gorbachev did not have a more convoluted strategy. It must be remembered that poison gas, not tear gas, was used on demonstrators in Georgia in 1988. And although shrouded in mystery, with or without *glasnost,* according to Georgian dissidents, the orders to use it came from Moscow. Gorbachev has permitted the release of the long unpublished (in the Soviet Union) secret protocols of the Hitler-Stalin Pact in which the two dictators agreed on German and Soviet usurpation of the independence of the three countries and their eventual domination by the Soviet Union. Nevertheless, Moscow spokesmen have still argued that the three countries have incorporated legally into the USSR—with its constitutional provisions that any member republic may secede. When Gorbachev visited Lithuania in early 1990, his arguments against local nationalism were a strange and ambivalent mixture of threats and concessions.

The question for realistic observers outside the country is how Gorbachev has dared to flirt with this kind of nationalism, with the possibility that it would spill over into other parts of the Soviet Union, particularly the neighboring Ukraine which—especially in the western Ukraine—shares historical and cultural identities with these societies. Or as events in early 1990 in Azerbaijan proved, into Muslim Central Asia. For the thrust of Gorbachev's strategy in using the Baltic states, one can look at the historical analogy of the 1920s, which suggests that the economic ability of the region in the Soviet context has always been far disproportionate to its size and population. When Lenin reversed disastrous Soviet policy and turned toward private initiative during the brief New Economic Policy period after 1923, "the emphasis was on concessions to Western entrepreneurs," writes Antony C. Sutton in his monumental work on Western technology transfer to the Soviet Union. Sutton continues: "The penetration of early Soviet industry by Western companies and individuals was remarkable. Western technical directors, consulting engineers, and independent entrepreneurs were common in the Soviet Union. In retrospect, perhaps the most surprising examples were the directorships held by General Electric affiliates on the boards of Soviet electrical trusts."[18] Those concessions in many areas of industrial activity relied disproportionately on the then newly independent Baltic states, either as sites for activity, as in the case of railroad repair, or as intermediaries in transferring Western goods and technology to the Soviet Union.[19]

Another way of expressing the political configuration of this problem is that the Soviets have decided to make the Baltic states their equivalent of Deng Hsiao-peng's Chinese Communist "foreign economic zones." A number of Soviet missions have investigated these Chinese operations in their visits to China in the new atmosphere of relaxation of tensions between Moscow and Peking. In these zones, which are adjacent to ports of entry into China, socialist economic principles are abandoned in favor of foreign entrepreneurs using Chinese labor and partners. They operate much as they would in so-called offshore manufacturing free ports around the world. Foreign investors and their technology can be attracted by special operating conditions that include not only government tax holidays and other incentives, but also a work force that closely resembles those of Western Europe, Japan, and the United States.

To effect that same sort of development, however, Moscow must lend authenticity to the talk of decentralization, loosening of controls, and *glasnost*. That has to mean, at least to some extent, meeting the nationalist demands of the Baltic people. In a 1989 Soviet Estonian article on economic problems, the writers say:

> A competent opinion on this topic [*perestroika*] of the recently elected Secretary of the Estonian Communist party Central Committee, sociologist Mikk Titma: "For Western entrepreneurs, the Estonian market is of no interest. For them, entering the capacious all-union market with us as intermediaries is lucrative. The time is near when all nations in our country will become aware even more profoundly that only within the Union of Socialist Republics we represent a superpower with which it is profitable for other countries to do business." Mikk Titma comes out in favor of creating a free economic zone in Estonia.[20]

Obviously there are risks in such a strategy. There is the centuries-old rivalry among the great powers of Europe for the shores of the eastern Baltic, their strategic importance to Leningrad, which is, in many ways, the Soviet Union's most important urban center, the fervent and often explosive nationalism of the Baltic people and its effect on the other ethnic groups within the Soviet Union. That is the reason that Gorbachev and his supporters draw on "Leninist principles"—the necessity to take risks, even risks that threaten the system—rather than go forward with the Brezhnev trends and their certain condemnation to ultimate catastrophe.

Gorbachev's game in the Baltic states is to be extended into Central Europe, attempting to create a belt of states between Moscow and Western Europe where there are still strong Communist minorities and which still have strong economic and political ties to Moscow, but that also reflect degrees of "liberalization" and "accommodation." These new "reformed socialist" states would be used in "bait and switch" tactics to enlist Western economic aid and draw down NATO defenses against a still largely intact Soviet conventional military superiority.

There are extremely difficult political problems that are not even defined, much less resolved, in any attempt to reconstitute the concept of Central Europe. A Czech defector, a former diplomat serving in Washington, writes:

> Compared to his successful handling of overall Soviet foreign policy and the East European role in it, Gorbachev's approach to internal developments in Communist countries remains beset with contradictions. It is the weakest point in his "new thinking." Gorbachev's present approach to Eastern Europe runs in two directions: He wants to have the area under stable Communist and Soviet control; at the same time, he would like to transform it from a liability into an economic and political asset for the Soviets. He has yet to figure out how to meld these two contradictory elements into a coherent policy. . . . and this is the greatest shortcoming of the Soviet and East European Communists' policies in Eastern Europe—the current official philosophy of reform contains no solution to the core problem: The withering away of the old system of governance is already well in train. There is no foreseeable way to make the smooth transition to a better system, leaving Eastern Europe in a quite unpredictable situation."[21]

In my conversations with Soviet academics and think-tank specialists in Moscow in May 1988, I found it difficult to get credible answers to any questions regarding economic relations among the members of the Communist Bloc. The deputy head of the Council for the Study of the Socialist World System, the principle think tank dealing with Bloc problems, for example, maintained that there was convertibility among Bloc trading partners until I protested, and he admitted that it was not true. Among all my conversations at that time, these were the most confused and showed the least evidence of a solid political "line."

Soviet leaders, academicians, and think-tank specialists, who have spoken to other Western visitors to Moscow, appear to underestimate the problem created in Central and Eastern Europe by the Gorbachev change of pace. The virtual collapse of the East German Communist regime in the fall of 1989 may well have gone faster and in a direction that Gorbachev did not anticipate when he gave the green light for Honnecker's ouster.

The lack of understanding permeates Soviet intellectual circles. In May 1989, for example, at a meeting of seventy writers from the Soviet Union, Central Europe, Western Europe, and North America—including the Nobel Laureate Czeslaw Milosz and the American left-wing commentator

Susan Sontag—there was an emotional outburst when Hungarian Gyorgy Konrad contended that Soviet writers "have to confront yourselves with the role of your country in a part of the world that doesn't want your presence in tanks but as tourists. . . . The first Soviet writer to respond was Alev Anninskii, a journalist, critic and writer, who said, 'Russian tanks came to liberate, so let's look at the causes before we talk about the effects.' In response, Tatiana Tolstaya, a Soviet writer and dissident and a descendant of Leo Tolstoy, said she found Mr. Konrad's proposition astounding. 'When am I going to take *my* tanks out of Eastern Europe,' she said. She denied that such a separateness existed."[22]

Moscow is now seeking to replace terror regimes formed by the Soviet military, the NKVD, and local Communist party political cadre (themselves remnants of a movement caught in the love affair and breakup between Stalin and Hitler) put together in the post-World War II chaos. The Kremlin's strategy is to exercise a sophisticated, subtle bureaucratic control by the International Commission of the Communist Party of the USSR over the affairs of Central Europe by manipulating local Communists within the more pluralistic regimes that are coming into existence. Academicians have told these Western visitors that it is Moscow policy to deliberately refuse to define precisely the meaning of "socialism", which Moscow earlier had said must remain as the hallmark of these regimes, or to draw distinct limits to Russian intervention (the Brezhnev Doctrine). Later Soviet spokesmen made formal statements against any direct Moscow intervention. The role of the Party, which Gorbachev has said is still sacrosanct in the Soviet Union itself, can be different in the satellites, which could have a multiparty system, they said. And conversations by Westerners with members of the Soviet Politburo, more ethnically Russian than at any time in the history of the regime, suggest a vast ignorance of the mood in the Eastern and Central European states, and a lack of understanding reinforced by old pan-Slavic attitudes toward the Poles, the Czechoslovaks, and the Balts as deeply Russian nationalist as they were before the revolution.[23] Furthermore, most of the Central European states emerge from their forty-five-year cocoon of Communism with most of their pre-1939 problems still unresolved, and are further demoralized because their traditional institutions have been eroded by Communist totalitarianism.

Nevertheless, it already is evident that any Soviet initiative to create a belt of semiautonomous, "reformed" states on her Western border would be met with considerable enthusiasm in Western circles. The so-called Sonenfeld Doctrine of the Nixon administration years, a proposed tacit agreement to permit Moscow to stabilize Central and Eastern Europe beyond Soviet borders with the consent of the West, is emerging in a new form. It is now to consist of a "condominium," a stability under the tacit military dominance of Moscow and the economic input—that is, investment and technological transfer—from the West.

". . . [A] posture of delayed and uncoordinated reaction to Soviet initiatives would enable the Kremlin to define the East-West agenda and serve primarily Soviet interests," states a draft report to the Trilateral Commission from Valery Giscard d'Estaing, Yasuhiro Nakasone, and Henry A. Kissinger.[24] The report goes on to say:

> Mr. Gorbachev's phrase, "a common European House," ignores the fundamental differences between Western Europe, Eastern Europe, and the Soviet Union. . . . The countries of Central and Eastern Europe have a special character. . . . For these countries, it is therefore important to devise a category of association with the European Community based on Article 238 of the Treaty of Rome. This kind of association should be regarded as a new type of relationship adapted to the special circumstances of the countries concerned.

In a parallel proposal made directly to the Bush review of foreign policy strategies, Kissinger's thoughts have been presented as ". . . [T]he basic concept of the new arrangement would be for Moscow to loosen its hold over the region in exchange for a pledge by the United States and its Western allies not to exploit the new environment in a way that threatens the Soviet Union."[25] A "leak" that such a policy was being considered by the Bush administration in its review of policy toward the Soviet Union was met shortly afterward by a statement from the newly installed Hungarian Communist Party chief on his return from an interview with Gorbachev in Moscow to the effect that "Analyzing the historical lessons of 1956 [the invasion of Hungary by Soviet troops] and 1968 [the invasion of Czechoslovakia] Mikhail Gorbachev said that there must be maximum guarantees today that outside force should not be used to resolve the internal affairs of socialist countries."[26]

Kissinger has said:

. . . The Soviet Union—if it is realistic—is condemned by circumstances to seek a realistic accommodation, provided always that the West is able to give a concrete content to its concept of peace through a series of precise political arrangements. Were foreign policy a science and not an art, this is what would happen. But it remains to be seen whether Americans can be brought to see foreign policy in terms of equilibrium rather than as a struggle between good and evil, or whether Russia can abandon its historical expansionism.[27]

As Kissinger pointed out in another context, however, there is a crisis of confidence in U.S. leadership of the Western alliance, encouraged by an overly optimistic view of Soviet intentions in Western Europe and in some American circles. It is a crisis, he says, which he anticipated fifteen years ago but which could not be dealt with then because of European fear of American domination and what he calls "tactical mistakes on my part."[28] Can it be solved, however, by an attempt at a "deal" on Central Europe with the Russians—an arrangement that might turn as sour as many other post-World War II attempts at establishing spheres of influence with the Soviets—or by Western policies that attempt to reward the Soviet "good guys" as opposed to the Soviet "bad guys"?

Joseph Churba writes that:

The failure to apprehend the profoundly alien and aggressively violent nature of Soviet and Russian political culture has prevented the United States from achieving the intellectual resolve to develop and commit to a long-term, far-reaching strategy against the USSR. The Soviets appreciate how American ambivalence about the nature of the Soviet character can be used as a weapon against the United States. Since 1918, the Kremlin has periodically floated reports about closet moderates besieged by radicals within the Soviet leadership; of radical wings of the Communist Party waxing in power because moderates were not given the ammunition by the West to justify a more accommodating policy; of new leaders, most recently Yuri Andropov and Gorbachev, who were closet "liberals" and admirers of Western literature and art; and of current leaders whose recent appreciation of Western liberalism, efficiency, or capitalist-style incentives needs only a few concessions to become a flame that would sweep away the debris of the Communist bureaucracy. What is astonishing is not that after seventy years credulous American officials and experts swallow such lines and adjust America's policies accordingly. This sort of behavior becomes rampant in times of superpower rapprochement, when the political fortunes of Western national leaders become inextricably linked with the "success" or "failure" of openings to the USSR . . . The Soviets are aware of this, of course, and they used such rumors to gain tactical and strategic advantages, including the paralysis of an American consensus and, for themselves, room and time to maneuver.[29]

If we now deal with the crisis that Kissinger identified as long as a decade ago through an agreement on a plan for stabilizing Central Europe (short of at least a complete Soviet military withdrawal, for their mere geographical proximity gives the Russians an enormous advantage), it may simply be another version of Yalta, which again abandons the interests of the Central Europeans in favor of promises by Moscow to behave differently. Furthermore, it sets Germany adrift in her old dreams of aggrandizement in Middle Europe, which has led to so much bloodshed and destruction in Europe, even in our century. Surely nothing Gorbachev has so far accomplished—as distinguished from what he and his supporters have said they want to do—yet invites that kind of confidence and commitment, given the long Soviet record of broken promises, broken treaties, and disinformation.

NOTES

CHAPTER 1

1. See Lloyd C. Gardner, *A Covenant with Power: American and World Order from Wilson to Reagan* (New York. Oxford University Press, 1984); H. G. Wells, *Marxism and Liberty, an Interview* (New York: International Publishing Co., Inc., 1935); Eugene Lyons, *The Red Decade: The Stalinist Penetration of America* (New York: Bobbs-Merrill Co., 1941); Robert A. Nisbit, *Roosevelt and Stalin* (Regenery Gateway, 1988); "NATO—The Next Thirty Years," [original] remarks by the Honorable Henry A. Kissinger, Palais d'Egmont, Brussels, Belgium, September 1, 1979.

2. Take for instance an interview from the once hack Soviet organ *Argumenty I Fakty* (No. 11, March 18–24, 1989) with S. Bovin, political commentator with *Izvestia*, entitled "The Basis of the Program is Life Experience": ". . . I meet with increasing frequency people who already in kindergarten unmasked Stalin's 'personality cult' and revealed Khrushchev's 'voluntarism' when still in first grade at school, and then Brezhnev's and Chernenko's labels when they were in senior grades. Such people, of course, decisively refuse to regard themselves as responsible for the state of the society in which they lived and still do live."

3. George F. Kennan, "After the Cold War", *New York Times Sunday Magazine*, February 5, 1989.

> Such differences as remain (between the Soviet Union and the United States) are not such that preclude a normal relationship, particularly when leadership on the Russian side is in the hands of a man such as Gorbachev. . . . What could we, from our side, do to promote the normalization of this relationship (Soviet-U.S.) and to shape its future in a manner commensurate with its positive possibilities? It would seem obvious, to this writer at least, that our first concern should be to remove, insofar as it lies within our power to do so, those features of American policy and practice that have their

origins and their continuing rationale in outdated cold war assumptions and lack serious current justification.

4. "Giving Gorbachev a Hand," *Washington Post,* December 29, 1988.

The real question is whether the Western world is willing to extend a helpful hand in a timely way to Gorbachev in the hope that he means what he says on disarmament and can stay in power. . . . Let's face it: for the West to respond affirmatively to Gorbachev's initiative is a gamble. He might take the aid he seeks and not deliver on his promises. Or he might want to deliver on his promises and be frustrated by the Red Army generals. Or he might take the help offered by the West, and, as Pepsico's Donald Kendall has suggested, still face Herculean problems that will take two generations to solve.

5. Gorbachev has specifically rejected this term, arguing "It may seem that our current *perestroika* could be called a 'revolution from above'. True, the *perestroika* drive started on the Communist Party's initiative, and the Party leads it. . . . [I]t is a distinctive feature and strength of *perestroika* that it is simultaneously a revolution 'from above' and 'from below'." But earlier: ". . . the restructuring effort started with the Party and its leadership. We began at the top of the pyramid and went down to its base, as it were." Gorbachev, *Perestroika: New Thinking for Our Country and the World,* rev. ed. (New York: Harper & Row, 1988).

6. "How Should America Respond to Gorbachev's Challenge? A Report of the Task Force on Soviet New Thinking," [monograph], Co-chairmen, Joseph S. Nye, Jr., Whitney MacMillan (New York: Institute for East-West Security Studies, 1987).

7. See "U.S.-Soviet Détente: The Collision of Hope and Experience," Seymour Weiss, *Strategic Review,* Winter 1988–89, for an insightful comparison of present events to the Khrushchev period. A writer for Radio Free Europe/Radio Liberty points out that an article defending the good name of the KGB and its personnel in a 1989 issue of the Soviet weekly *Nedelya* "is peculiarly reminiscent of one published by the same weekly nearly 27 years earlier, in 1962, some six years after Nikita Khrushchev's secret speech on Stalin's crimes . . . Both these *Nedelya* articles appeared during periods of political liberalization and thus were designed to tailor the KGB's image to the changing times." "Personnel Changes in KGB as Public Relations Campaign Continues," *Report on the USSR* I, no. 10 (March 1989).

8. John J. Dziak, *Chekisty: A History of the KGB* (Lexington, Mass.: Lexington Books, 1988).

9. I refer here, of course, to Solzhenitsyn's *Gulag Archipelago* (New York: Harper & Row, 1985), a detailed account of the other world within the Soviet Union—that vast network of prisons, torture chambers, and points of internal exile where millions have been condemned to slow deaths or a prison life since the regime was founded. But, on second thought, perhaps what is much more

applicable here is that final anecdote from what is probably Solzhenitsyn's best novel, *The First Circle* (London: Collins & Harvill Press, 1968). There, as the prisoners are being carted away from a sophisticated prison, where their scientific and engineering talents are being used under prison conditions to further the regime, the van marked "meat" in which they are being carried toward new prison horrors is sighted by a Moscow correspondent for the Paris newspaper *Liberation* (for most of the post-World War II a faithful Stalinist sheet). "He remembered having seen several trucks like this today in various parts of Moscow. Taking out his notebook he wrote with his dark red fountain pen: 'Now and again on the streets of Moscow, you meet food delivery vans, clean, well-designed and hygienic. One must admit that the city's food supplies are admirably well organized.' "

10. "Why You'll Never Have Fun in Russian," excerpts from a conversation between Richard Lourie and Aleksei Mikhalev, *New York Times Book Review*, June 18, 1989.

11. Walter Laqueur, *"Glasnost* & Its Limits," *Commentary* (July 1988).

12. "Représentation de l'Occident et guerre psychologique dans les media soviétiques", Françoise Thom, *L'astrolabe*, No. 89–1988–II, l'Association pour la Russie Libre, Paris, 1988.

13. *Sovietskaia Kultura,* Dec. 16, 1986, as quoted by Thom.

14. Thom, "Représentation de l'Occident."

15. Ibid.

16. David Remmick, "Soviet Journal Attacks Party: Monthly Publishes Call for Accountability," *Washington Post,* February 9, 1989.

17. William Pearl, "Gorbachev's Legal Reformer is Anything But," *Wall Street Journal,* June 30, 1988.

18. Cathy Young, "Let's Not Praise Glasnost, Just Now: New Laws Could Signal a Crackdown on Dissent," *New York Times,* May 14, 1989.

19. Don Ritter, "Cloud Over Glasnost," *Washington Post,* May 26, 1989.

20. William D. Zabel, *"Perestroika* Bypasses the Legal System," *Wall Street Journal,* February 10, 1989.

21. Ken Ringle, "From Russia, With Law: For 17 Soviets, a Taste of Freedom in a Unique Internship Program," *Washington Post,* October 11, 1989.

22. Viktor Suvorov, *Soviet Military Intelligence* (London: Hamish Hamilton, 1984).

23. Quoted from *Izvestia,* Bill Keller, "Soviet Aid Admits Maps Were Faked for 50 Years," *New York Times,* September 3, 1988.

24. Bill Keller, "Soviet Libraries Purge Books Giving Pre-Gorbachev Views," *New York Times,* August 17, 1989.

25. *Disinformation: Soviet Active Measures and Disinformation Forecast,* no. 13 (Fall 1989).

26. Anne Williamson, "Leisure and Arts: Tatyana Tolstaya: A Soviet Author Speaks Out, Loud," *Wall Street Journal,* May 11, 1989.

27. Walter Laqueur, "Party Favors," a review of *The Long Road to Freedom: Russia and Glasnost* in *The New Republic*, June 19, 1989.

28. Andrei Navrozov, "Letter from Albion: Prison-Pencil, Supermarket Crayon," *Chronicles* (February 1989).

29. Sergei Grigoriants and Ludmilla Thorne, "In Conversation with Sergeï Grigoriants," *Freedom At Issue* (September-October 1989).

30. Walter Laqueur, "Glasnost and its Limits," *Commentary* (July 1988).

31. Vasilii Seliunin and Grigorii Khanin, "Cunning Figures," *Novy Mir*, no. 2 (February 1987).

32. Ibid.

33. See what was then considered a highly unorthodox view: "Soviet Dependence on Foreign Trade," Professor Vladimir Treml, External Relations of CEMA Countries, *The NATO Colloquium*, Brussels, 1983.

34. "Djilas on Gorbachov," *Encounter* (November-December 1988).

35. The absurdity of this kind of "science fiction" was only partly facetiously alluded to by *The Economist* (June 25, 1988) of London:

> Since central planning has allowed the Soviet Union only one factory that makes condoms . . . Poorer working women in Russia's unequal society probably average between four and six abortions in their lives. All of these unnecessary abortions are then counted as part of doctors' gross production, and therefore swell Russia's reported national income. Most Western attempts to translate fictitious Communist growth figures into real ones, including one by America's Central Intelligence Agency, have been far too kind to the Communists. That has long been known by readers of the mainly mimeographed papers from some fine economists still working in Hungary and Poland. *Glasnost* has now permitted the publication in English of a book by Warsaw's brave Professor Jan Winiecki called *The Distorted World of Soviet-type Economies*, Routledge and Kegan Paul, London, 1988, and any scholarly discussions of planned economies should henceforth start from it.[36]

36. For a compendium of how financial transfers to the East have been ignored, even in some U.S. official reporting, see Judy Shelton's *The Coming Soviet Crash: Gorbachev's Desperate Pursuit of Credit in Western Financial Markets* (New York: The Free Press, 1989).

> Estimates of total Soviet indebtedness to the West were roughly doubled overnight in May 1984. . . . the joint report issued by the OECD and the Bank for International Settlements (BIS) for loans outstanding as of the end of June 1983 showed that the Soviet Union ranked as the third largest hard-currency debtor in the world, excluding the 16 industrial countries plus Liechtenstein who report to the OECD. . . . The most astonishing aspect of the report, though, was that the Soviet Union ranked first in the world in loans subsidized by Western governments.

37. *Western Technology and Soviet Economic Development*, 3 vols. (Stanford, Calif.: Hoover Institution Press, 1968, 1971, 1973).

38. Anthony Read and David Fisher, *The Deadly Embrace: Hitler, Stalin and the Nazi-Soviet Pact, 1939–1941* (New York: Norton, 1988).

39. The invasion of Afghanistan was accomplished in part with the use of trucks built at the famous Kama River Truck Factory, a dramatic instance of U.S.-German technological transfer to the Soviets during the détente period.

40. An example: "Upon inspection, industry will not have produced one-fourth of the scheduled additions [to the current five-year plan] in physical reality. This is not an assumption. For example, in the last Five Year Plan, the planned increase in coal production was 54–56 million tons; the actual increase constituted 10 million tons. It was anticipated that the production of rolled ferrous metal would increase 14–17 million tons in practice; the addition was 5 million tons." Vasilii Seliunin and Grigorii Khanin, "Cunning Figures," *Novy Mir* no. 2 (February 1987).

41. Anders Aslund, "How Small is the Soviet National Income?" (Stanford University: Hoover-Rand Conference on the Defense Sector in the Soviet Economy, March 1988).

CHAPTER 2

1. See his monumental work, *Oriental Despotism: A Comparative Study of Total Power,* Karl-August Wittfogel, (New Haven, Conn.: Yale University Press, 1951).

2. "Solzhenitsyn: The Russian Liberal," Mikhail S. Bernstam, *Chronicles* (October 1988).

3. "The National Liberation of Russia," David Moro, *Policy Review* (Winter 1988).

4. "Letters: Moro's Misconceptions," *Policy Review* (Summer 1988).

5. Leon Trotsky, *The History of the Russian Revolution* (Ann Arbor, Mich.: University of Michigan Press, 1957).

The not-infrequent disputes among Russian histories of the newest school as to how far Russia was ripe for present-day imperialist policies often fall into mere scholasticism, because they look upon Russia in the international arena as isolated, as an independent factor, whereas she was but one link in a system. India participated in the [World] war [I] both essentially and formally as a colony of England. The participation of China, though in a formal sense "voluntary," was in reality the interference of a slave in the fight of his masters. The participation of Russia falls somewhere halfway between the participation of France and that of China. Russia paid in this way for her right to be an ally of advanced countries, to import capital and pay interest on it—that is, essentially, for her right to be a privileged colony of her allies—but at the same time for her right to oppress and rob Turkey, Persia, Galicia, and in general the countries weaker and more backward than herself. The twofold imperialism of the Russian bourgeoisie had basically the character of an agency for other mightier world powers.

6. Constantine FitzGibbon, "Introduction", Werner Keller, *East Minus West = Zero: Russia's Debt to the West* (New York: G. P. Putnam's Sons, 1961).

7. See Martin Gilbert, *Atlas of Russian History* (New York: Dorset Press,

Marboro Books Corp., 1972), which presents in brief pictocartographic form a mind-boggling array of these migrations.

8. Nicolas V. Riasanovsky, *A History of Russia,* 4th ed. rev. (New York: Oxford University Press, Inc., 1984).

9. Andrezej Walicki, *A History of Russian Thought: From the Enlightenment to Marxism* (Stanford, Calif.: Stanford University Press, 1973).

10. Ibid.

11. Ibid.

12. "Peter the Great not a Revolutionary Innovator," Sergei F. Platonov from *Leksii po Russkoi Istorii (Lectures on Russian History),* I. Blinmov, ed. (St. Petersburg, 1904), translated by Mirra Ginsburg. Mark Raeff, ed., *Plans for Political Reform in Imperial Russia, 1730–1905* (Englewood, N.J.: Prentice-Hall, 1960).

13. B. H. Sumner, "Peter the Great," *History* 32 (March 1947).

14. M. N. Pokrovsky, "The Reforms of Peter," in *History of Russia: From the Earliest Times to the Rise of Commercial Capitalism,* trans. and ed. J. D. Clarkson and M. R. Griffiths, 2nd ed. (Bloomington, Ind.: University Prints and Reprints, 1966).

15. Ibid.

16. Ibid.

17. Theodore H. von Laue, "The State and the Economy," *Russian Economic Development from Peter to Stalin,* ed. William L. Blackwell (New York: Columbia University Press, 1963).

18. Ibid.

19. Ibid.

20. Ibid.

21. Theodore H. von Laue, *Sergei Witte and the Industrialization of Russia* (New York: Columbia University Press, 1963).

22. Ibid.

23. Ibid.

CHAPTER 3

1. Quoted in Keller, *East Minus West = Zero.*

2. See Arthur Koestler and others, *The God that Failed,* ed. Richard H. S. Crossman (New York: Harper, 1949).

3. George F. Kennan, *Russia, the Atom and the West* (New York: Harper, 1949).

4. E. H. Carr, *The Bolshevik Revolution, 1917–23,* vol. II (New York: Macmillan, 1951–53).

5. The concept was explored and developed by the German, and later Ameri-

can, anti-Stalinist Marxist philosopher-historian, Karl-August Wittfogel, in his *Oriental Despotism.*

6. Ypsilon, *Pattern for World Revolution* (New York: Ziff-Davis Publishing Co., 1947).

7. Keller, *East Minus West = Zero.*

8. The Hoover Institution on War, Revolution and Peace, *Western Technology and Soviet Economic Development,* 3 vols. (Stanford, Calif.: Hoover Press Publications, 1968).

9. Ibid.

10. Quoted in Richard B. Day, *Leon Trotsky and the Politics of Economic Isolation* (Cambridge: Cambridge University Press, 1973).

11. Ibid.

12. Mikhail Heller and Aleksandr M. Nekrich, *Utopia in Power* (New York: Summit Books, rev. 1985).

13. "Les Soviets et les concessions aux étrangers," *Revue de Deux Monde* 35, 1926, quoted in Sutton.

14. Mikhail Heller and Aleksandr M. Nekrich, *Utopia in Power.*

15. A. Shoikhet, "The Heart of Soviet Darkness: An Abomination of Desolation," *Glasnost* (September–October 1989).

CHAPTER 4

1. Robert C. Tucker, *Stalin as Revolutionary, 1879–1929* (New York: W. W. Norton & Co., 1973).

2. David Yul'yevich Dallin, *Soviet Espionage* (New Haven: Yale University Press, 1944).

3. Keller, *East Minus West = Zero.*

4. Alec Nove, *An Economic History of the U.S.S.R.* (New York: Penguin Books, 1982).

5. J. P. Nettl, *The Eastern Zone and Soviet Policy in Germany* (London: Oxford University Press, 1951).

6. Keller, *East Minus West = Zero.*

7. Ibid.

8. Nove, *An Economic History of the U.S.S.R.*

9. Quoted in Jan Winiecki, *The Distorted World of Soviet-Type Economies* (London: Routledge, 1988).

10. Ibid.

11. I rely here on an unpublished paper, Karel Kaplan and Petr Pribik, "Czechoslovakia and the Marshall Plan." Kaplan was a junior official in the Czechoslovak planning organization.

12. Ibid.

13. Ibid.

14. Winiecki, *The Distorted World of Soviet-Type Economies*.

15. Petre Nicolae, *CEMA in Theory and Practice* (Falls Church, Va.: Delphic Associates, Inc., 1984).

CHAPTER 5

1. I have appropriated this title from a French author, André Fontaine, whose *Un seul lit pour deux rêves: histoire de la "détente", 1962–81* (Paris: Fayard, 1981), is a very good explanation of the scope of the Western disenchantment with the Nixon-Kissinger experiment.

2. Eric Laurent, *La Corde pour les Pendre* (Paris: Librarie Artheme Fayard, 1985).

3. I met Nixon briefly with a group of reporters while he was in transit at the Bangkok airport on one of his whirlwind tours of Asia during this period while I was a foreign correspondent in the area for a major publication. Several local reporters and I had a somewhat informal press conference with him, and were impressed with his knowledge of Southeast Asia affairs, especially as compared with so many political birds of passage whom we had seen in the area. I might add that none of us was disposed to see Nixon in this light, so we were pleasantly surprised.

4. A phrase very current in CIA circles at the time as used in several conversations with me in Southeast Asia during the period with station chiefs in the area.

5. Mike Bowker and Phil Williams, *Superpower Détente: A Reappraisal* (London: The Royal Institute of International Affairs, Beverly Hills: Sage Publications, 1988).

6. Herbert S. Levine, "Industry," in *Prospects for Soviet Society,* ed. Allen Kassof (New York: Frederick A. Praeger, 1968).

7. Bowker and Williams, *Superpower Détente: A Reappraisal*.

8. "Détente: an evaluation," article reprinted for the use of the Subcommittee on Arms Control of the Committee on Armed Services, U.S. Senate (Washington, D.C.: Government Printing Office, 1974).

9. Aleksandr Solzhenitsyn, speech to the AFL-CIO, New York, 1975, quoted in *Peace Endangered: The reality of Détente,* R. J. Rummel (Beverly Hills: Sage Publications, 1976).

10. Lester A. Sobel, ed., *Kissinger & Détente* (New York: Facts on File, Inc., 1975).

11. Robert J. Pranger, ed., *Détente and Defense: A Reader* (Washington, D.C.: American Enterprise Institute for Public Policy Research, 1976).

12. Gregory Grossman, "The Economics of Détente and American Foreign Policy," in *Defending America,* Introduction by James R. Schlesinger (New York: Basic Books, San Francisco: The Institute for Contemporary Studies, 1977).

13. Ibid.

14. Samuel Pisar, "Trade, the Heart of East-West Détente," *New York Times,* quoted in Morris Brafman and David Schimel, *Trade for Freedom: Détente, Trade and Soviet Jews* (New York: Shengold Publishers, Inc., 1975).

15. Robert Conquest, "A New Russia? A New World?" *Foreign Affairs* (April 1975).

16. *Détente, National Security, and Multinational Corporations,* foreword by Gen. Andrew J. Goodpaster, U.S. Army War College, Thomas Y. Crowell Co., 1976.

17. G. Warren Nutter, "Kissinger's Grand Design," in *Détente and Defense: A Reader,* ed. Robert J. Pranger (Washington, D.C.: American Enterprise Institute for Public Policy Research, 1976).

18. Eric Laurent, *La Corde pour les Pendre.*

19. John Lloyd, "Showpiece car plant falls victim to glasnost," *Financial Times,* October 10, 1988.

CHAPTER 6

1. Robert C. Tucker, *Stalin as Revolutionary, 1879–1929: A Study in History and Personality* (New York: W. W. Norton & Co., 1973).

2. Alexander Barmine, *One Who Survived: The Life Story of a Russian under the Soviets* (New York: G. P. Putnam, 1945).

3. Robert C. Tucker, *Stalin as Revolutionary.*

4. Vasilii Seliunin and Grigorii Khanin, "Cunning Figures," *Novy Mir,* no. 2 (February 1987).

5. Nove, *An Economic History of the U.S.S.R.*

6. Jan Winiecki, *The Distorted World of Soviet-Type Economies* (Pittsburgh, Pa.: University of Pittsburgh Press, 1989).

7. Seliunin and Khanin, "Cunning Figures."

8. Winiecki, *The Distorted World of Soviet-Type Economies.*

9. Ibid.

10. Ibid.

11. Igor Birman, *Personal Consumption in the USSR and the USA* (New York: St. Martin's Press, 1989).

12. Ibid.

13. Mikhail S. Bernstam, "Anatomy of the Soviet Reform," *Gobal Affairs* (Spring 1988).

14. Sergei Freidzoin, *Patterns of Soviet Economic Decision-Making: An Inside View of the 1965 Reform* (Falls Church, Va.: Delphic Associates, Inc., 1987).

15. Ibid.

CHAPTER 7

1. Mikhail Gorbachev, *Perestroika: New Thinking for Our Country and the World* (New York: Harper & Row, Perennial Library Edition, 1988).

2. Vladimir Solovyov and Elena Klepilova, *Behind the High Kremlin Walls* (New York: Dodd, Mead & Co., 1986).

3. Andrew A. Michta, *An Émigré Reports: Fridrikh Neznansky on Mikhail Gorbachev, 1950–1958* (Falls Church, Va.: Delphic Associates, Inc., 1985).

4. Ibid.

5. Ibid.

6. Thomas G. Butson, *Gorbachev: A Biography* (New York: Stein and Day, 1986).

7. "In the 1970s and 1980s, the center of the prerogative state moved from the party to the defense committee, on which the party had a representative, but which it did not control. A similar process has been taking place throughout the Soviet empire. The Soviet authorities created a body to manage crises in Eastern Europe two years after the invasion of Czechoslovakia in 1968 (they realized that the invasion had been a nervous and unsound reaction to the Prague Spring). Now this body has been transformed into a center for coordinating the current changes in Poland, Hungary, and the Soviet Union. In my opinion, this center— which is close to the KGB and the globalists, the party faction that views the current situation in the context of the world-wide interests of the Soviet empire— has concluded that the Soviet Union must reverse the decisions that were made in the 1920s if it is to retain its empire. Back then, it was held that the state ownership of the means of production would prevent foreign capital from penetrating the country; by the same token, allowing the market to regulate the economy would turn the Soviet Union into a colony of the capitalist countries. Now the decision to cut the Soviet economy off from the capitalist world is considered a mistake: as a result, the communist countries are on the periphery, while capitalism dominates the world. Moreover, the communist countries are dependent on the capitalist world, but in a negative sense—that is, the communist countries pay dearly for an economic system that isn't regulated by the market, yet they don't receive the benefits that normally accrue to colonies. Foreign capital penetrates dependent countries in the Third World, but it makes the economies of

these countries more rational. That's a benefit. It seems to me that the imperial staff of the socialist bloc now believes it necessary to move from a negative situation to something I would call dependent development."

Q. "When you say 'staff' are you speaking literally?"
A. "Yes, in connection with the defense committee."

Q. "What evidence is there that such a staff exists?"
A. "The changes taking place in the socialist bloc are coordinated—both chronologically and conceptually—to a significant degree. The reform-oriented elites in intelligence, state security, and defense are similar to each other.

"Everything is centered in the defense committees. These committees undoubtedly include people who are assigned to manage the permanent crisis besetting the communist countries. An analogous crisis staff, I'd imagine, is on permanent duty in Moscow so that hasty actions aren't undertaken like the invasion of Czechoslovakia. That decision was made on the basis of information supplied by the Soviet ambassador, who wanted to provoke an invasion because he failed to take control (conceptually, it seems, as well as politically) of the course of events, a career-threatening situation for him."

Q. "Do you think the current changes in the socialist bloc were planned?"
A. "I believe they were, although their realization is to a large degree a spontaneous process. The 'revolution from above' is supposed to do away with collective property in certain sectors of the economy—to the extent necessary, that is, to allow Western technology and capital to flow in so that dependent development can begin. . . ."

Excerpts from an interview in *Tygodnik Solidarnose,* October 27, 1989, entitled "Fragment wiekszag oalosoi," with Jadwiga Staniszkie, former Polish Communist senator, sociologist.

   8. Solovyov and Klepikova, *Behind the High Kremlin Walls.*

   9. *MacNeil/Lehrer Newshour,* Wednesday, December 21, 1989, WNET, New York, New York.

   10. Milovan Djilas, "Between Revolution and Counter-Revolution," A conversation with George Urban, *Encounter* (November-December 1988).

   11. "That Mikhail Gorbachev's remedies for the Soviet system sound like nothing so much as the nostrums of Margaret Thatcher, contains a message to the world about the failed utopia of Marxism-Leninism," Milovan Djilas, "Between Revolution and Counter-Revolution," A conversation with George Urban, *Encounter* (November-December 1988).

   12. Ilia Zemtsov and John Farrar, *Gorbachev: The Man and the System* (New Brunswick, N.J.: Transaction Publishers, 1989).

   13. Murray Feshbach, "The Structure of Soviet Population: Preliminary Analysis of Unpublished Data, *Soviet Economy* 1, no. 2 (1985).

14. Murray Feshbach, "Soviet Military Health Issues, Gorbachev's Economic Plans, Study Papers, Joint Economic Committee, Congress of the United States, Government Printing Office, Washington, D.C., 1987.

15. Zhores A. Medvedev, *The Nuclear Disaster in the Urals* (New York: Norton, 1979).

16. James M. McDonnell, "SDI, the Soviet Investment Debate and Soviet Military Policy," *Strategic Review* (Winter 1988).

17. Donald R. Carter, "NATO Theater Nuclear Forces: An Enveloping Military Concept, *Strategic Review* 9, no. 2 (Spring 1981).

18. Edward N. Luttwak, "Gorbachev's Strategy, and Ours," *Commentary* (July 1989).

19. Zemtsov and Farrar, *Gorbachev: The Man and the System.*

20. Sol W. Sanders and Yosef Bodansky, "Using Arms Talks to Gauge U.S. Intentions," *Wall Street Journal,* March 12, 1985.

21. Michael Tsypkin, "Turmoil in Soviet Science," *Report on the USSR* I, no. 29 (July 21, 1989).

22. In a sense, there is a parallel here with Mao Tse-tung's attempt with the Cultural Revolution to revitalize China's Communist system. Mao believed, and historical evidence has been corroborated by events since his death, that the centuries of Chinese cultural heritage would ultimately return the population to old ways unless it was periodically ruthlessly shaken up and prevented from falling back into familiar sociological and economic patterns of behavior. His answer was to turn loose the juvenile delinquency of the Red guards on the population until the country had to be rescued from chaos by the People's Liberation Army. Events during the summer of 1989 suggest that the problem remains and that Mao's successors have not found an answer to it.

23. Michta, *An Émigré Reports.*

24. *"Istoki* (Roots)," *Novy Mir,* no. 5 (1988).

25. Vera Tolz, "Soviet Author Critically Evaluates Role of CPSU," in *Report on the USSR* I, no. 13 (March 31, 1989).

26. Mikhail Gorbachev, *Perestroika: New Thinking.*

CHAPTER 8

1. Anders Aslund, *Gorbachev's Struggle for Economic Reform* (Ithaca, N.Y.: Cornell University Press, 1989).

2. *Encounter,* "Djilas on Gorbachev," November–December 1988.

3. Zemtsov and Farrar, *Gorbachev: The Man and the System.*

4. Mikhail Gorbachev, *Perestroika: New Thinking for Our Country and the World* (New York: Harper & Row, Perennial Library, 1987).

5. There is a rather stupid penchant of Western journalists and social scientists for ascribing substance to pseudoscientific methodology. A prime example is the belief that public opinion polls have any meaning in a Soviet society that has undergone for hundreds of years bitter repression and secret service activity that has included all sorts of provocation.

6. The title of this chapter is taken from an old cliché, variously attributed to Lenin and almost all other old Bolshevik and Western fellow-travelers visiting the Soviet Union during the past seventy years: You cannot make an omelet without breaking eggs, that is, to make a better society, there must be violence, a rationale for the cruelty of the regime.

7. "Is There Privatization in Soviet Agriculture?", Karl-Egon Wadekin, *Perestroika: A Socioeconomic Survey,* A Conference Sponsored by Radio Free Europe/ Radio Liberty, Inc., July 7–10, 1989, Munich, Federal Republic of Germany.

8. Anders Aslund, *Gorbachev's Struggle for Economic Reform.*

9. Abel Aganbegian, *Inside Perestroika: The Future of the Soviet Economy* (New York: Harper & Row, 1989).

10. *Pravda,* October 17, 1987, quoted in Aslund's *Gorbachev's Struggle for Economic Reform.*

11. D. J. Peterson, "Unemployment in the USSR," *Report on the USSR* (August 25, 1989).

12. Aganbegian, *Inside Perestroika.*

13. "Topical Dialogue: Hand on Exports," [interview at an unknown place and date], Faminsky's interlocutor is A. Shabashkevich, *Pravda,* May 5, 1989.

14. "USSR Law on Amendments and Additions to USSR Law 'On the Cooperative System in the USSR,' " *Pravda,* October 21, 1989.

15. V. Badov, "Topic of the Day: Give us a Billion," *Pravda,* April 9, 1989.

16. Igor Birman, *Secret Incomes of the Soviet State Budget* (The Hague: Martinus Nijhoff, 1981).

17. V. Badov, "Topic of the Day: Give us a Billion."

18. *Soviet Labour Review,* 7, no. 3 (October 1989).

19. David Marples, "Why the Donbass Miners Went on Strike," *Report on the USSR* (September 8, 1989).

20. Ibid.

21. M. Kushinski, "Flight from Money: Why Lines Are Forming at Jewelry Stores," *Izvestia,* October 6, 1989.

22. "Deputy's Stance: How to Cure the Economy," *Ivestia,* September 11, 1989.

23. Martin Feldstein, "Why Perestroika Isn't Happening," *Wall Street Journal,* April 21, 1989.

24. Abel Aganbegian, *Inside Perestroika: The Future of the Soviet Economy* (New York: Harper & Row, 1989).

25. Excerpts from an exchange between a Gosplan representative and Wayne Angell, Federal Reserve governor. *Wall Street Journal,* October 5, 1989.

26. *The Economist,* October 21, 1989.

27. The Report presented by Mikhail Gorbachev to the first meeting of the newly elected Congress of the People's Deputies of the USSR on May 30, 1989, The Kremlin, Moscow.

28. "The Emerging Economic Strategy," *Soviet Labour Review,* 7, no. 1 (June 1989).

29. Herbert Norman, *The Emergence of Japan as a Modern State* (San Francisco: Institute for Pacific Relations, 1940). A basically Marxist interpretation, but an authoritative study of the first years of Meiji Restoration, makes this abundantly clear.

CHAPTER 9

1. Abel Aganbegian, *Inside Perestroika: The Future of the Soviet Economy.*

2. Lawrence Brainard, "Will *Perestroika* Pay?" *The International Economy,* July/August 1988.

3. Ibid.

4. Ibid.

5. *Wall Street Journal,* October 5, 1989.

6. Roger Robinson [testimony], House Foreign Affairs Subcommittee on International Economic Policy and Trade, November 17, 1987.

7. Lawrence Brainard, "Soviet International Financial Policy: Traditional Formulas or New Innovations?" January 5, 1987.

8. Padma Desai, *Perestroika in Perspective: The Design and Dilemmas of Soviet Reform* (Princeton, N.J.: Princeton University Press, 1989).

9. *Argumenty I Fakty,* no. 42 (October 15–21, 1989).

10. Judy Shelton, *The Coming Soviet Crash: Gorbachev's Desperate Pursuit of Credit in Western Financial Markets* (New York: The Free Press, Macmillan, 1989).

11. *American Foreign Policy Newsletter* (New York: National Committee on American Foreign Policy, Inc., October 1988).

12. Edward Mortimer, "Foreign Affairs: The rebirth of Central Europe", *Financial Times,* June 27, 1989.

13. Josef Joffe, "The Revisionists: Moscow, Bonn, and the European Balance," *The National Interest* (Fall 1989).

14. Henry Kissinger, "The Search for Stability," *Foreign Affairs* (New York: Council on Foreign Relations, 1959).

15. In 1974, I was being guided through the Hadrany Castle in Prague by a very earnest young Czech woman. She showed us the castle and repeatedly spoke of certain parts of the design as being "great examples of Slavic" architecture, painting, statuary, and so forth. She spoke in English for a group of about fifty visitors, mostly German. As we entered one hall, she turned to the group and said

in German, "Would my German friends please come over here with me." She then turned to the English-speakers, and asked us to wait for a few moments. I moved with the German-speakers as we approached a window of the castle, and the guide said, "This is the window." An immediate chorus of "Ah zoh!'s" came from the assembled Germans. I was puzzled for a moment, until I remembered that at this window—in this center of Slavic art—perhaps the most important movement in German history, the *Kulturkampf,* the Catholic-Protestant conflict, had started when priests were thrown from the window.

16. It is to be remembered that the market's members are synonymous with NATO save for Ireland which, while officially neutral, has a longtime cooperative relationship with the Brussels NATO command that lends at least communications assets to the alliance.

17. Vienna observers I spoke to during a visit in October 1988 believed that the Russians did, in fact, encourage the whole idea.

18. Peter Riddell, "Bush Review Urges Caution on Gorbachev," *Financial Times,* April 13, 1989. Gerald F. Seib, "Bush Spells Out Aid to Poland; Urges Reforms," *Wall Street Journal,* April 18, 1989.

19. See Jan Winiecki, *The Distorted World of Soviet-Type Economies* (London: Routledge, 1988).

20. Sol W. Sanders, "Trying to Understand West Germany's Sovi-euphoria," *Christian Science Monitor,* November 29, 1989.

21. Milan Svec, "Communist Reformers Need Our Help," *Washington Post,* April 10, 1989.

22. Patrick Glynn, "The Dangers Beyond Containment," *Commentary* (August 1989).

23. David Marsh, "Man in the News: Hans Dietrich Genscher; Exposing Germany's Faustian Dilemma over NATO," *Financial Times,* April 24, 1989.

24. "West German President Upholds Assertive Stance," *New York Times,* May 25, 1989.

25. Nathaniel Nash, "Brady Asks Germans, Taiwan for Debt Aid," *New York Times,* July 20, 1989.

26. "W. German Trade with Communist Countries Soars," *Financial Times,* July 17, 1989.

27. Lawrence Brainard, "Eastern Europe in U.S.-European Community Relations: The Economic Dimensions," October 12, 1989.

28. Ibid.

29. "Make Way for the Germans," *The Economist,* October 14, 1989.

30. Ibid.

CHAPTER 10

1. Rowland Evans and Robert Novak, "Gorbachev's Pitch to Baker," *Washington Post,* August 9, 1989.

2. Stuart Auerbach, "U.S. Relaxes Computer Sales Curbs," *Washington Post,* July 19, 1989.

3. William P. Schneider, "Small Computers in the Army: An Apple a Day to Keep the Soviets Away," *Signal* (February 1982).

4. "Transfer of Technology to the Soviet Union and Eastern Europe," Selected Papers, Permanent Subcommittee on Investigations, Committee on Government Affairs, U.S. Senate, Washington, D.C.: U.S. Government Printing Office (September 1977).

5. "U.S.–Soviet Accord on Science Signed," [unsigned], *New York Times,* January 13, 1988.

6. Malcolm W. Browne, "Russians Claim Computer Knowledge," *New York Times,* February 16, 1988.

7. "Soviet Science in 'Stultifying' State," United Press International, *Washington Post,* July 18, 1988.

8. Takov M. Rabkin, *Science Between the Superpowers,* A Twentieth Century Fund Paper, New York: Priority Press Publications, 1988.

9. Evelyn Richards, "Soviets Offer to 'Referee' HDTV Race," *Washington Post,* February 23, 1989.

10. Philip J. Hilts, "Soviet Satellites Radiation Distorts Scientific Observation," *Washington Post,* April 4, 1989.

11. Richard F. Staar, "The High-Tech Transfer Offensive of the Soviet Union," *Strategic Review,* Washington, D.C.: U.S. Strategic Institute (Spring 1989).

12. "Prepared Statement of Richard N. Perle," "Transfer of Technology," Hearings, Permanent Subcommittee on Investigations, Committee on Governmental Affairs, U.S. Senate, 98th Congress, Second Session, April 2, 3, 11, 12, 1984 (Washington, D.C.: U.S. Government Printing Office, 1984).

13. *Soviet Acquisition of Militarily Significant Western Technology: An Update,* CIA-Department of Defense, 1985.

14. David Wigg, "Considering National Security in East-West Trade Policy," *Policy Forum* (February 15, 1989).

15. Prepared Statement of Richard N. Perle.

16. Norman A. Bailey and Roger A. Robinson, "Norway's Forgotten Contribution," *Journal of Commerce* (September 4, 1987).

17. "Soviet Oil and Gas: Exploding Exports," *The Economist* (June 17, 1989).

18. "Intelligence Collecting in the U.S.S.R. Chamber of Commerce and Industry," Washington, D.C.: Department of State-Central Intelligence Agency.

19. Ibid.

20. "Sovjetiskt Industriespionage Och Illegal Teknologioverforing," *Fokus Ost,* Stockholm, Sweden, September 1986.

21. John Williams, "Why is Prime Minister Hawke in Moscow?" *News Weekly,* Melbourne, Australia, December 2, 1987.

22. "Soviet Emigrants Arrested by Bonn," [unsigned], *New York Times,* March 29, 1988.

23. William C. Triplett II, "Crimes Against the Alliance: The Toshiba-Kongsberg Export Violations, *Policy Review,* Washington, D.C.: The Heritage Foundation (Spring 1988).

24. Kumagai published these details in an article, "Soviet Aircraft Carriers which Western World Constructs; Second Note of Accusation by Leading Actor in the Toshiba Case," *Bungei Shinju* (Tokyo, September 1987).

25. Ibid.

26. Ibid.

27. "Commentary: Paul Freedenberg on U.S. Export Control Policy and the Toshiba/Kongsberg Episode," [unsigned], *Japan Economic Survey* (April 1988).

28. *World Briefing,* London, February 1989.

CHAPTER 11

1. Dimitri Simes, "Even if Gorbachev Falls, Détente Will Last," *New York Times,* March 20, 1989.

2. Arkady N. Schevchenko, *Breaking with Moscow* (New York: Alfred A. Knopf, 1985).

3. Margaret van Hattem, "Ambiguities of Gorbachev," *Financial Times,* February 24, 1989.

4. *The Economist,* March 11, 1989.

5. Charles Wolf, Jr. et al., *The Costs of the Soviet Empire* (Pasadena, Calif.: Rand Corporation, September 1983).

6. Zemtsov and Farrar, *Gorbachev.*

7. "The Soviet Economy in 1988: Gorbachev Changes Course, A Report by the Central Intelligence Agency and the Defense Intelligence Agency," Subcommittee on National Security, Joint Economic Committee, The Congress, April 14, 1989.

8. Ibid.

9. Richard F. Staar, "The High-Tech Transfer Offensive of the Soviet Union," *Strategic Review* (Spring 1989).

10. Robert M. Gates, "Recent Developments in the Soviet Union and Implications for U.S. Security Policy," speech to the American Association of Science, Colloquium on Science, Arms Control and National Security, Washington, D.C., October 14, 1988.

11. Bernard E. Trainor, "Soviet Maneuvers: A New Strategy?" *New York Times,* November 4, 1988.

12. N. Ogarkov, "A Feat Never Previously Known in History," *Zarubezhnoye Voyennoye Obozreniye* (Foreign Military Review), no. 4 (April 1988).

13. Leon Gouré, "The Soviet Strategic View: Ogarkov on the Persistent Danger of War," *Strategic Review* (Summer 1989).

14. James T. Hackett, "Gorbachev's Arms Reduction Proposals: A Siren Song for the West?" *National Security Record,* The Heritage Foundation, Washington, D.C. (January–February 1989).

15. "Theater Warfighting Concepts," [unsigned] in *Soviet Military Power: Prospects for Change 1989* (Washington, D.C.: U.S. Department of Defense, September 1989).

16. Sanders and Bodansky, "Using Arms Talks to Gauge U.S. Intentions," *Wall Street Journal,* March 12, 1985.

17. "U.S. Economists Are Ready to Advise the Soviets," *New York Times,* October 10, 1989.

18. Antony C. Sutton, *Western Technology and Soviet Economic Development: 1917 to 1930* (Stanford, Calif.: Hoover Institution for War, Revolution and Peace, Stanford University, 1968).

19. Ibid. For example, delivery of repaired railway equipment was paid for by the Soviets partially in disabled czarist locomotives, partially in cash advances, and the remainder in cash at the Latvian–USSR border in the early years of total absence of Soviet international credit.

> The [Soviet] locomotive stock at this time [August 1920] was about 16,000 of which only about 6,000 were able to operate at all. In August 1921, of a listed rolling stock of 437,125 cars, only 20,000 were in first-class condition, and fewer than 200,000 were able to run at all. The equipment and locomotive problem was solved by purchasing European and American locomotives; sending defective locomotives to Latvia, Estonia, and Berlin for repair; and importing German technicians and railway materials for wagon repair. . . . The first Estonian contract was with locomotive-building plants in Reval for repair of 2,000 "sick" locomotives. . . . Payment was in American dollars. . . . All steel and parts, except copper fire-boxes, were the subject of a separate agreement between the Estonian companies and Krupp of Germany. The latter also arranged financing of the program from Deutsche Bank. The British Vickers-Armstrong Company participated in the repair contract by leasing the Russo-Baltic works through a specially formed subsidiary, the Anglo-Baltic Shipbuilding and Engineering Co. The major portion of the order was divided between Anglo-Baltic, the Dvigatel [plant], and the Peter shipyard [all in Reval]. The plants were kept busy for one and a half years.

20. Valerii Badov and Viktar Shirokov, "Does Narva Need a Customs Checkpoint?" by *Sotsialisticheskaia Industriia* (March 2, 1989).

21. Milan Svec, "The Prague Spring: 20 Years Later," *Foreign Affairs* (Summer 1988).

22. Paul Delaney, "Soviet Bloc Writers Clash at a Conference," *New York Times,* May 10, 1988.

23. Remarks by Ambassador William Luers, Conference on Human Rights, Security, and Economics in Eastern Europe, School of International Affairs, Columbia University, April 13, 1989.

24. *"East-West Relations: A Draft Report to the Trilateral Commission,"* April 1989.

25. Thomas L. Friedman, "Baker, Outlining World View, Assesses Plan for Soviet Bloc," *New York Times,* March 28, 1989.

26. James Blitz from London and Quentin Peel from Moscow, "Gorbachev pledges no interference in East bloc countries' affairs," *Financial Times,* March 30, 1989.

27. Henry Kissinger, "Dealing with Moscow: A New Balance," *Washington Post,* February 7, 1989.

28. Henry Kissinger, "Kissinger: A New Era for NATO," *Newsweek,* October 12, 1989.

29. Joseph Churba, *Soviet Breakout: Strategies to Meet It* (Washington, D.C.: Pergamon-Brassey's, 1988).

INDEX

Abalkin, Leonid, budget deficit, 134; reform stalled, 128, 129

Abuldze, Tengiz, popularity of anti-Stalinism, 22

Academy of Sciences (Soviet), new exchanges, 170. *See also* Standard of living (Mozhina)

Adenauer, Konrad, Stalin's reunification offer, 152

Adenauer Stiftung (Konrad), seminar, 164

AEG, NEP assistance, 47

Afghanistan, Carter policy changes after, 84, 175; computer military applications, 168; inflationary effect, 134; stinger missile, 181; withdrawal saves Soviets money, 195

Aganbegian, Abel G., alcoholism, 127; Lenin, 117; not Gorbachev's principle economic adviser, 122; price reform, 130; Siberian rivers project, 149

Agriculture, Brezhnev's promises, 124; collectivization, 92; destruction of traditional, 56; Gorbachev's early attention, 124; Gorbachev's performance, 119; *Gosagoprogr,* 124; industrialization of, 92; Leninist principles, 124; NEP, 92; privatization, 124, 125; Stalin's program, 54, 55; thread of peasant, broken, 126; yields, 55

Aid, Soviet strategy for Western, xiii; U.K. World War II, 60; UNRRA, 60; U.S. data collection, 200. *See also* NEP

AIDS, disinformation campaign, 16

Alcan Highway, built for Soviet aid, 58

Alcoholism, Gorbachev's program, 126, 127

Allied Control Council (Germany), reparations, 61

American Association of Science (Colloquium), 225

American Enterprise Institute for Public Policy Research, 216

Amtorg (Soviet Purchasing Mission), wartime activities, 58

Andropov, Yuri, Gorbachev intimacy, 109; Novosibirsk Report, 122; Romanov as protégé, 123; succession, 104; "testament", 109; visits to spa, 109

Angell, Norman, *The Great Illusion,* 81

Angell, Wayne, ruble, 139

Anglo-Baltic Engineering Co., 226

Anninskii, Alec, writers' meeting, 204

Apparatchiki, Gorbachev as typical, 108, 111; opposition to Kosygin/Brezhnev reforms, 75

Armenia, inflation effects, 134

ACKNOWLEDGMENTS

The author wishes to thank his many American friends and colleagues who patiently helped him unsnarl his thesis and debated many of these issues over the past several years, as well as friends and colleagues in Austria, Britain, Canada, Finland, France, Germany, and Sweden. Especially helpful and long-suffering were Walter Hahn, Leo Labedz, and Vladimir Rudolph. In addition, the author wants to thank Soviet émigré scientists, engineers, and factory officials and workers in the New York and Boston areas who consented to interviews. The author also wishes to express his gratitude to Frank R. Barnett and the National Strategy Information Center.

The U.S. Institute of Peace helped through partial financing of the project.

Special thanks are due to Charles Lean and Lynn Gemmell at Madison Books, and Carol Clark, my copy editor. They were extraordinarily helpful in their care and attention during the publishing process.